Literacy, Culture and Identity

American University Studies

Series XIV
Education

Vol. 42

PETER LANG
New York • Washington, D.C./Baltimore • Boston
Bern • Frankfurt am Main • Berlin • Vienna • Paris

Jill Sinclair Bell

Literacy, Culture and Identity

PETER LANG
New York • Washington, D.C./Baltimore • Boston
Bern • Frankfurt am Main • Berlin • Vienna • Paris

Library of Congress Cataloging-in-Publication Data
Bell, Jill.
Literacy, culture and identity / Jill Sinclair Bell.
p. cm. — (American university studies. Series XIV,
Education; vol. 42)
Includes bibliographical references.
1. Second language acquisition. 2. Literacy. 3. Chinese language—Study
and teaching—Foreign speakers. 4. Language and culture. I. Title.
II. Series: American university studies. Series XIV, Education; vol. 42.
P118.7.B45   418'.4—dc20   96-42924
ISBN 0-8204-3656-9
ISSN 0740-4565

Die Deutsche Bibliothek-CIP-Einheitsaufnahme
Bell, Jill Sinclair:
Literacy, culture and identity / Jill Sinclair Bell. –New York;
Washington, D.C./Baltimore; Boston; Bern; Frankfurt am Main;
Berlin; Vienna; Paris: Lang.
(American university studies: Ser. 14, Education; Vol. 42)
ISBN 0-8204-3656-9
NE: American university studies / 14

Cover design by Andy Ruggirello.

The paper in this book meets the guidelines for permanence and durability
of the Committee on Production Guidelines for Book Longevity
of the Council of Library Resources.

© 1997 Peter Lang Publishing, Inc., New York

All rights reserved.
Reprint or reproduction, even partially, in all forms such as microfilm,
xerography, microfiche, microcard, and offset strictly prohibited.

Printed in the United States of America.

For my father, Ronald K. Sinclair (1912-1996).

Acknowledgments

I will always be grateful to Cindy Lam for the many hours she devoted not only to teaching me Chinese, but to discussing my progress, listening to my ideas, reading my drafts and giving me the benefit of her thoughtful insights. Without Cindy, this book could never have been written.

The other person who played a critical role in the development of this work was Michael Connelly, whose creative and incisive thinking had a significant impact on the study and on myself. I am grateful also to a number of colleagues and friends who shared their insights and gave me encouragement. Chief among them are Tara Goldstein, Jessie Lees, Barbara Burnaby, Patrick Allen, Carola Conle and Carol Mullen.

Finally, I would like to thank my husband, Bob, and my daughters, Thalia, Kirsten and Karen, for their ongoing love and support.

* * *

Excerpts from the Introduction appeared in J. S. Bell (1997). Shifting Frames: Shifting Stories. In C. P. Casanave & S. Schecter, (Eds.), *On Becoming a Language Educator*. Hillsdale, NJ: Lawrence Erlbaum Associates.

Chapter 3 of this book first appeared in *Curriculum Inquiry 23: 2*, pp. 131-153, (1993), under the title "Finding the Commonplaces of Literacy."

Excerpts from Chapters 8 and 9 appeared in a somewhat different form in *TESOL Quarterly 27: 3*, pp. 467-475, (1993) and *TESOL Quarterly 29: 4*, pp. 687-704 (1995).

The development of this study was supported by a grant from the Social Science and Humanities Research Council of Canada.

Table of Contents

Introduction:	Different language, different literacy	1
Part One:	**Studying Literacy**	
Chapter 1:	A pilot study	9
Chapter 2:	Trying to come to terms with the literature	29
Chapter 3:	Using commonplaces to come to terms with the literature	43
Chapter 4:	Coming to a personal view of literacy	73
Part Two:	**Studying Chinese**	
Chapter 5:	The stories before the story	93
Chapter 6:	The story of learning Chinese	103
Chapter 7:	Other versions of the story	145
Part Three:	**The Experience of Learning Chinese**	
Chapter 8:	Stories shaping the literacy experience: Cindy's Story	159
Chapter 9:	Stories shaping the literacy experience: Jill's Story	175
Chapter 10:	The impact of the experience on the learner	197
References		223

Introduction

Different language, different literacy

The first indication that Cindy and I conceptualized literacy quite differently came up during a social lunch before she actually began to teach me Chinese. We had met to talk about the possibility of her tutoring me in Chinese literacy, but we both felt that we wanted to get to know each other a little better before committing ourselves, so the conversation had been largely social. My first impressions were of a very sophisticated young woman, whose English I would have presumed was that of a native speaker if she hadn't told me differently. I knew she had a lot of experience teaching English language literacy to Chinese learners, especially senior citizens in bilingual classes, but somehow it seemed hard to imagine her in those surroundings, she seemed so thoroughly Canadian in the settings in which I had met her. I wondered whether she might have moved too far away from her Chinese origins to be able to teach me the Chinese culture which I assumed would underlie the Chinese characters.

I tried to explain to her why I wanted to learn Chinese and what I thought I might learn from the experience. Nearly all of my teaching experience in Canada had been with adults who had fairly low levels of proficiency in English, and who were unable to work well with the standard textbooks which were available. I had become used to developing my own teaching materials because the students I taught could not make sense of the grammatical explanations or even the simple dialogues which were a staple of so many ESL textbooks. Most of the students I worked with could not turn such printed text into speech. Some did not recognize the alphabetic shapes at all and were as baffled by a page of English as I would have been by a page of Sanskrit. Others had some familiarity with the alphabet but were unsure as to what sounds were associated with the letters in English. A few knew the basics of English pronunciation and could sound out the more straightforward words but had insufficient vocabulary to make much sense of what they were reading. All of these students needed large amounts of contextual support before they could recognize the purpose of a piece of text, much less understand its specific message. Instead of using the textbook dialogues therefore, I worked with real-life objects, pictures, street signs and so on, helping them to recognize and produce the written form of words they already knew orally.

As I had gained more experience in working with such students I had become increasingly unhappy with a narrow definition of literacy as simple coding and decoding skills. Although in one sense I had been pleased with the progress my students had shown in developing the ability to sound out a brief piece of text such as a subway station name, I was also aware that these apparent signs of progress were not always as useful outside of the classroom as I had originally hoped. (In the case of the subway sign, for instance, the students later pointed out to me that if one had to sound out the subway sign before deciding whether to get off the train one would miss the stop. It was more efficient to learn the colours of the tiles at the various stations.) It seemed that my attempts to put literacy use into a real context were not successful—at least partly because I did not understand the ways in which literacy was used and understood. Limiting the understanding of literacy to the ability to sound out words seemed to encourage both teacher and learner to focus on only the surface manifestations of interacting with print rather than considering the understandings on which such use is based.

By focussing solely on the sound symbol correspondence, I felt I was teaching a literacy which was very language specific. It seemed self evident that this specifically English pattern of symbols and sounds rested on a much more complex web of knowledge and assumptions about how print operates but I did not know what that web consisted of, nor how much of it was specific to English and how much might be common to other languages. While intuitively feeling that there must be some common base to all literacies, simultaneously I was aware that different cultures use and perceive literacy in different ways. Even those learners highly fluent in another script could not, therefore, learn a new literacy merely by learning a new set of encoding conventions. Instead they would have to learn the complex of cultural assumptions and attitudes which we teachers had not yet consciously acknowledged for ourselves, much less learned how to teach.

I had struggled with this problem in my recent ESL classes which had grouped highly literate but non-Roman alphabetic students with those who had never attended school. My expectation was that the learners who were fluent in another script would be able to transfer over some of their knowledge about literacy systems and hence would make more rapid progress in learning to read and write in English. To a considerable extent, my practical experience suggested that there was indeed some correlation between prior exposure to education and progress in English but the relationship was not as clear cut as I had expected, and there were a number of cases where I found that I had completely misjudged my students' mother tongue literacy abilities. I wanted to know more about what it was like to attempt literacy in a new language as an adult.

Although I had begun to read widely on the topic of literacy I had not found anything which helped me understand the actual experience of the second language literacy learner, which seemed to me to be crucial in comprehending what happens when we become literate in a new language. In the course of my Ph.D. work I had thus planned on making an intensive study of one or two ESL learners and had in fact carried out a pilot study with two Afghan refugees. My pilot study had not been very successful. It proved impossible to find learners with no prior English language literacy who were also orally fluent. The result was that I could not ask these men to describe their experience directly, but had to rely on observation or interpretation. I realized too that to expect such learners to document their progress, expectations, strategies, assumptions and emotions as they progressed with the language was asking from them a degree of commitment and metalinguistic awareness that was unrealistic.

Hence I conceived the notion of an autobiographical study. By studying my own experiences in attempting literacy in Chinese I hoped that I would gain a better understanding of just what the experience is like of attempting a new literacy as an adult. As I explained to Cindy, I recognized that the problems I would face in learning Chinese characters were not necessarily applicable to learners of English, but I hoped that I might get some sense of what understandings were common to both literacies. I imagined too that I would discover some of my assumptions about English language literacy—that I would become aware of some of those aspects which were "taken for granted" in Schutz's (1973) terms. By trying to become literate in another language, the unacknowledged assumptions of my current literacy would surely become evident.

Cindy was intrigued by the idea, and interested in participating. We discussed the merits of the various dialects of Chinese and decided that she should teach me Cantonese—the dialect in which she herself had first become literate. Cindy was at pains to point out that she had no prior experience in teaching Chinese literacy, and wanted me to be aware that she would not consider herself to be an expert. In some ways I welcomed this lack of prior experience as I did not want the experience to be neatly packaged for Western learners. I wanted to share something akin to the experience learners from other cultures have when they find themselves in a Canadian classroom being taught by Canadian methods, which may or may not match their expectations of what education should be. If anything, I was concerned that Cindy's considerable experience with ESL literacy would make her so conscious of Western methodology that she would shape the Chinese literacy into unduly familiar patterns.

I was very soon to receive my first hint that this fear was groundless. Our conversation moved onto the logistics of the study and the amount of time we would spend on it.

"How much of your time will be spent on the research side of things and how much on the actual learning of Chinese? Will you have time to do work on your own?" she asked me. I explained that in addition to her tutorials, I would be attending an oral Cantonese course at the university and that I would be committed to a considerable amount of work transcribing the tapes of both the oral and the literacy classes, so the demands of the research side would take up a fair proportion of the time.

"But I will have time for assignments," I added, "so if you would set me some work each time we meet, I'll certainly do it. I should have about an hour a day for home-study, I think. Plus of course, I spend two hours a day commuting on the subway, so I thought I could use that time to work on the characters."

"What!" Cindy looked astonished. "You can't—you can't do characters on the subway!"

I was baffled. I had had many ESL students who would carry a set of index cards around with them to study on buses and trains at odd moments. I had thought this would be an excellent way of learning characters. I didn't expect to be able to produce good writing under those conditions, but I could surely learn the order of strokes, and the basic pattern of the characters. I suppose my face showed my bafflement, because Cindy began to laugh. "Oh, I'm sorry," she said, "but you just can't learn characters like that. It's a matter of balance. You can't write characters in those conditions."

"Well, yes, I know, it's kind of bumpy, but just to learn the shapes?"

"No, I don't mean that kind of balance. You have to have balance inside to be able to learn them. You'll never learn them properly if you don't have the proper conditions."

I didn't understand what Cindy meant at that time, and I was not sufficiently convinced to let go of the idea that I could use subway time to learn to recognize the characters even if I could not produce them. I was surprised too, not merely by the content of what Cindy said but by the immediate and decided way in which she said it, which contrasted sharply with the flexible open-minded tone she had taken in discussing English language literacy. My surprise must have been evident because suddenly it seemed as if Canadian Cindy resurfaced as she distanced herself from the pronouncement.

"Maybe things have changed now," she said. "For all I know, children in China sit in front of the TV set to do their homework, these days. But when we were children, homework had to be done at a clean desk in peace and quiet so you could concentrate—our parents thought that was very important and the teachers insisted on it. Even in a very poor house, the parents will make sure there is a good quiet table for the children to study on. I really don't think you can write good characters without those conditions—otherwise there won't be any balance."

Over the next year, the terms *balance* and *concentration* were to become very significant to me as I struggled to learn to write in Chinese. It is hard now, in retrospect, to recall how strange Cindy's words seemed to me then, or how little I understood of what she was trying to say to me. As a potential learner, I found her speech rather daunting. But as a researcher I found it a reassuring beginning in that it demonstrated very clearly that, despite Cindy's and my common experience with ESL literacy, we certainly did not share the same assumptions about literacy in Chinese.

PART ONE

STUDYING LITERACY

Chapter One

A Pilot Study

At the point when I met Cindy, I had worked in the field of second language education for about fifteen years. Some of this time had been spent as a regular classroom teacher in England and in the Caribbean. Later, in Canada, I had worked with adult immigrants in part-time settings focusing on the teaching of literacy. Gradually, I had moved from direct teaching into materials development, teacher education and research. Eventually, in my late thirties, I decided to go back to school and work towards my doctorate.

I was keen, however, not to lose touch with classroom literacy teaching. I wanted to keep my hand in as a teacher but without having to give up my commitment as a student to do so. I decided to approach contacts at a government-sponsored language program that catered to large numbers of refugees and recent arrivals, to ask if I would be able to volunteer my time as a teacher assistant while simultaneously doing some observational research. At that point in my studies, I was envisaging that the major research for my doctoral dissertation would be an observational study of a literacy class. I planned to teach the class for a year, simultaneously observing and recording the progress and strategies demonstrated by the learners. I was not entirely sure how I would go about this, or what I would be trying to document, so this initial session as a participant observer was designed to function as a pilot study, which would help me shape the full thesis proposal.

I was fortunate to be able to make arrangements with a teacher at Arrival Place[1], to spend one day a week working with her students. We agreed that for the morning session I would act as her teacher-aide and we would maintain the class as one group. In the afternoon session I would take a small group of those with the lowest literacy levels for intensive literacy work. I began work in late April, and our arrangement continued throughout the summer until mid-August when the classes ceased.

1 The name of the school has been changed.

Background to the class

Arrival Place is a government funded facility that provides support to many newly arrived immigrants. It provides a range of services such as translation, counselling and a day nursery in addition to English classes. A high proportion of the learners in this program are accepted into Canada on the basis of either their refugee status or their family relationship to previous immigrants. There are no language or education requirements for people admitted in these categories, so their previous experience of education tends to be limited. Full-time language education courses, which last either six or twelve weeks, are offered at seven levels of difficulty. The class in which I was working was classified as the pre-basic class, with learners being grouped mostly on the basis of oral command of English. Literacy levels thus varied widely. Students could be accepted or promoted at any point during the course so the class character changed considerably over the twelve weeks I was there. The average class size was around fifteen students, although the numbers fluctuated from a minimum of twelve to a high of twenty-seven at one point.

The class was mixed in terms of age with two senior citizens and a couple of teenagers representing the extremes. The majority were, however, in their twenties or thirties with a fairly even mix of men and women. Ethnic backgrounds included Tamil, Afghan, Ecuadorean, Sino-Vietnamese, Turkish, Iranian, and Yugoslav. Despite the pre-basic label on the class, a variety of abilities were obvious, with some of the students having strong educational backgrounds and command of three or four other languages. Mostly, such students were rapidly promoted, leaving the more basic students as the core of the class.

Instructional practices

The activities in class were, for the most part, selected by the teacher as part of her ongoing program. Although theoretically I had the responsibility for the literacy group in the afternoon sessions, in practice the teacher commonly influenced the activities, with a request to cover a particular item or to complete unfinished work from the morning session.

The activities presented or chosen by the teacher were drawn from a number of text books such as *Side by Side* (Molinsky & Bliss, 1983), or *New Routes to English* (Sampson, 1979). They fell into two broad categories: those that presented vocabulary and those that practised a particular sentence pattern. For vocabulary work, the teacher would normally present the material in a question-and-answer format, using an illustration from a textbook, poster or realia in the case of such items as clothing. Students would be asked to identify an item, their response would be confirmed or corrected and the correct term would commonly be written up on the blackboard. The writing on the blackboard was normally done in uppercase letters, which the teacher felt was easier for the newer students. (Almost all textbooks provided used lower case, however.) The words were not normally arranged on the board in any particular order, with the teacher writing on the nearest available piece of free space. Literate students had no problem with this and in most cases would arrange the words in long lists in their notebooks along with native language translations. Students with minimal literacy skills in their own language did not normally make any attempt to copy down these randomly arranged words but instead focused on oral production.

One textbook, which the teacher used regularly, provided a variant on the above procedure with detailed pictures of scenes on which various items were numbered. Below the picture the appropriate vocabulary was provided in random order for the students to match number and word. When working with this text the teacher would first identify the vocabulary for the entire picture orally then repeat the procedure, writing the words and their numbers up on the blackboard, and asking the students to complete the exercise in similar fashion in their notebooks. The major task for the literacy level students was, therefore, that of copying a list of approximately twenty-five words. These were the only writing tasks that students attempted in the whole group sessions.

Work on sentence patterns was normally presented by way of a dialogue that was read to the class a number of times, firstly by the teacher and subsequently by the more advanced students. Students with minimal literacy abilities were never asked to attempt reading aloud. Oral activities designed to focus attention on the pattern followed a similar format to vocabulary presentation, with individual students being asked to manipulate a sentence pattern in some way and oral feedback being provided regarding their success. Occasionally, students would be asked to work in pairs to practice a short dialogue, possibly with some substitutions for the more fluent speakers. This provided the first opportunity for the literacy level students to attempt reading a sentence. One of two patterns was commonly apparent here. Either the students had memorized the dialogue as a result of the numerous readings and were able to recite it quite well, or they remained silent until a more fluent reader provided a model for repetition. The dialogues were selected to give an opportunity for sentence pattern practice rather than communication of information, as in this example:

> "Are you wearing a red shirt?"
> "No, I'm not. Are you wearing blue pants?"
> "Yes, I am."

Given this type of reading assignment it was difficult to identify whether the students had developed such skills as using physical or semantic context to predict meaning.

Very little reading or writing work, therefore, took place in the morning sessions, with copying being the primary print-related activity. The data gathered in this pilot study reflects this preoccupation. In those afternoon sessions where I was able to choose the content, I could ask the students to attempt a wider variety of literacy-related tasks. A number of techniques were used, the most common being a global approach of taking a meaningful unit, which was then broken down into individual words. I had hoped to be able to develop language experience stories with the learners, in which after a discussion of a topic of interest, I would transcribe their own words for them. Such learner-dictated material would be ideal, I thought, as reading texts. However, these learners had virtually no productive oral ability and consequently could not build up even the simplest of stories. Accordingly, I had to provide the text for all reading encounters. I used sentences such as:

> My name is _____.
> My address is _____.
> My telephone number is _____.

I wrote the individual words in large print (lower case with initial capital for the first word) on index cards and provided sufficient extra cards for the personal details of all class members. I presented the words as sight words with no attempt to sound them out and followed the comprehension and production stages with work on reordering the cards after shuffling, picking out the appropriate missing card from a pile of three or four distracters, and identifying the appropriate personal card. Once the students were familiar with the basic sentence and all students could recognize and identify the words of the sentence, I introduced the appropriate question (e.g. *What is your name?*), which was presented in similar fashion. Students would then make their own cards, and work in pairs arranging the cards to make the appropriate dialogue or hiding one card in a sentence for the other to identify.

Other activities included working with simple forms, some phonic work on initial consonant recognition and working with captions to pictures. On one occasion, I brought in illustrated advertising flyers from the local supermarket, hoping the combination of photographs, prices and food labels would provide valuable context.

On a number of occasions I attempted tasks that, in the event, I proved totally unable to explain to the students. An attempt to develop a language experience story based on a series of pictures produced nothing but my own descriptions of the pictures. An attempt to complete an exercise on opposites provided in Wigfield (1982) involved as the first example *good–bad*. This produced the pairing *good–bye* from the whole class, a misunderstanding I was unable to clear up.

Although these afternoon sessions included a wider range of activities, they yielded fairly limited data. Reading from word cards gave hints of certain patterns. For instance, wrong card choices normally reflected a word of similar length or appearance, allowing the observer to hypothesize about the features of the word that were being identified. The work with the advertising flyers presented the students with an authentic text, which enabled them to use context clues to support their reading predictions, but the limitations of vocabulary made it difficult for the researcher to distinguish difficulties with lexis from difficulties in reading. The greatest problem was that the average group size was nine people, none of whom had any significant English competence, and who thus could not be assigned task work. The demands on me as a teacher were too time-consuming for much research or observation to take place and, consequently, I gathered even less data from the afternoon sessions than from those of the morning, since the type of activity selected did not leave an end product that could be scrutinized at leisure.

Overall, the combination of the teaching practices outlined above with the minimal oral proficiency of the students made it very difficult to observe learners interacting with print in all but the most controlled contexts. The students' writing work at this early stage consisted almost entirely of copying and the case histories described below thus show a disproportionate interest in the copying process. While, at first sight, this copying may seem a very limited introduction to the writing process, in fact a close examination of their copying work over this period shows considerable progress and a growing knowledge and understanding of the conventions and expectations of print.

Students selected for the pilot study

Very few of the original group of students whom I began to observe were still attending classes by the end of the twelve-week period. Some were promoted, some dropped out; others changed to different programs or attended only sporadically. Two Afghan students, however, were present for the bulk of the time and they form the focus of this preliminary study. When the programme started the two men were absolute beginners in English with no known previous exposure to literacy at all. Over the twelve weeks during which I worked with these men, they moved from treating writing as a form of drawn icons, to a recognition of the basics of sound-symbol correspondence and a familiarity with letter forms.

Yusefi[2] was a Farsi speaker, who had worked as a kitchen helper in his native country of Afghanistan. He arrived in Canada, as a refugee, one month before I met him in class. He spoke no English at all when he first came to Arrival Place and was put in the pre-basic

---

2 As so much of the work done by my students in this class related to personal information, I have not been able to give them the anonymity I would have preferred. I have, however, obliterated pieces of the text samples in order to hide their family names and addresses.

class. At that time he was thirty-four years old.

The most striking feature of Yusefi was the enthusiasm that he brought to his work. He was a keen participant in all the activities that the teacher suggested, joining in oral work with volume and enthusiasm. He had a good ear for sound and had less trouble with English pronunciation than most of the other students in the class. Even in the first weeks of the course, he was able to repeat phrases and sentences of seven or eight words with considerable accuracy, although he did not normally retain them. He often volunteered to answer questions, point out named objects or demonstrate required actions. He had an outgoing personality, and would attempt to make jokes even with his minimal English. He appeared to have some ability in Arabic and often provoked laughter among the other Arabic speakers.

To the best of my knowledge, Yusefi had had no prior experience with formal education, and had no literacy skills before he began classes at Arrival Place. Initially, his teacher assumed that he could read and write since he copied down words from the blackboard with a fair degree of accuracy. After the oral presentation of a dialogue, he would read sentences aloud, running his finger along underneath the words as he articulated them. It took some days before the teacher noticed that he was in fact reciting from memory and was pointing to quite different words on the page.

Yusefi was remarkable for the confidence and determination that he brought to the literacy process, qualities that were demonstrated by his interest in borrowing and copying materials. On one occasion we had been working with index cards on which I had written the words of basic sentences. Yusefi asked if he could borrow the cards and take them home. The next day he proudly demonstrated that he had copied all the cards onto squares of paper. A similar event took place when I took in a child's set of alphabet cards. This motivation to work at home gave me considerable difficulty as a researcher because I had great difficulty persuading Yusefi to part with his notebook long enough to allow me to take it away for photocopying.

He did not seem to be discouraged by failure or by publicity and would commonly volunteer to write information on the blackboard in response to the teacher's request. I found such occasions suggestive of his learning strategies. He would begin by looking intently at the word in his notebook, presumably trying to fix the letter shapes in his memory. He would then stride confidently to the board and write the first two or three letters, but then pause, unable to recall the rest of the word. Other students would often call out the names of the subsequent letters but Yusefi got little apparent help from this and normally preferred to look again at his notebook for further input. We can hypothesize from this either a preference for visual input, or more likely, a lack of knowledge of the letter names. Yusefi rarely forgot the beginning letters of a word but quite often forgot the final letters. This suggests he had developed some sense of left-right directionality. A similar pattern could be seen in the letters he omitted when copying words, where again it was the final letters of words that gave difficulty. Quite commonly, his copied work showed an increasing degree of inaccuracy towards the end when, presumably, he was tiring.

As Figures 1 and 2 show (week three of the course), Yusefi was prepared to copy any material that the teacher put up on the blackboard, irrespective of its likely relevance for his learning. He would copy down long vocabulary lists of items that he was unlikely to

17	TOOTH BRUSH	18 GLASS
19	WASH CLOOTE	20 NAIL BRUSH
12	TOOTH PASTE	22 TOWEL
23	TOWEL RACK	24 BATHROOM SCALE
25	EAT MAT 26 STONGE 27 SOAP	
28	HAM PER 29 TILE 30 CURTI rod	
31	STOWER CURTAIU	

Figure 1: Yusefi's copybook, Week 3 (reduced).

need to identify. He did not normally use such lists to refer back to, but he did demonstrate an understanding that the symbolic representations referred to specific objects. Where he was clear as to the meaning of the words he was writing, he would sometimes add small illustrations as a memory aid, as in the list of household items (Figure 1), which the teacher presented by way of a picture. Such drawings were apparently helpful to Yusefi both in fixing the meaning in his mind and in focusing his attention on the word. Some weeks after he wrote the list in Figure 2, I was doing some phonics

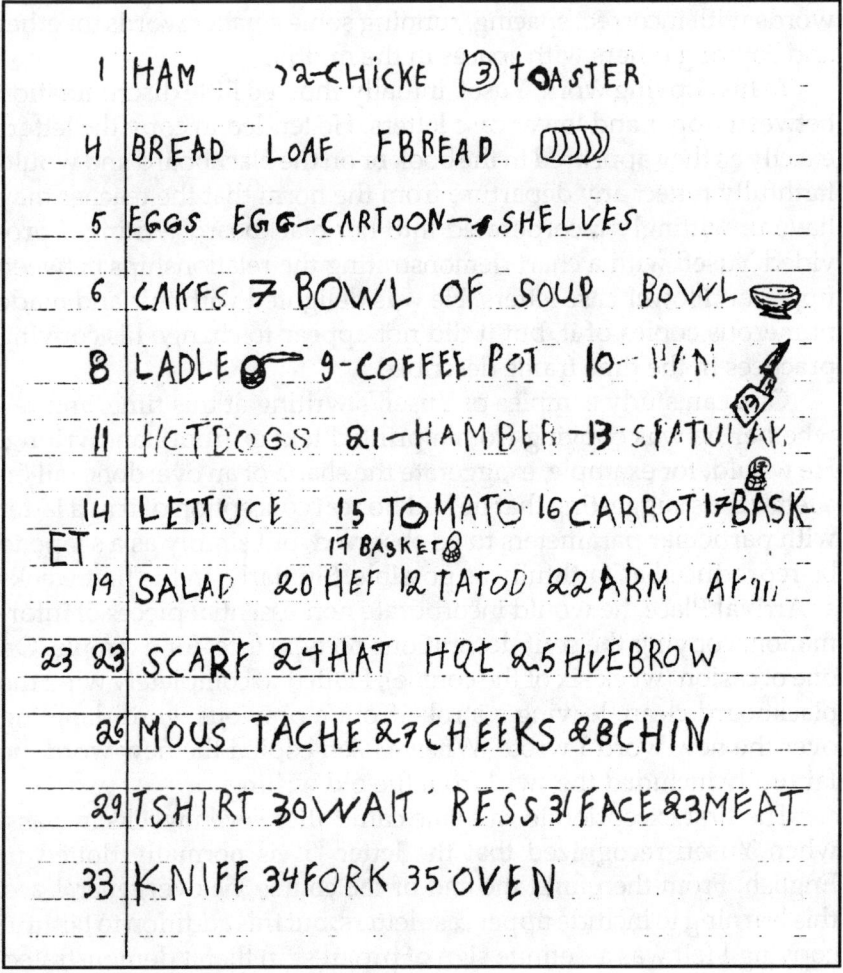

Figure 2: Yusefi's copybook, Week 3 (reduced).

work with him on single syllable words with "-an", and drew quick pictures on the board of "man," "van" and "pan." Yusefi picked up on "pan" immediately and began to search his notebook. Eventually, he came up with an almost identical sketch, accompanying the word "ladle" and demanded an explanation of the relationship between the two words. This was, however, the only occasion on which he used his notebook for reference that I observed.

Not all the material that Yusefi copied appeared to be as meaningful to him. Even by the end of the twelve-week course, he did not always demonstrate a clear idea of word boundaries and would copy words with incorrect spacing, running some smaller words together and copying others with spaces in the middle.

In his copying work, Yusefi initially showed little discrimination between upper and lower case letters. He tended to copy the letters exactly as they appeared in the book or on the blackboard and would faithfully reflect any departure from the norm that the teacher may have unwittingly incorporated into her blackboard writing. I provided Yusefi with a chart demonstrating the relationships between upper and lower letters. He was delighted with this and made numerous copies of it, but it did not appear to change his copying practices in the time frame described.

One can study samples of Yusefi's writing at this time, and tell whether he was copying from a printed text or from handwriting. He would, for example, exaggerate the shape of an overdone tail on a letter thus suggesting that he had no real conception of it as a letter with particular parameters to be observed, but simply as a shape to be reproduced as faithfully as possible. Similarly, in his first weeks at Arrival Place, he would incorporate non-essential pieces of information, copying the serif decorations on type face, for example. On one occasion (week six of the course), I failed to completely wipe the blackboard clean, leaving a stroke from a previous word dangling over the new word I wrote. When Yusefi copied the new word, he faithfully included the swirl from the old writing.

The first exception to this rule came after seven weeks in class, when Yusefi recognized that the letter "i" is normally dotted in English. From then until the end of the course, he overgeneralized this learning to include upper case letters, but this addition to faithful copying I felt was a definite sign of progress in that it demonstrated his recognition that there is an essential element of "i-ness," which he was attempting to reproduce, rather than simply drawing whatever meaningless shape another writer produced for him. It seemed to me that this recognition of a constant underlying the many physical variants of a letter was an important stage in his literacy development.

With regard to the simple matter of pen control, Yusefi found it hard, throughout the course, to keep letters straight and even in size, whether writing on paper or on the blackboard, although some progress could be seen in this over the period of the study. The amount of small muscle control that is needed for the writing process is presumably developed, at least in part, by practice and does not automatically develop with physical maturity.

Another area of difficulty for Yusefi concerned layout conventions. His early work demonstrated minimal knowledge of normal Western conventions for page layout. When copying a list of words that the teacher had put up on the blackboard, for instance, he did not arrange the items in a list, or attempt to line them up in any way. His pages appeared to be justified as much to the right as to the left margin and many words were thus broken and continued on a new line. There were no dates or titles in evidence on any of his work.

He also appeared not to have any expectations of the conventions of filling in forms. He had done work with me for two weeks on the phrase, "My name is Yusefi," when I introduced a simple form that asked for name and telephone number. On seeing the descriptor "Name" on the form he immediately wrote "SI [is] Yusefi." This was the first piece of spontaneous print that Yusefi produced. He remembered many of the letters of his name and produced them accurately, but reversed the letters of the word "is." His error thus allowed me to hypothesize both about his concept of the conventions of writing in relation to form completion, and his memory of word shapes.

Yusefi's reading strategies were less easily described than those which he employed in writing. This problem also occurred with the other student described in the pilot study and was an indication of a flaw in the research design.

It did not prove possible to give attention to student reading performance in any detail while simultaneously teaching six or eight other students. In the morning sessions, little reading was done by the identified students other than choral recitation or repetition. What was noticeable for Yusefi was that he wanted to appear as a reader and would recite from memory while running his finger along under the words. The finger did not necessarily point to the right words; indeed on occasion, Yusefi was on the wrong page. He found work with phonics very difficult, and would rarely be able to identify a three-letter word from letter recognition alone. Sight word recognition was stronger but appeared to be based on shape recognition rather than decoding. When working with a number of word cards, for example, Yusefi could normally find the cards for unusually long or short words but would guess wildly when trying to identify words of five or six letters. After about six weeks, he began to demonstrate some knowledge of using phonic skills to sound out the initial letters of words, thus restricting the scope of his guesses.

The second learner on whom the pilot study focused was Fazli, an Afghan who was then thirty-eight years old. Fazli's registration records show him as having had secondary education. However, he demonstrated no evidence of literacy or experience with education and it seemed unlikely that the record was correct. When classes began, he had virtually no oral English, and hence could not volunteer any information about himself. There are no formal interpreter services available at Arrival House, so that the teacher's and my only source of information from Fazli was the indirect route of asking a Turkish student to use Arabic to speak to Yusefi, who would then translate into Farsi. By the time the answer had followed a similar route in reverse the validity of the information was sometimes a little doubtful.

Fazli was quiet in temperament and did not volunteer information about himself or volunteer responses in class. However, he took his learning seriously, attended regularly and did his best to fulfill the teacher's expectations.

An early page (Figure 3) from Fazli's notebook (week two of the course) shows his ability to do close copying. The teacher had asked the class to copy the numerals one to ten from a list on the blackboard. Fazli had worked slowly, copying faithfully, but was still writing number nine when the list was wiped clean from the board. He sought confirmation that his effort at nine was correct and asked for help with "ten." He then borrowed a neighbour's exercise book to check that he had the other numbers correct. His neighbour, however, a Spanish-speaking woman, had transliterated the numbers into a semi-cursive style. Fazli copied down this second set of numbers carefully reconstructing and in fact unwittingly exaggerating such features as the tail on the letter "t." See, for example, the word "fourteen" in Figure 3. This suggested to me that he had not at that point developed the idea of a constant underlying the different letter variations but was producing drawn icons.

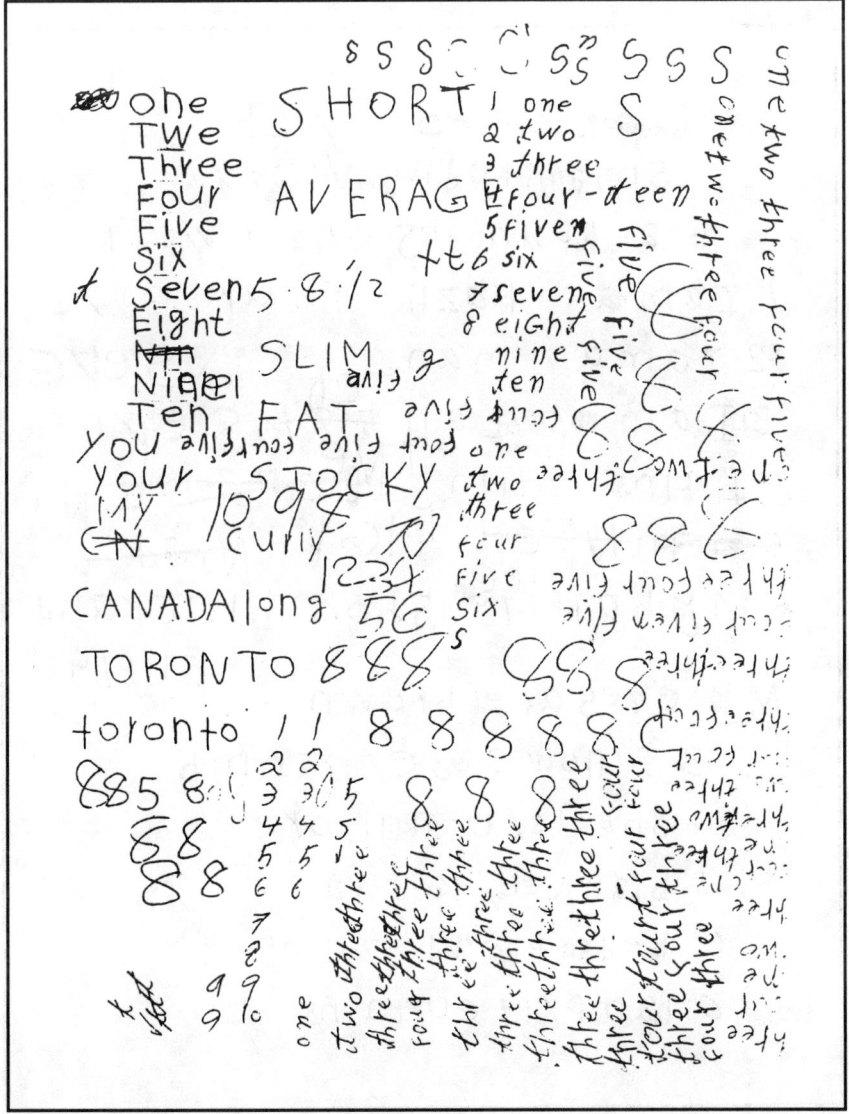

Figure 3: Fazli's copybook, Week 2 (reduced).

Following this attempt, Fazli proceeded to spend the rest of the lesson practising the new letter forms over and over in all directions on his page. It is interesting to note here that, although he did not observe the convention of writing in a single direction, he did consistently begin at the left margin of the page as it is held at any given moment.

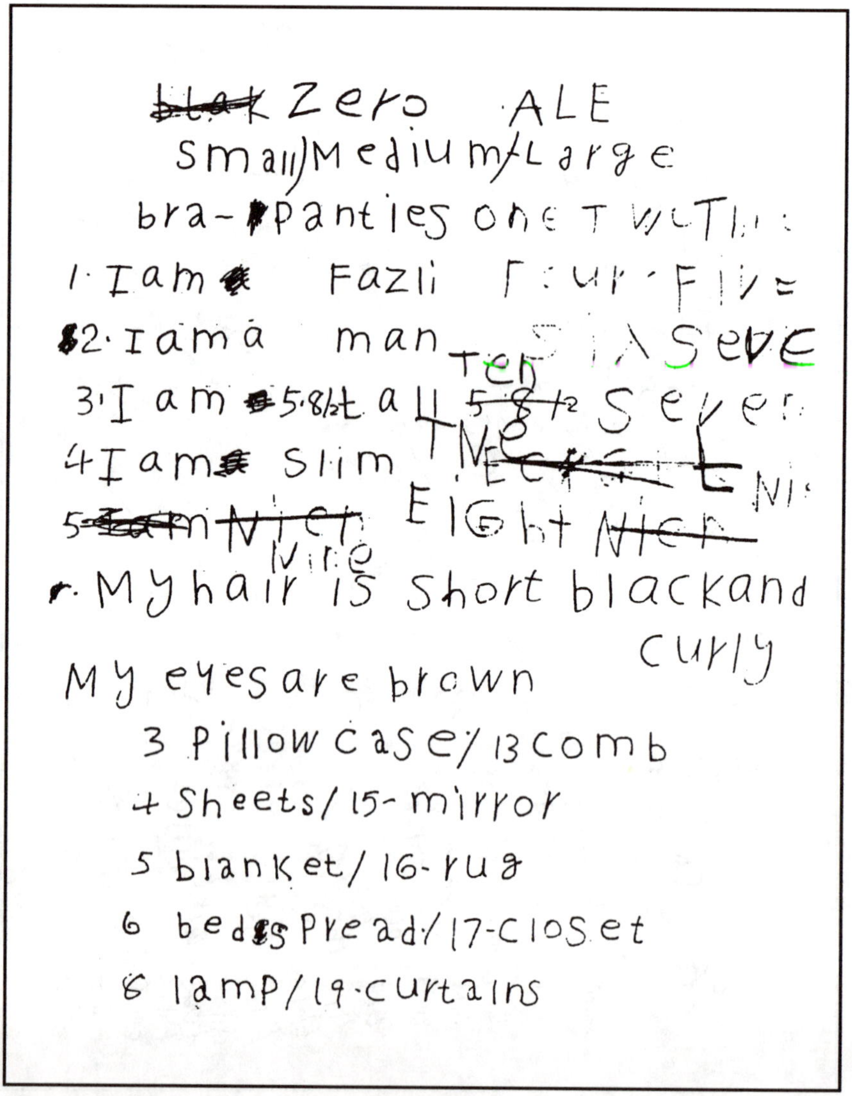

```
black  Zero      ALE
Small/Medium/Large
bra-Panties  one T wcTh
1. I am    Fazli  four·Five
$2. I am a   man     Seve
                   Ten
3. I am 5.8½t all 5-8½ Seven
4. I am slim
                 Eight Nier
5.          Nire
r. My hair is short black and
                            curly
My eyes are brown
    3 pillow case/ 13 comb
    4 sheets/ 15- mirror
    5 blanket/ 16- rug
    6 bedspread/ 17-closet
    8 lamp/ 19-curtains
```

Figure 4: Fazli's copybook, Week 5 (reduced).

It is difficult to know how much meaning these shapes had for Fazli. He had a good enough eye to recognize when his drawn shape did not match the model provided and spent a long time struggling with the digit "8" trying to get the curves correct. However, he made no attempt to match word and digit except for the original copying task when both were copied simultaneously. The general impression is more one of handwriting practice than of any attempt to use written repetition as a way of learning the words or of relating the two forms.

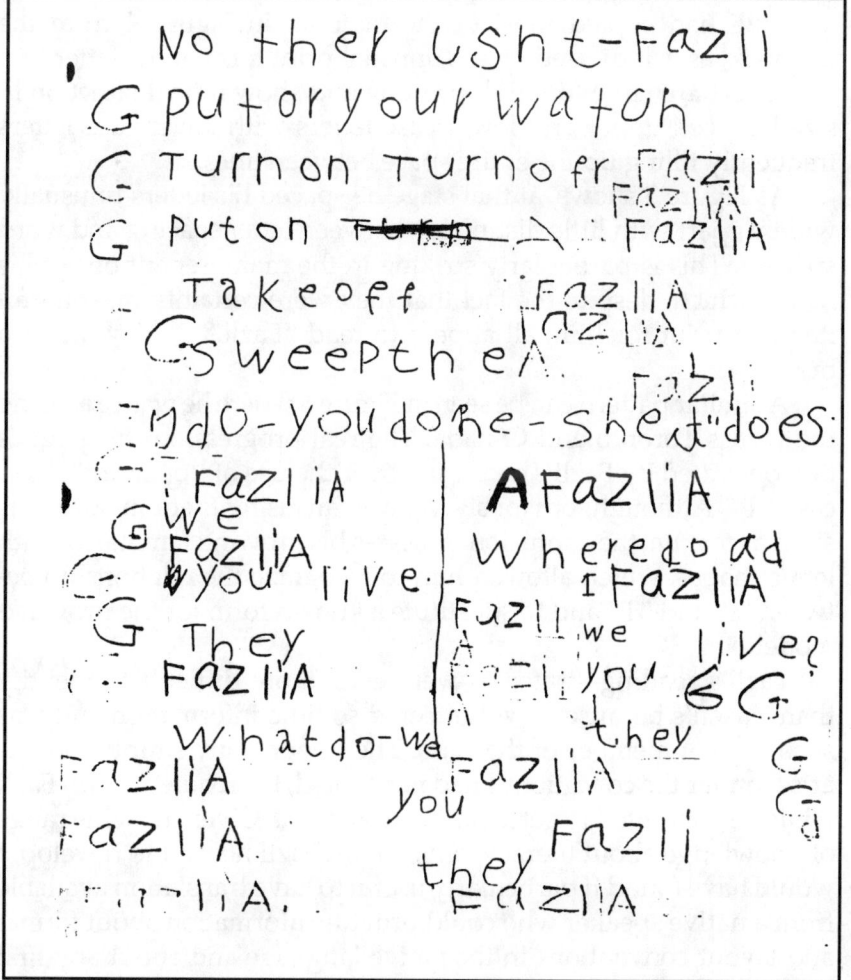

Figure 5: Fazli's copybook, Week 5 (reduced).

On his later work, some progress is apparent. The page is no longer rotated and he has attempted to work along the lines. As Figure 4 demonstrates, by the fifth week of the course, he was still not observing the conventions of layout, which would suggest a new line for each new item. The attitude to blank space demonstrated in this example may, of course, be culturally determined by a thrifty use of paper and perhaps should not be taken as being too significant. However, it was a pattern that none of the literate class members demonstrated, no matter how poverty-stricken their backgrounds.

Fazli had copied most of the material in Figure 4 from the textbook, as is indicated by the unusual print form of the letter "a." His letters are large for adult printing and show little distinction in size between upper and lower case letters with lower case letters frequently filling up the entire space between lines.

As Figure 5 shows, at that stage he spaced his letters unusually widely apart with little distinction between letter spacing and word spacing. This is particularly striking in the many repetitions of his name, which, despite the fact that they were certainly meaningful items of print for him, all appear to read "FazliA____" without a break.

A similar pattern can be seen in Figure 6 where he was practising the words Toronto and Canada. The real progress on this page is demonstrated by Fazli's confusion over the use of upper and lower case "T." Although, obviously, he was misusing them in such versions as *toronto*, the confusion indicates his growing familiarity with letter shapes, which allowed him to recognize the relationship between "t" and "T" and to substitute a known form for the provided model.

Fazli's reading strategies were even more difficult to identify than Yusefi's because he volunteered so little information and was such a quiet member of the class. The opportunity simply did not arise, under the conditions I had negotiated, to sit quietly with Fazli while he attempted to get meaning from print. Given the wide range of knowledge about literacy, which I felt Fazli needed to develop, I would have found it particularly useful to have translation available from a native speaker who could provide information about format and layout conventions in the native language and about any first language literacy skills that Fazli may have had.

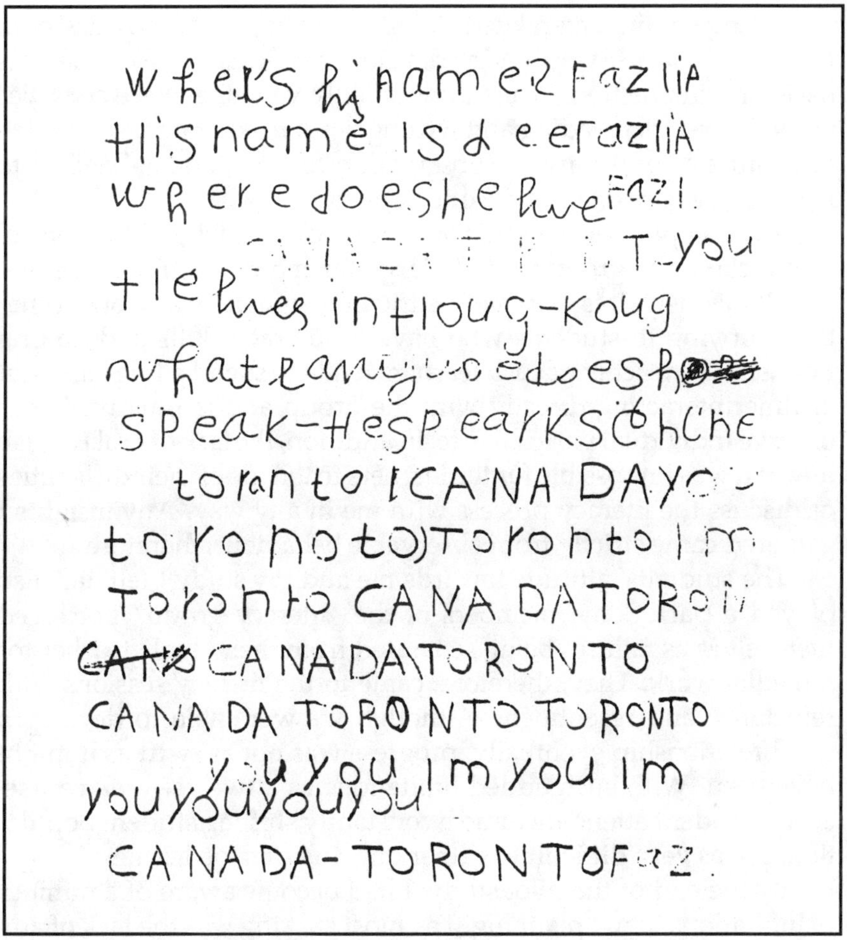

```
wheI's hi name? FazliA
tlis name is d eerazliA
where doeshe hveFazl.
                    T-you
tle hies intloug-koug
what ranyu·s edoesho
speak-Hespearkschche
toronto ICANA DAYo-
to ro no to)Toronto Im
Toronto CANA DATOR·N
CANS CA NA DA\TO RO N TO
CA NA DA TORO NTO TJ RONTO
         you you Im you Im
youyouyouyou
CA NA DA- TO RON TOFaz.
```

Figure 6: Fazli's copybook, Week 8 (reduced).

Summary of results of the pilot study

This study did not give me the kind of information about literacy that I had hoped I might be able to obtain. In particular, I felt very disappointed with the superficial picture of the students' progress, which was all that I was able to gather. I ascribed the problem to a number of flaws in the design of the study, which had restricted the type of data to which I had access. My position as teacher aide for another teacher meant I had little control over the content that was being presented to the class or the instructional practices. Activities such as language experience stories, which would have involved a wide range of literacy-related skills, were not part of the classroom routines. Instead, vocabulary development was stressed, as was basic oral interaction. While undoubtedly valuable, these activities tended to restrict reading and writing work to copying tasks, which gave little opportunity for observation of the students' ability to make sense of print or to decode or encode.

Another problem was that on those occasions when I had control of the class, the group was too large for me to teach and observe simultaneously. It is extremely difficult to assign "seat work" other than copying to students who have no literacy skills and no oral English. The teacher of such learners tends to spend a large amount of time interacting directly with the group and is thus unable to observe individual performance. In addition, the lack of oral English meant it was impossible for the learners to tell me of their difficulties or discuss the literacy process with me in any way. Any insights I gathered came strictly from observable behaviour, therefore.

The students' attitude towards me and my study I felt had also played a part. Some members of the "literacy group" perceived themselves as failures being separated from their "real" teacher for remedial work. They, therefore, came to the literacy sessions with reluctance and resentment. Although we were able to develop a good relationship eventually, progress was not as swift as it might have been. With such added limitations as a twelve-week course, erratic student attendance and a constantly shifting student population, it was very difficult to gather ongoing data on learners.

By the end of the pilot study, I had become aware of a number of limitations in my planning. The most striking was the lack of any acknowledgment that literacy is more than simply a possession. Literacy was understood as something you have, not something you are. There was no suggestion that literacy is something that is lived out in people's lives; and consequently there was an apparent lack of interest in the lives of Yusefi and Fazli outside of the classroom. There was minimal acknowledgment that literacy may have an individual or personal component, but instead an assumption that literate patterns of behaviour developed in one language would manifest themselves with little or no change in the second language. The attitudes I manifested in planning this study were in essence those that I had depicted in a book for teachers, which I had co-authored in 1984, *A Handbook for ESL Literacy* (Bell & Burnaby, 1984).

My understanding of literacy did not appear to have grown in the interim.

At the time I carried out the pilot study, I was just beginning my doctoral studies and had never really felt a need to think through what literacy was, or what it entailed. My work in teacher education had rested on the assumption that I, and the teachers I worked with, all shared a common sense understanding of the topic. We focused on methods and materials without ever considering exactly what it was we were trying to teach. These assumptions about literacy, it appears, operated almost as a folk-model (D'Andrade, 1987) in that they seemed to be part of an unquestioned stock of cultural knowledge. I am amazed in retrospect that my own experiences as an ESL teacher did not alert me to some of the limitations of this model of literacy. Where did this common sense understanding come from? I imagine there must have been an individual experiential component, based on my own literacy development, but in large part I find that my assumptions about literacy are reflected in the way the topic is presented in the popular media.

Whether such media coverage shapes a society's perceptions or merely reflects them is not of critical importance here. However, I would suggest that the way in which we understand literacy is culturally determined. As I shall explore in the next chapter, the understanding of literacy demonstrated in the popular press of North America demonstrates most of the assumptions that underpinned the pilot study quoted above.

Chapter Two

Trying to come to terms with the literature

The understanding of literacy demonstrated in the popular press

As I suggested in the last chapter, when I look back at the assumptions about literacy that shaped the pilot study, it seems that my understanding of the term was influenced less by personal experience than by its use in common parlance. The terms used in the pilot study suggest that if I had been asked to offer a definition of literacy at that time, I would have focused on the skills of reading and writing and their use to allow for the transfer of a piece of information.

I might then well have come up with a definition such as, "Literacy may be defined as the ability to read and write a simple message," (Fondacaro & Higgins, 1985. 73), or "A person is literate who can with understanding both read and write a short simple statement on his daily life" (Thomas, 1983. 19).

By endorsing such definitions, I would, I think, have been making a number of unstated assumptions. Primarily, I would have been assuming that literacy can be defined in terms of skills and of actions. Locating literacy in this way makes it comparable to a learned physical skill such as learning to swim. I would have acknowledged that it is possible to read or write more or less fluently and efficiently, just as it is possible to swim at a variety of degrees of proficiency. However, just as common parlance acknowledges a point at which a person can swim—that is, he or she can stay afloat and not sink—so I think I would have argued for a point at which a person could "read."

I might even have taken the analogy one step further and compared the ability to swim in different water conditions as being comparable to working with different texts, or the ability to use a variety of swimming strokes as paralleling reading and writing in different languages, thus allowing myself to explain how a person could be literate in one context and not in another.

As I will be exploring in this chapter, any definition of literacy that describes it as merely a set of skills is highly restricted. Where did I develop such a restricted understanding of the term and why did I hold to it, despite my classroom exposure to a variety of learners, which might have brought me to recognize the numerous other factors that play a part in literacy? Essentially, this view of literacy is the traditional one, which has been in common usage for many years. The definition of how complex a task one might be asked to perform in reading or writing in order to earn the label "literate" has changed historically (Graff, 1979, 1981), but the understanding of literacy as being manifested in print skills has largely remained standard.

To a large extent this is also the understanding of literacy that we see in the popular press and other media of North America. The current resurgence of interest in the "back-to-basics" movement in education has caused the term "literacy" to be freely used in the media, thus affecting what we might call the layman's definition, and making literacy a sensitive area prone to political pressure. Although literacy in this context is understood to relate strictly to interaction with print (almost always alphabetic print), and describes the ability to sound out and take meaning from a written message and to encode a message in a format that can be understood by others of the community, it is commonly presented as part of a much larger economic and political package.

Literacy in this context is normally set in opposition to "illiteracy," defined as the inability to fulfil societal demands related to print. Illiteracy itself is commonly presented as a deficiency state remedied by the introduction of formal education.

The language used in media discussions of literacy

It is noticeable that the pervasive metaphor for this discussion in the media is one of battle. A survey of newspapers, journals and television broadcasts will routinely demonstrate examples as "the war against illiteracy," "literacy crusade," and "ways of combating workplace illiteracy," amongst many more.

Lakoff and Johnson's work (1980) would suggest that the use of language like this shapes our understanding of the topic. It is difficult to conceive of literacy as a broad continuous spectrum of human activity and thought when it has been split into opposing factions in a war situation. The combatant metaphor thus encourages the sense of a clear divide between literacy and illiteracy, and hence a distinction between those with and without literacy skills. War also implies an enemy, commonly an enemy that dangerously threatens our way of life. Illiteracy thus becomes a dangerous and threatening condition that should be attacked and destroyed before it damages the very fabric of society.

The surface rationale for portraying illiteracy as a threat to society relates to the fact that in North American society, low levels of education correlate with poverty (Ross, 1981), and crime (US Department of Justice, 1983), and there has been a tendency to see this association as a causal relationship.

Alden (1982) argues for a different purpose that this perception of a causal relationship has directly affected the way in which literacy education is offered. He suggests that the predominant philosophies of recent years assume that an individual's lack of literacy excludes him or her from the labour market and thus from the opportunity of financial advantage. The provision of literacy training is thus seen as "a neutral technical matter of remedial skill acquisition" (Alden, 1982. 10) to remedy a deficit position. However, because the need for literacy education is seen in this view as tightly related to the labour market and thus to the demands of the economy, the kind of education likely to be offered under such philosophies will focus on socializing the learner to perform more adequately within the work force rather than on individual development.

Attempts to define literacy and illiteracy

Language such as that drawn from the combatant metaphor, which postulates a divide between literacy and illiteracy, forces an attempt to designate some point on the spectrum of literate behaviour where one ends and the other begins. Such a split is also encouraged when literacy education is designed to serve the interests of business rather than the individual. Programs will then tend to be shaped to fit financial and temporal commitments on the part of funders, leading to restrictions on acceptable candidates for entry, easily measured criteria for program success, etc.

One key result of this type of language and of the resulting search for easily defined categories is that we are encouraged to see not merely a distinction between literacy and illiteracy but between literate and illiterate people. Although we might not yet be in a position to offer a satisfactory definition of exactly what literacy might involve, we are surely already able to recognize that such distinctions are artificial and of limited value. Nonetheless, the assumption that it is possible to draw such a distinction between literate and illiterate people is so deeply held that much of the debate has centred on the accuracy of the distinction rather than its value.

A variety of approaches have been demonstrated by those who attempt to specify where such a boundary might lie, ranging from statistical data, through expert witness to formal testing. As I will attempt to demonstrate, the idea of a split between literate and illiterate is so deeply ingrained in our thinking that we do not discard the notion lightly. Instead we seek to rephrase the distinction or to argue for a different approach to it.

One common way of determining the boundary of literacy is to use the criterion of years of completed education. Writers have suggested variously that one should be able to access most print material on completion of grade five (see Thomas, 1989; Johnson, 1985), or that the complexity of such everyday documents as government forms or newspapers would demand a minimum grade twelve education (Kozol, 1985; Chall, 1984; Draper, 1985).

The advantages of this use of grade level as a yardstick relate to the ease with which data can be gathered from existing statistical sources, such as the Census, or immigration documents. Grade school equivalencies are also terms that are widely familiar to the general public, thus allowing for easy reference in government speeches, or easy quotability in media reports. Even proponents of this method of defining literacy acknowledge, however, that years of attendance in school do not necessarily guarantee the meeting of any particular reading or writing standards even as measured by academic tests.

When I first started to use the term literacy to refer to the kind of basic level reading and writing I was doing with my students, as far as I can tell, the meanings I attributed to the term were those described above. Certainly in my co-authored text, *A Handbook for ESL Literacy* (Bell & Burnaby, 1984), I make use of similar statistics to argue the need for literacy education.

> Of Canadian residents whose first language is neither English nor French, 88.8% have less than a grade eight education, which is normally considered the minimum for functional literacy, or sufficient reading and writing skills to cope with daily life. This refers of course to first language literacy and we can safely assume that the proportion of functional literacy in English is even less. (p. 1)

Later in the same text, I acknowledge the limitations of using grade equivalency scores to assess adults and suggest instead that, "It can be helpful when assessing [students'] needs to consider them as falling into one or more of the following groups" (p. 3).

I go on to provide descriptions and student profiles for illiterate, semi-literate, non-functionally literate, and non-Roman alphabetic students. An interesting point related to this section concerns the use of terminology. When I wrote the first draft of this text, I labelled these profiles, "Illiterates," "Semi-literates," and so on. More than one of the people who reviewed my manuscript put me straight in no uncertain terms, that by using such adjectives as nouns, I was offensively defining people as if their literacy abilities were the only significant feature about them. My use of the terms reflected, I think, the common language used in the media.

I am still a little ambivalent about the offensiveness of such terms. We commonly define people as adolescents, immigrants, non-swimmers, Chinese and so on, without offence. The offensive element lies not in the grammatical feature but in the negative stereotype attached to literacy problems. This links directly back to the use of war language and the sense of a divide between literates and non-literates.

In using the four categories of illiterate, semi-literate, non-functionally literate and non-Roman alphabetic to describe literacy skills I was, of course, demonstrating that such divisions were embedded in my thinking. I not only parroted the division between literate and illiterate but tried to carve up those divisions even more closely. The rather confusing and inconsistent descriptions of what features are associated with different levels of literacy suggest that I found this categorization task difficult, especially when I tried to address the question of functional literacy.

The term "functional literacy" is, as far as I am aware, first defined by Gray in a UNESCO publication (Gray, 1956). Drawing on the worldwide experience of literacy programs in many countries, Gray acknowledges openly the tremendous difficulties in prescribing standards for such varied situations. Talking of potential candidates for literacy programs, he writes, "Their level of achievement, needs, and aspirations vary widely in relation to anthropological and geographic factors, and the social, political and economic forces that act within and upon the community" (Gray, 1956. 22). Gray goes on to suggest that the minimum standards for literacy, which had been in use prior to that time, be replaced with an understanding of the need for functional literacy. He suggests that the criterion be:

> A person is functionally literate when he has acquired the knowledge and skills in reading and writing which enable him to engage effectively in all those activities in which literacy is normally assumed in his culture or group. (Gray, 1956. 24)

A later UNESCO publication contrasts the minimal literacy demand of reading and writing, with the functional demand of using literacy to interact with the community. However, the circularity of the definition limits its usefulness:

> A person is literate who can with understanding both read and write a short simple statement on his everyday life. A person is functionally literate who can engage in all those activities in which literacy is required for everyday functioning of his group and community and also enabling him to continue to use reading, writing and calculation for his own and the community's development. (Thomas, 1983. 19)

To define the state of being literate by saying it allows one to engage in activities in which literacy is required does not of itself increase our understanding of the term. The definition, therefore, addresses the level of functionality rather than the meaning of literacy itself.

More recently attempts to determine functional literacy have been competency-based and essentially tried to identify the kind of activities for which literacy is required. The *Southam Report on Illiteracy* (Creative Research Group, 1987), which made Canadian headline news in 1987, attempted to "...provide a comprehensive assessment of the literacy performance of adult Canadians, which both recognizes the complexity of information processing skills and provides a relevant context in which to assess these skills" (p. 5). The survey's definition of functional literacy was, "...the ability to use printed and written information to function in society," (Calamai, 1987) with a jury of twenty-four Canadians functioning as expert witnesses in selecting tasks that they felt were fundamental to daily life in North America.

In the report this definition was then used to justify an announcement that an "astonishing" twenty-four per cent of the Canadian population is illiterate, with the proportion being as high as forty-four per cent in Newfoundland. It would appear to be self evident that such a large proportion of the population cannot be deemed incapable of fulfilling the demands of daily life when the individuals concerned continue to function and support themselves, hence the validity of the Southam measure must be queried as well as the assumptions that underlie their approach.

Assumptions demonstrated in the popular press

The texts I have drawn on so far are all written for the general reader and they reflect the broad understanding of the term "literacy," which I held when I began graduate study in this area. As I have tried to show, the non-specialist press presents a picture of literacy that rests on a number of unexamined assumptions. Essentially these are:

1. Literacy stands in opposition to a condition known as illiteracy;

2. Literacy can be defined in terms of skills and abilities;

3. These skills and abilities relate to printed or written material;

4. Illiteracy presents a danger to society;

5. People can be classified as literate or illiterate and a division between these two states can be defined.

When I first turned to the specialist literature, as far as I can now tell, I was just beginning to challenge some of these assumptions. My classroom experience suggested that literacy might include more than simple print skills. My struggles and inconsistencies in attempting to categorize degrees of literacy had made me question the divisions of the popular press. I had not yet reconstructed a new meaning of literacy, so I turned to texts in psychology, anthropology, history and other disciplines, looking for a new way of understanding literacy.

Considering the academic literature

I was initially somewhat daunted to discover that one of the most striking aspects of discussions of literacy is the lack of agreement regarding the use of the term. It seemed that I read text after text which began by asking what literacy might be. "Just what is literacy? What are its functions and aims?" (de Castell, Luke & MacLennan, 1986. 3). "What is literacy? The task of definition now becomes devilishly difficult" (Thomas, 89. 3). "What is Literacy?" (Gee, 1991). "Although literacy is a pressing national concern we have yet to discover or set its boundaries" (Scribner, 1984. 6).

I found also that other writers ask the same question less directly, challenging instead what they see as the simplistic assumption that we do understand literacy. Langer (1987) writes,

> Many scholars, as well as the general public, have regarded literacy somewhat narrowly—as the ability to read and write and get on at some minimal 'functional' level in day-to-day life and work...because of this restricted view, our solutions to very pragmatic issues of literacy learning and instruction have suffered, as have national interpretations of literacy-in-society for policy and planning. (p. 1)

Street comments that,

> A surprising number of general arguments about society, language and thought appear to rest upon claims made, whether implicitly or explicitly regarding the nature of literacy. It is assumed that we 'know' what literacy is and can therefore appeal to it in the resolution of more uncertain areas of knowledge. (1984. x)

Olson (1986) extends this argument, noting that as early as 1951, Harold Innis "...pointed out that our relentless concerns with achieving and improving literacy have blinded us to any clear analysis of the nature and consequences of literacy." He continues, "Rather than see literacy as a solution to every other problem, Innis helped turn literacy into a problem, indeed a central problem in understanding ourselves and our modern world" (Olson, 1986. 109).

Following Innis, an upsurge of interest in literacy has been reflected in a spate of publications in fields including education, psychology, sociology, classical studies, philosophy and anthropology. However, each discipline appears to have its own understanding of what it means to be literate. In part, this confusion over terms reflects the complexity of the phenomenon. Levine comments that on attempting to define literacy,

> An endless series of disagreements and controversies will be encountered, which reflect the fact that we are dealing with a complex amalgam of psychological, linguistic and social processes layered one on top of another like a rich and indigestible gateau. Different varieties of academic specialists cut slices out of this cake with the conceptual equipment their disciplinary training has taught them to favour. (Levine, 1986. 22)

The risks of these incomplete definitions are pointed out by Scribner:

> The definitional controversy has more than academic significance. Each formulation of an answer to the question, 'What is literacy?' leads to a different evaluation of the scope of the problem (i.e. the extent of illiteracy) and to different objectives for programs aimed at the formation of a literate citizenry. Definitions of literacy shape our perceptions of individuals who fall on either side of the standard (what a 'literate' or 'non-literate' is like) and thus in a deep way affect both the substance and the style of educational programs. (Scribner, 1984. 6)

Because definitions will directly affect the way in which literacy education is viewed, it becomes particularly important that our understanding of literacy be as well rounded as possible. The evidence seems to be that much of the debate has been conducted along multidisciplinary lines rather than interdisciplinary ones. Klassen (1988) comments on, "...the lack of theoretical integration in discussions of literacy," while Levine claims that, "The topic's sprawl across several disciplines results in identical issues being discussed in quite separate contexts with different vocabularies" (Levine, 1986. 6). In this fragmented discussion, it appears that there has been an ethnocentric division as well as a disciplinary one.

Narasimhan (1987) argues that the debate has so far focused almost exclusively on Western models of literacy. Citing the work of a varied mix of historians, classicists, and psycholinguists, he asks, "To what extent would these conclusions remain valid if other non-Western traditions are analyzed along similar lines?"

Scollon and Scollon make a similar point. "It is striking how little Asian literacy is mentioned in general discussions of literacy . . . this is in itself an indication of the nearly complete identification of literacy with the European essayist style" (Scollon and Scollon, 1981. 45).

Ong comments that, "Almost all the work thus far . . . has contrasted orality with alphabetic writing rather than other writing systems (cuneiform, Chinese characters, the Japanese syllabary, Mayan script, and so on) and has been concerned with the alphabet as used in the West" (1982. 3).

This compartmentalized approach to understanding the phenomenon, and the tendency for writers in various disciplines to use the same words to represent quite different meanings has considerably hampered fruitful research or discussion, as has been noted by those like Graff (1986), and de Castell, Luke and MacLennan (1986), who attempt to place the term within a contextual or historical perspective. Graff claims that, "Discussions about literacy are surprisingly facile. . . they have no appreciation of the conceptual complications that the subject of literacy presents" (1986. 63).

Trying to situate my study within such a widespread literature posed a distinct problem for me. When I first began to read the academic literature it seemed that it organized itself according to the discipline of the authors; those with backgrounds in sociology argued for a view of literacy as a process of socialization; cognitive scientists discussed strategies and concepts involved in literate performances; educators argued over the existence of predetermined stages in literacy development.

Anthropologists, historians, philosophers and classical scholars also seemed to have their own conception of what literacy might be.

I was reminded of the story of the blind men asked to describe an elephant, where each one offers a contradictory description based on whether he happened to touch the tail, the trunk or the leg. Rather than holding all these views in opposition to each other, I wanted to see them as related—to get some sense of the whole elephant by at least recognizing the relationship between the parts being described.

I began a second attempt to organize the literature, this time grouping writers according to the questions they had framed regarding literacy. Essentially, it seemed to me that in addition to the attempt to define form, which I have already discussed, the literature on literacy could be subsumed under three questions:

1. How does literacy develop?
2. What are its functions?
3. What are its effects?

The development of literacy

As one would expect from such a multidisciplinary literature, writers and researchers have addressed the development of literacy from a number of viewpoints. Whereas traditionally literacy has been considered to begin with letter recognition in the primary school grades, a relatively recent development has been the acknowledgment that literacy learning begins at a much younger age, and a resultant inquiry into literacy practices among very young children.

Writers such as Schieffelin and Cochrane Smith (1984), Cochrane Smith (1986), Heath (1982), and Anderson and Stokes (1984), have used ethnographic approaches to suggest that children are socialized to literacy at a very young age through exposure to societal patterns of interaction with print.

Other writers, such as Ferreiro and Teberosky (1982), Ninio and Bruner (1978), Snow and Goldfield (1982), and Curtis (1986), have looked at the relationship between literacy and cognitive development in young children, exploring the strategies and concepts that such children demonstrate as they attempt to read or write.

Other writers on the development of literacy in pre-school children, such as Wells (1986), Harste, Woodward and Burke (1984), and Taylor (1989), do not restrict their observations to either a psychological or a sociological viewpoint, but attempt to observe the overall picture looking at young children's linguistic and cognitive growth within a social setting.

The writers cited above have largely focused their attention on the early development of literacy, that is the period in which learners cannot use print independently to express or understand meaning. Those aspects of literacy development that involve increasing confidence and fluency in the use of print have, of course, attracted the attention of educators for many years, and there is a considerable literature that describes ways in which reading and writing skills may be developed and/or taught. (See for instance, Chall, 1983a, 1983b; Clay, 1979; Mason & Au, 1986.)

Other writers who have focused on increasing fluency in reading and writing have looked less at teaching methodologies than at attempts to identify the cognitive strategies that are employed. Kintsch and VanDijk (1978), Flower and Hayes (1980), Just and Carpenter (1980), and Kintsch and Greene (1978), suggest cognitive models by which the process of reading might be understood, while others such as Scardamalia and Bereiter (1983, 1985), Scardamalia, Bereiter and Steinbach (1984), attempt to identify specific cognitive strategies, and link those to educational practice. A third aspect to the literature on the development of literacy argues the position that literacy skills develop in accordance with linguistic or metalinguistic development. (Herriman, 1986; Kaplan, 1983)

Functions of literacy

Once literacy has developed, what is its function? This question tends to be addressed comparatively. Historians, such as Stock (1983), and Graff (1979, 1981), have looked at the uses of literacy in different eras, using evidence such as surviving documentation to trace changes over long time periods.

Others such as Hoggart (1957), Levine (1986), Hamilton and Stasinopoulos (1987), Hunter and Harman (1979), have focused on those who have limited literacy development in an implicit comparison with the mainstream societies in which they live.

A similar comparative approach underlies the work of anthropologists and ethnographers who have demonstrated the wide variety of functions for which different communities use literacy. (See for instance, Delgado-Gaitan, 1994, 1996; Heath, 1983, Fishman, 1988; Kulick & Stroud, 1993; Schieffelin & Gilmore, 1986; Smith, 1986; and Street, 1984, 1993.) At an individual level, Neilsen, (1989) compares functions of literacy for three mainstream Canadians.

The functions of literacy have attracted relatively little interest from the field of psychology, although a point that is interesting for me as a second language researcher is made by Scribner and Cole (1981), who note that individuals who are literate in more than one script or language tend to have different functions for literacy in each system.

Effects of literacy

In the literature on the effects of literacy, we find once again that the academic background of the writers affects the kinds of questions that they ask. The issue of whether literacy has cognitive effects on individuals has been discussed by Olson, (1977, 1978, 1986), Vygotsky (1978), Goody (1977), and Scribner and Cole (1981), among others. While some suggest that we may be confounding the effects of formal education with those of literacy, others claim a clear cognitive effect, which has in turn affected society, a position in which they are supported by classical scholars such as Havelock (1963, 1987), Ong (1977), and anthropologists such as Goody and Watt (1963).

Historians have tended to look more directly at the effects of literate practices on society, citing the ways in which institutions such as the judicial system or the church changed in response to the widespread adoption of literacy (Stock,1983; Graff, 1981), or the effects of the printing press (Eisenstein, 1979).

The effects of literacy on language have also been considered. Feldman (1987), Lord (1960), and Havelock (1987), have drawn their conclusions from comparisons with languages or literary forms, which are predominantly oral. Others such as Tannen (1982a, 1982b), Chafe (1985), Hildyard and Hidi (1985), and Stubbs (1980), have compared written and spoken text in current usage.

Reassessing the literature

In my attempts to relate my study to the literature, I found it reassuring to discover that some of the relationships among this vast literature could be demonstrated in this way, but I did not find that such an organizational scheme was totally successful. Where, for instance, would one locate writers such as Innis (1951) and McLuhan (1962)? They have challenged the assumption that societies can be classified as literate or oral, suggesting instead a shifting pattern of predominantly oral or literate behaviour. Are the writings of Hirsch (1987), or Estes, Gutman and Estes (1989), relevant to this debate, when they discuss the kinds of background knowledge that should be considered a concomitant of literacy?

Many of the writers I was attempting to categorize did not fall neatly into a single pigeonhole. Their studies may have tried to link, for instance, the forms of literacy with its effects, and recognizing such relationships was critical to understanding their position. Without a clear understanding of how the literature related, it was not possible for me to place my own work within that literature.

I began to look for another way of characterizing the literature—one that would avoid oversimplifying complex arguments, but that would still allow me to express arguments simply. Above all I wanted a method of conceptualization that explored the relationships among this massive literature rather than one that merely listed differences.

The answer seemed to lie in the development of commonplaces for literacy. Commonplaces, which have their roots in Aristotle's *Topica*, are the set of fundamental elements that are essential to any complete discussion or description of a topic. As I describe in the next chapter, I felt that if I could identify those elements that are common to all discussions of literacy, I would have a valuable tool to help me see the relationships in this complex literature.

Chapter Three

Using commonplaces to come to terms with the literature

Developing commonplaces

As outlined in the previous chapter, my attempts to place my study within the massive literature on the subject of literacy were hampered by the variety of terms, assumptions and approaches exhibited in the writings. Before I could see my own study in relation to the literature, I needed to feel more confident that I had a clear understanding of what the relationships might be among this multidisciplinary body of writing.

In "The Nature of Scientific Enquiry," Herron (1971) discusses a somewhat similar problem he faced in conceptualizing the various modes of scientific inquiry. He describes how a review of the literature allowed him to recognize that most accounts of scientific inquiry were built around certain common terms—"a lexicon of elements that may be said to be essential to any complete characterization of scientific enquiry" (p. 178). Herron designated these elements "commonplaces" and went on to describe their potential value through the following metaphor.

> The situation might be likened to a game of 'mosaic-making' in which all participants must use the same given universe of pieces. A player is not required to construct a 'complete' mosaic and hence need not use all the pieces at his disposal. The individuality of each 'artist's' mosaic resides in the permutations and combinations of the pieces set *in relationship to one another* [my italics]. Our position in this 'game' would be to identify and describe each of the available pieces in such a way that our account will be useful in characterizing any one of the mosaics in terms of the pieces used in its construction and the manner in which they relate to one another. (Herron, 1971. 178)

Herron goes on to suggest that the set of terms must be "...patient of a variety of points of view. This is a most important restriction, for it follows that such a set of terms must be as nearly devoid of inherent specialized meaning as possible" (p. 178).

Herron was able to demonstrate that his set of terms could be used not only to describe (with minimal bias) alternative models of scientific enquiry but also to demonstrate the commonalities and the differences of a variety of models. Such an approach seemed very attractive for a literature as complicated as the one with which I was attempting to deal, and I consequently decided to attempt the development of commonplaces for literacy.

Methodology in developing commonplaces

It should be stressed that I was already familiar with the literature before I attempted to find commonplaces. In the proposal for my thesis, I had summarized much of the literature, grouping writers according to their academic disciplines. As outlined in the previous chapter, I had attempted to reformulate this understanding by considering literacy in terms of form, function, development and effects.

I had done some preliminary exploration also with the idea of grouping writers according to the metaphor that their assumptions seemed to embody. In this I was influenced by the recognition that my personal metaphor had changed dramatically over the course of this study and also by the suggestions of Scribner (Literacy in Three Metaphors, 1984) and Smith (A metaphor for literacy: Creating worlds or shunting information, 1985). None of these approaches seemed to offer me the same potential for locating my own study within the literature, or of understanding how the various writers on literacy could be seen in relation to each other, as that offered by commonplaces.

My first step was to remind myself of how commonplaces worked and what I might expect of them. As well as rereading Herron, I read Enns (1982), who had used commonplaces to conceptualize crisis research. Through Enns, I was reminded of Aristotle's suggestions regarding the use of commonplaces mnemonically and as checklists, and for some time I struggled with this approach but without success. I was not trying to evaluate a literature as being appropriately thorough or not, I was searching for a way to conceptualize it and to explore its relationships.

One experience with commonplaces, which was useful to me, was thinking back to course work I had done in the early days of doctoral study, when we had been asked to work with the four commonplaces of curriculum: *Learner, Teacher, Subject Matter and Milieu*. We had not used these commonplaces to decide whether curriculum writers had covered all the appropriate bases, but as ways of summarizing complex arguments. We had classified writers as being concerned primarily with the interaction of perhaps learner and milieu. We had grown used to defining writers' starting points and their goals in terms of commonplaces. If I could do this for the literature on literacy, I felt I could really come to terms with it.

I selected three preliminary texts to consider in depth, consciously trying to choose pieces that would represent different disciplines and forms of inquiry. The first was Olson's "The cognitive consequences of literacy," (1986), which as its name suggests comes from the discipline of cognitive science and focuses on literacy's effects. The second piece was Freire and Macedo (1987), *Literacy: Reading the Word and the World*, which presents an argument for a particular pedagogical approach informed by critical theory. The third piece was Heath's *Ways With Words* (1983), which is an ethnographic account of the language and literacy practices in two small communities in the Carolinas.

Having read and reread these pieces many times, I listed the terms that seemed to be key for each author. I also wrote out each premise they laid down and searched to identify whether those premises rested on assumptions that were taken for granted. I wrote and rewrote their arguments in more and more general terms and I began to search for commonalities among the various writers. It was obvious, for instance, that *text, interpretation, context, society, hermeneutics* and *epistemology* were important terms for Olson.

Freire seemed to be using the term *word* in a way that matched Olson's *text*, but where was *interpretation*? Could the conceptual shift suggested in Olson be related to the *conscientizaçao* of Freire? Obviously these were not the same concept but could they both be subsumed under some commonplace such as *differentiation*, which implied the learner's discovery of the relationship between subjectivity and objectivity?

My first working hypothesis was that there were four commonplaces for literacy: *Agent, Society, Text and Differentiation*[1]. In my working paper I described the commonplaces as follows:

> *Agent* is the term I am using for the individual demonstrating the literate behaviour under scrutiny. This would include the individual as reader or author of a text. It could also include dictator, scribe, literate thinker, learner, student, and so on. For some writers, agent includes the entire literate segment of a society.
>
> *Society* is the social setting, culture or environment in which the literate behaviour is developed or displayed. Society is commonly perceived as affecting agents and texts in various ways. Society in turn may be affected by agent or by differentiation. Society may have a temporal element as well as a geographic or sociological one.
>
> *Text* is the object of the agent's literate behaviour. This will normally include some form of print or writing but may be defined to include oral language under scrutiny or reflection.
>
> *Differentiation* is the least well defined of the posited commonplaces. I am using the term to suggest a development (usually on the part of the agent) of a recognition that topics formerly considered uniform can be seen as being composed of separate entities. This differentiation commonly relates to the recognition of the dialectical relationship between subjectivity and objectivity.

I began with the assumption that all discussions of literacy would be based on the interplay of these four concepts, with the differences between different writers being suggested by the commonplaces they highlight, their starting points and the direction of interaction or dialectical relationship that they perceive between the commonplaces.

If, for instance, I applied these commonplaces to the Southam survey of adult literacy described in an earlier chapter, I would

---

1 When terms are used as commonplaces, they will be capitalized and italicized.

characterize it as being primarily concerned with *Agent* and *Society*. The report does not demonstrate a sense of literacy as a developmental process, which might imply the kind of personal growth or conceptual change that I was including under *Differentiation*. *Text* is presented as merely the tool by which the literacy user demonstrated his role in society, and is not conceived of as being significant in itself. So, the commonplaces would have allowed us to characterize this piece as focusing on the interaction of *Agent* and *Society*.

One would then go on to ask, "How does this report understand these two commonplaces? What is the relationship it posits between them?" In the case of the Southam report, we might answer by saying that *Agent* is generally understood as a reader or responder to others' literacy, rather than a writer. The report focuses largely on those users whom it classifies as lacking literacy skills. We might thus characterize the report's conception of *Agent* as adult Canadians with minimally developed literacy.

The Society that provides the context for the study is harder to characterize. Readers of Southam Press newspapers were addressed as if they comprised the "mainstream" of Canada, and thus the *Society* against which the literacy performance of the *Agent* is discussed. However, the jury, which Southam Press selected to decide on what level of literacy was required to function in Canadian society, was weighted towards those with expert status. The "problem of illiteracy" is described against an economic background of unemployment, literacy difficulties in the work place, inability to complete government forms, etc. We can thus see that the conception of *Society* found here is not the general Canadian public but the commercial, industrial and bureaucratic sector, which needs to be able to interact with its clients and employees through a print medium.

What relationship does the Southam Report posit between these two commonplaces? Does *Agent* affect *Society*? Can we expect to see government forms written in simplified English and other steps being taken to adapt *Society*'s literacy demands to the abilities of *Agent*? With a few exceptions, Southam assumes the opposite relationship; that is, that *Society* affects *Agent*. The assumption is that *Agent* was given the opportunity of education and if that education proved defective or inadequate for the demands *Society* is now making, *Agent* must adapt to the new demands or suffer marginalization.

Refining the commonplaces

The four commonplaces I originally posited were adequate for at least a preliminary overview of a relatively simple piece such as the Southam Report. However, when I tried to apply the commonplaces to more complex arguments, it was apparent that I had not yet defined an adequate set of terms.

In particular, *Differentiation* was giving me problems. Freire and Olson are not alone in suggesting that the ability to interact with text can produce a new way of thinking. Wells, for instance, argues that the epistemic mode of engagement, in which one "interrogates" the text by considering alternative interpretations, allows one to "make advances in one's intellectual, moral or affective understanding to an extent that would otherwise be difficult or impossible to achieve" (1990. 374).

Langer discusses how literacy makes us "...conscious of the distinctions between discourse meaning and...interpretation," which "...leads to the spiralling change that comes about when people use their literacy skills to think, rethink, and reformulate their knowledge and their worlds" (1987. 4).

I felt that *Differentiation* could include also Bruner's argument that literacy, as a symbolic mode of representation, served as a cultural amplifier (Bruner, 1966, 1972). All these writers, and others, postulate a different way of viewing the world, which arises from the ability to distance oneself from text and see it critically.

It seemed to me that this notion might well be a critical part of literacy and I wanted a commonplace that represented this powerful mental shift. But was this process a commonplace of literacy or did it merely represent a potential that literacy possesses but that is not necessarily realized?

Bereiter and Scardamalia suggest that over 90% of students are on the "low road" to composition, that is, they are not using writing as "an organizing force in their mental development" (1983. 31). Wells (1990) similarly comments that few classroom situations encourage learners to engage text in the epistemic mode, suggesting that one can indeed interact with print without this kind of differentiation.

My doubts about the appropriacy of this fourth commonplace were confirmed when I could find nothing in the Southam Report that related to *Differentiation* at all. Although I did not intend my commonplaces as a checklist, I had nonetheless expected to find some recognition in any text of the components I had defined as key. I was prepared to find that various writers took the presence of such components for granted and failed to explore or define them (as, for instance, the Southam Report does with the commonplace *Text*). However, the total lack of any place for one of my key terms made me suspicious. I was also concerned that this term was too closely tied to *Agent* to be ranked as of equal importance. In my journal, I wrote at the time, "I am aware that this term is somewhat different in kind from the other three, in that it is an attribute of *Agent*, and concerns *Agent's* view of the other two commonplaces."

Other qualms about the tentative commonplaces related to the absence of certain factors such as meaning that seemed intuitively to me to be important. Should *Meaning* be a commonplace, or was the ability to make meaning already included in differentiation? What about learning? Was the term *Agent* adequate? Would it be better replaced by *User*, or should I go back to what had been my original notion of *Reader* and *Writer*?

The only way to discover how useful the commonplaces would be was to use them. Despite some reservations, I went ahead and developed a working paper in which I attempted to consider in depth how Olson and Freire's arguments could be expressed and related to each other through the four tentative commonplaces originally identified.

Rethinking

I was fortunate in having a number of colleagues who were prepared to read my paper and consider the viability of the commonplaces I was proposing. I received a number of suggestions for alternative commonplaces, including *teacher, culture, environment, cultural practice, community, learner, skill, author,* and *development,* each of which I tried to fit into my understanding of the literature in general and my own study in particular.

Through discussion and reflection, a number of points became clearer. The first related to the controversial *Differentiation* commonplace. I had been misled by the coincidence that both Olson and Freire discuss objectivity and subjectivity into assuming that this was a key part of a literacy discussion. *Differentiation* did not merit status as a commonplace; instead, it was a particular author's way of characterizing the interaction of *Agent* with *Text*, or *Agent* with *Society*. One reader suggested that I might consider the more general term *Interaction*, which would embrace differentiation without being restricted to it.

Some of the additional commonplaces suggested to me such as *Culture, Milieu, Setting* and *Environment* all seemed related to my original commonplace of *Society*. I had originally tried working with the term *Culture*, but had replaced it because *Society* seemed to better embrace the fact that the setting for literacy could be a unit as small as the family, for which *Culture* seemed inappropriate.

I began to consider what differences would be implied by the selection of one term over the other. Those terms that had the ability to embrace a temporal notion as well as a geographic one would be valuable for characterizing such aspects of the discussion as historical effects. *Milieu* had the advantage that it could apply to the immediate setting such as the family home, the community or to society at large, which was a critical notion in the discussion of literacy. Another suggestion was that I consider including two societal terms, to cope with the comparative notion found in many literacy discussions. Exploring these ideas made me aware that I had two separate notions embedded in my commonplace *Society*. The first related to the situation in which the *Agent* uses or develops literacy, while the other related to the situation in which the *Text* is encountered.

I reflected on all these suggestions and then went back to the selected texts. It was surprisingly difficult to determine which concepts were key to any understanding of literacy and which ones were specific to particular authors. Obviously, the authors did not necessarily use the same words to refer to the concepts under discussion so that it was not always clear whether one was dealing with a new concept or simply a new label for one particular aspect of an already defined commonplace.

The first stage of attempting to define commonplaces had essentially been one of searching for and identifying concepts that were key to all the authors under scrutiny. For this second stage, I worked in the opposite direction, beginning with a larger number of possible commonplaces and discarding those that could not be identified as being key for my authors. The new list had seven commonplaces in it: *User, Text, Community, Society, Meaning, Context* and *Process*.

Only one commonplace from the original list, i.e. *Text*, remained unchanged in both term and concept. A second commonplace, *User*, was essentially a change of name for the original category *Agent*, the change having been made because *User* seemed a more neutral term. A third term from the original set, *Society*, remained on the list but had changed in its conception.

As suggested earlier, many authors who write about literacy in specific incarnations compare the literacy they are describing with other manifestations of literate behaviour. Sometimes the comparison is explicit, as when ethnographers describe two communities, or historians compare societies over a time span. Frequently, however, the literacy behaviour under scrutiny is implicitly compared with the writer's own assumptions about mainstream practices in the Western world. To allow for this split to be characterized, the original term *Society* was divided into *Community*, (the specific arena of literacy use under discussion) and *Society* (the larger framework of use against which *Community* might be set.)

Another new term I considered was *Context*, or the relation of the part to the whole. Any piece of text sits within a larger context spatially, temporally and conceptually and cannot be meaningfully considered without recognition of that context. The reader or writer both recognizes the context in which the text is implicitly placed, and also brings his or her own context to bear on the text to interact with it according to prior knowledge and expectations that are both socially and individually determined.

Meaning was a term that had been on and off the original list many times. If text could be understood as the form of a message, then the existing commonplaces did not seem to account for meaning. Some of the key arguments in the literature seemed to relate to how meaning was made, and where meaning came from. It seemed that such a key term should be considered for the commonplaces.

The final term was *Process*. None of the original commonplaces allowed for any suggestion of the temporal notion inherent in a developmental view of literacy, and the introduction of this term was an attempt to allow for such a view to be adequately portrayed.

Having drawn up my new list of potential commonplaces, I combed through the selected texts to determine the words and phrases that were key to understanding each author's argument. Then I tried to match each of these key words to one of the chosen or possible commonplaces, noting mismatches, and areas of difficulty. Thus I categorized Olson's term "inference" as an example of my commonplace *Meaning*, but noted that it could also fall under *Process*.

The next stage was to approach the same task from the other angle, that is, I attempted to write out how each of my potential commonplaces had been characterized by each of the authors under discussion. Heath's use of *Process* was thus characterized as the socialization of community members to specific patterns of interaction. Once again areas of difficulty were noted, as in the attempt to determine *Context* for some authors.

Finally, I tried to express each author's argument in terms of my commonplaces and the interactive forces they posited among those commonplaces. Freire was thus summarized as arguing that only when *User* was able to shape *Community* could the *Process* of interacting with *Text* become successful. Once this *Process* was initiated, *User* would begin to shape *Text*, *Community* and *Society*.

Final selection of commonplaces

Having worked through the exercises described above, I re-evaluated my commonplaces, and determined which terms had been key to helping me conceptualize the various arguments under consideration. After considerable thought, I rejected *Context* as a commonplace because it was too vague to be helpful. Valuable though the notion of context is to understanding literacy, it seemed to be better understood as a function of the relationship between two or more of the other commonplaces than as a stand-alone concept.

I also rejected *Meaning* as a commonplace for much the same reasons. It seemed that *Meaning* was essentially subsumed under *Process*, and could be better characterized as a relationship between *Process* and another commonplace.

Finally I recombined my two societal terms, *Society* and *Community*, back into the original commonplace, *Society*. *Community*, I found, was unnecessary, since I could express the necessary arguments within the terms *User* and *Society*, given the flexibility of both notions.

My current hypothesis is, therefore, that there are four commonplaces by which we can understand the literature on literacy. Through these four terms of *User, Text, Society* and *Process*, we can find the common ground in arguments from a variety of academic backgrounds. As I shall shortly attempt to demonstrate by a detailed consideration of works by Olson, Heath and Freire, these terms allow us to explore the relationships between apparently diverse positions, without being misled by different use of vocabulary.

I must acknowledge that this position is still hypothetical. Obviously the attempt to bring such a large and varied literature to terms warrants considerably greater attention than I have had the opportunity to give it in this context. However, I feel that the commonplaces I have identified can serve a valuable heuristic function, even at this relatively rudimentary stage. Certainly this conceptualization has been valuable for my own struggle to place my work within the literature and has allowed me to understand the literature and my contribution to it in a new way.

Using the commonplaces to bring writers to terms

In this section I will try to explore the common ground in the arguments of Olson, Freire and Heath by expressing them through the commonplaces that I have identified above. Following Adler and van Doren, I have called this process of rewriting authors' arguments into a common language, "bringing authors to terms" (Adler & van Doren, 1940/1967. 318).

David Olson

The first piece I will consider is, "The cognitive consequences of literacy," by David Olson (1986). As the title suggests, Olson, a cognitive scientist, is interested in whether (or rather how) the development of literacy produces cognitive change at an individual or societal level. This question has of course been discussed by, among others, Ong (1982), Havelock (1987), and Goody and Watt (1963). By exploring Olson's position in some detail, I shall thus hope to cast light also on those authors who write about literacy with a similar conceptual approach.

Olson's basic argument is that the exposure to literacy leads to a distinction on the part of literacy users between the written form of a text and the variety of interpretations that can be attached to that form. This distinction between what is fixed and what is open to interpretation provides a cognitive concept that is applicable in other areas of life. Olson suggests that historically this cognitive mechanism was used to distinguish between fact and theory, thus allowing for the development of modern science (fact) and modern philosophy (theory).

Olson begins by citing the position developed by a number of historians and classicists that, if considered historically, societies can be seen to have changed as a result of the widespread adoption of literacy. He also cites anthropological evidence from predominantly oral societies to suggest that literate societies have developed cognitively in ways that oral societies have not. He then searches for a mechanism that might explain how both differences could have come about. Based on his own and others' research into the development of young children, he suggests what the missing cognitive mechanism might be.

Before we go on to examine this argument more closely, we can see some assumptions at work here. The first assumption is that the changes that can be documented as having occurred after the widespread adoption of literacy can be assumed to have been caused by that adoption. His task is thus determined to be one of explaining how the causal relationship was effected, rather than considering whether it existed.

> Let us summarize the argument to this point. Even if there was no agreed theory on the role of literacy in social and cognitive change, there was and continues to be a general agreement that literacy, printing and the alphabet, however they did it, were fundamental to those changes.... But how does literacy produce its effects? (p. 111)

A similar assumption of causality is at work when he cites the anthropological evidence.

> The point to note is that the Azande make little distinction between what is said and its interpretation. This is not because they are 'primitive' or 'childlike' but because that distinction is a literate one—one shaped up for dealing with texts. (p. 114)

His third assumption is that some mechanism can be identified that caused those developments or changes, and that that mechanism will be cognitive in nature. (As changes of a cognitive nature can only be assumed to occur at an individual level, there is a further unstated assumption here that cognitive change in sufficient individuals will lead to changes in societal patterns of functioning.)

Olson thus approaches the topic of literacy with certain assumptions about it, which seem to reflect his background and training in cognitive science. He draws, however, on evidence from a variety of sources to support his argument, so that this piece of writing is far more than an account of a psychological experiment. If we consider this argument in terms of the commonplaces, how might we understand what Olson is saying?

Because Olson marries more than one discipline in this argument, his characterization of the commonplaces changes as the argument progresses. For the first part of his argument, he conceives of *User* as the general population of Western Europe in the Middle Ages. As *User* exists within the *Society* of Western Europe at that time period, *User* and *Society* thus become closely allied for this portion of the argument. He follows *User* over a temporal span during which time, he argues, *User* is increasingly exposed to and interacting with *Text*.

> In a word, writing, reading and printing ushered out an oral society and ushered in a literate one, bringing in its wake such dramatic changes as the Reformation and Counter-Reformation, the rise of modern science and modern Cartesian or 'mentalistic' psychology....Why and how did writing, printing, the alphabet and literacy contribute to such a change? That problem, I believe, remains largely unanswered. There is no 'mechanism' as we cognitive scientists say to explain the development...How could literacy generate, cause, produce or invite such things as the Reformation, modern science and Cartesian mentalism, the theory of mind that originated with Descartes and Locke and that remains predominant to this day? (Olson, 1986. 110)

Text is initially conceived of by Olson as a piece of language that can be considered by a *User*. Examples cited include written and printed items such as Lutheran sermons and legal documents but the key example is the Bible. (It should be noted that Olson also uses the word "text" to include oral utterances such as oracles. Thus, we have to distinguish between the commonplace *Text*, which within the bounds of his argument must be printed, and his particular use of the word, which can include oral speech.)

Olson conceives of *Process* as the development of a conceptual distinction between fact or text, and its interpretations.

> A written text preserves only part of the language. What is preserved is the form and the meaning has to be regenerated from that form by the reader.... Writing preserves what is said, the very words, while the meaning or intention is lost and must be reconstructed from the text, context and the like. With writing, meaning and interpretation become a problem. Writing invited the distinction between what a text said and what it meant; the first part is taken as a 'given' the second is taken as the 'interpretation.' (p. 113)

Having argued that *Text* forces a *User* to distinguish between what is given and what is implied, Olson transfers his argument to a different sphere, in which he reconceptualizes the commonplace of *Text*. *Users* who are able to differentiate between text and interpretation he argues, will then apply this conceptual skill elsewhere. *Text* thus becomes the entire world with which *User* interacts, and differentiation allows for the development of hermeneutics and epistemology.

> The hypothesis connecting hermeneutics with scientific epistemology is that hermeneutics provided the conceptual distinction between something taken as fixed or given and something else taken as interpretation. The scriptural text and its interpretation was seen as exactly parallel to the natural world and its interpretation.... Modern science was the product of applying the distinctions needed for the understanding of the book of Scripture, namely that between the given and the interpreted, to the book of nature. For modern science, the given was the world of observed facts; all the rest, hypotheses, final causes, interpretations and inferences, were invented, made up by man. These distinctions are fundamental to scientific epistemology. Modern science rests on the distinction between observation and inference, observations being objective and reliable whereas the inferences are theoretical interpretations of those observations. (p. 115)

As I have mentioned earlier, this extensive discussion of the cognitive effects of literacy at a societal level is only part of Olson's argument. Having hypothesized from historical and anthropological evidence that literacy leads to the ability to distinguish between fact and interpretation, Olson turns to psychology to explain that process, reporting on his own research and that of other cognitive scientists. As he admits, "The account I have given of the relation between hermeneutics, epistemology and subjectivity has some of the properties of 'just-so stories' (e.g. How the tiger [sic] got his spots). One begins with a modern conclusion and looks back to see if the story can be told in such a way as to make the conclusion appear inevitable without doing damage to the historical record." He admits that the historical record may not provide the necessary information to allow one to judge the hypothesis adequately, but claims that the "psychologist can make a unique contribution to our understanding of these issues." By asking the right questions the experimental psychologist can "determine the relations between the phenomena in question—interpretation, objectivity and subjectivity" (p. 116).

Olson's research attempts to prove that the ability to distinguish between text and interpretation can be seen to develop in individual children simultaneously with the ability to distinguish between inference and perception. Hence, he claims that the conceptual categories required to distinguish fact from interpretation are the same as those required to distinguish objectivity and subjectivity, though he does acknowledge that ,"We must note that the relation of these 'literate' distinctions to the actual process of learning to read and write is indirect" (p. 119).

Expressed in terms of the commonplaces, Olson now has as *User* the developing child in the process of being exposed to text. *Text* once again is not closely defined, and must be presumed to include the range of learning materials to which the child is exposed in school, so that the learning takes place within a *Society* that is defined largely by its text use, that is the formal educational system. The three commonplaces of *User*, *Text* and *Society* are thus characterized quite differently in this section of the argument, suggesting that Olson is not particularly interested in close exploration of these terms, but is using them as placeholders to allow him to focus on the aspect that does interest him, i.e. *Process*.

In this final stage of his argument, Olson is focusing closely on the idea of a developing conceptual distinction by which *User* separates what is said from what is meant, and what is seen from what is known. Thus the commonplace of *Process* is extended hypothetically to embrace the notion of subjectivity and objectivity as the child learns to distinguish between various sources of knowledge and inference.

Olson thus provides varying exemplifications of the commonplaces but holds to a consistent relationship between them. Essentially, in his theory, *User* is affected by the *Process* of exposure to *Text*. The *Process* is explored and presented as a cognitive mechanism that allows for conceptual development on the part of *User*. In turn this change in *User* shapes the kind of *Society* in which *User* lives. As I shall hope to demonstrate by a discussion of other writers on literacy we shall find that significant differences between opposing theories come down to the directional relationship suggested between those commonplaces and the degree of focus on particular commonplaces.

Paulo Freire

The second writer whose arguments I would like to examine is Paulo Freire, particularly his views as outlined in his book on literacy, *Literacy: Reading the Word and the World* (Freire & Macedo, 1987). In Adler's terms (Adler & van Doren, 1940/1967), this is an entirely practical book in that its purpose is to change the practice of its readers. Freire is less concerned with understanding literacy than he is with changing the way people view it, teach it and learn it. Most of all he wants to change society, and literacy is one of the tools he sees to be useful to this end.

Although Freire's purpose is practical, his discussion is invariably theoretical, a pattern that comes from both political and pedagogical beliefs. When asked about this seeming paradox, he writes, "I cannot write a text that is filled with universal advice and suggestions. When some educators criticize me on this point, they reveal how influenced they are by the dominant ideology they are fighting against, and how they fail to understand the ways in which they reproduce it" (p. 135).

Literacy: Reading the Word and the World is a book made up from a variety of sources. Some chapters are transcripts of discussions on the topic of literacy between Macedo and Freire, with Macedo's role being essentially restricted to that of interviewer. One chapter is largely autobiographical reminiscence on the part of Freire; another is a reprint of a Freire speech; a third is a reprint of a letter from Freire to the Minister of Education of Guinea Bissau where Freire was heavily involved in a national literacy campaign. Other chapters contain accounts of literacy campaigns with lengthy excerpts from the relevant teaching materials. In addition, there are introductory essays from Giroux and Berthoff. Because this text ranges over many aspects of literacy, it does not provide a clear argumentative thread that we can follow as we did with Olson. Instead we must build up Freire's case from his assumptions and recommendations.

Freire takes issue with the "notion that literacy is simply a mechanical process" because such an approach "overemphasizes the technical acquisition of reading and writing skills." He calls instead for "a view of literacy as cultural politics," suggesting that, in his analysis, "literacy becomes a meaningful construct to the degree that it is viewed as a set of practices that functions to either empower or disempower people."

Freire is primarily interested in the relationship between *User* and *Society*, which he portrays as dialectical. Freire sets up as parallel the *User-Text* interaction and the *User-Society* interaction claiming that one cannot "read the word until one can read the World." Essentially he is suggesting that the *Process* by which a *User* interacts meaningfully with *Text* is the same as that by which a *User* interacts with *Society*. For Freire, the *Process* is the development of the *User's* political ability to see himself as an agent within the world, shaping and being shaped by that world. Only when the agent has developed this consciousness *(conscientizaçao)* can printed text have any meaning for him.

There is obviously a point of commonality here between Olson's argument and Freire's in that both posit that the *Process* of interacting with *Text* produces change in the *User* although, of course, they conceive of *Text* differently. It is noteworthy that Olson, the cognitive scientist, looks for a cognitive mechanism to account for literate behaviour, while Freire, a critical theorist, assumes the change to be one of political awareness.

Literacy cannot be reduced to the treatment of letters and words as purely mechanical domain. We need to go beyond this rigid comprehension of literacy and begin to view it as the relationship of learners to the world, mediated by the transforming practice of this world taking place in the very general milieu in which learners travel. (p. viii)

Both Olson and Freire express their view of literacy primarily in terms of *Users, Society* and *Process*. The differences in their arguments rest in the relationship that they draw between those commonplaces. For Freire, personal change gives people a set of practices through which they can change their world and in the process change themselves. For Olson, cognitive development changes people, who in turn change the world they live in.

Freire suggests that illiterate people accept their world and their place in it as fixed and immutable. They do not see the world nor reflect on it. The process of becoming literate is thus the process of learning to look at the world and to become conscious of one's position in relation to it, and vice versa, and to shape that world by "reading" it and "writing" it.

> The transformation of objective reality, (what I call the "writing" of reality), represents precisely the starting point where the animal that became human began to write history.... It is precisely this world consciousness touched and transformed, that bred the consciousness of the self. (p. 50)

The process of conscientization is in part one of becoming aware of objective and subjective ways of viewing the world and the self. As a dialectician, Freire holds both these positions within the notion of conscientization. The learner has to become aware of him or herself as something quite separate from the world while simultaneously recognizing that he or she is part of society. Learners,

> ...discover for themselves in the process of becoming more and more critical that it is impossible to deny the constitutive power of their consciousness in the social practice in which they participate. On the other hand, they perceive that through their consciousness, even when they are not makers of their social reality, they transcend the constituting reality and question it. (p. 48-9)

Social transformation is perceived as a historic process in which subjectivity and objectivity are united dialectically. (p. 43)

Freire's characterization of the commonplaces

In contrast to Olson's shifting characterization of *User*, Freire has a clear and relatively fixed vision. He has in mind *Users* who are essentially the learners in his own literacy campaigns; adults with minimal exposure to formal education who work as fishermen, farmers and labourers. He discusses literacy in the context of national literacy campaigns, stating that he would not be interested in being associated with programs that did not serve to empower the people. His terms for *User* include: the people, learners, the illiterate, the dispossessed majority, the oppressed. As these terms suggest, *User* implies a large group of people rather than an individual.

The commonplace *Text* is rather less straightforward in its characterization in *Literacy: Reading the Word and the World*, the complexity being exemplified in Freire's assertion that *Society* is a text to be read and written. Indeed, for Freire, any object of attention that can be interacted with and interpreted is a manifestation of *Text*. Thus he insists that there is a "dynamic relationship between the reading of the world and the reading of reality" (p. 64).

For Freire, *Text* is never immutable, but is constantly affected by the conditions under which it was created and the conditions in which it is read. Thus, he refuses to "dichotomize reading the text from reading the context" (p. 64), insisting for instance that he cannot read Lenin without understanding,

> ...the historical, political social, cultural and economic moment, the concrete conditions that led Lenin to create the text in the first place. I cannot then, simply use Lenin's text and apply it literally to the Brazilian context without rewriting it, without re-inventing it. (p. 133)

Text can never be read without simultaneously being rewritten in the light of the reader's own context. Freire suggests that this is as valid for the single word plus picture "codifications," which he advocates for classroom teaching, as it is for the *Text* of cultural community in which learners interact, or the dominant society in which that community is located.

These two notions of immediate community and dominant society are both part of Freire's characterization of the commonplace *Society*, but his focus is less on the people who may comprise these groups than on the politics that determine the interaction between those people. Thus when he demands that learners rewrite the world, he is asking for a challenge to the existing social order and relationship between the "oppressed" and "the dominant class, which has the power to define, profile and describe the world" (p. 53).

Because "reading always involves critical perception, interpretation and rewriting of what is read" (p. 36), for Freire, literacy "serves as a set of cultural practices that promotes democratic and emancipatory change" (p. viii).

It is noteworthy that Freire describes literacy as a set of practices in contrast, for example, to Olson's use of terms such as "conceptual distinction," or "conceptual category." Freire's term has a temporal ongoing element that is largely lacking in Olson's terms. The *Process* of being literate is thus ongoing and developmental.

> In the literacy phase, what is attempted is not a profound comprehension of reality under analysis, but the development of a curious attitude to stimulate learners' critical capacity as subjects of knowledge who are challenged by the object to be known. What is important is the systematic experience of this relationship between the subject who searches and the object to be known. (p. 68)

Freire's characterization of *Process* is also different from Olson's in that Olson's is essentially an individual change, whereas Freire's notion of *Process* is both a social and an individual act.

> Consciousness is generated through the social practice in which we participate. But it also has an individual dimension. That is, my comprehension of the world, my dreams of the world—all of these are part of my individual practice; all speak of my presence in the world. I need all of this to begin to understand myself. But it is not sufficient to explicate my action. In the final analysis, consciousness is socially bred. (p. 47)

Thus Freire puts *Society* at the centre of his commonplaces, portraying it as dialectically linked with the *User*, and with the *Text*. The question he is attempting to answer is not Olson's question of what effect will literacy have on individuals and on societies, but the issue of how society can be best affected, using literacy as tool.

Shirley Brice Heath

Ways with Words (Heath, 1983) is an ethnographic exploration of language use (both oral and written) in two small communities in the Piedmont Carolinas. Heath documents the different ways in which the children of these communities learn to use language, and contrasts both patterns of language socialization with the patterns demonstrated by the group she designates the *townspeople,* that is the "mainstream" blacks and whites who hold power in the schools and work places of the region.

Through this ethnographic study of language use in the different communities, Heath argues that the skills of reading and writing are developed in accordance with the cultural practices that a community has developed. Children grow up being socialized into the patterns of their society, which shape the ways in which they view and use literacy just as they shape every other aspect of individual growth. Culture is presented as learned behaviour and literacy habits are seen as part of that shared learning.

Through detailed observations of language interaction, Heath demonstrates the way social context operates in practice to shape the language use. Heath argues that in these communities "the different ways children learned to use language were dependent on the ways in which each community structured their families, defined the roles that community members could assume, and played out their concepts of childhood that guided child socialization" (p. 11).

One example that Heath explores is the attitude towards *Text,* demonstrating how patterns at work in literacy interactions can be seen to be similarly present in other areas of life. She describes how in Trackton, a black community, the written word is used for "negotiation and manipulation—both serious and playful. Changing and changeable, words are the tools performers use to create images of themselves and the world they see" (p. 235). She documents how a letter is read aloud to neighbours, all of whom share in the negotiation of meaning, bringing individual stories and experiences to bear on the *Text.* Of this incident, she writes, "The question, 'What does this mean?' was answered not only from the information in print but from the group's joint bringing of experience to the text" (p. 197).

Heath relates this approach to the written word with the patterns shown in other arenas, such as religious life. She is able to demonstrate that similar shared constructions of meaning are common in the Trackton church where the congregation will "raise hymns" by spontaneously departing from the printed words to create a new chanted hymn. "The phrases offered by the leader who raises a hymn may become a formula that subsequent sets of phrases modify or play with, or the initial sets of phrases may only introduce a theme that other leaders comment on and vary throughout the raised hymn"(p. 204). Through this and other similar examples, Heath is able to show that this approach to words is not a specific instance of literacy use but is part of deeply embedded patterns of interaction.

Heath contrasts this attitude to *Text* with the patterns found in Roadville, a nearby white community of similar size where, as in Trackton, the workers are mostly employed in the area's textile mills. In Roadville, the *Text* is seen as more authoritative and is rarely considered open to negotiation. Heath relates this to the different religious practices demonstrated in the neighbourhood.

> In Roadville, the absoluteness of ways of talking about what is written fits church ways of talking about what is written. Behind the written word is an authority, and the text is a message that can be taken apart only insofar as its analysis does not extend too far beyond the text and commonly agreed upon experiences. New syntheses and multiple interpretations create alternatives that challenge fixed roles, rules and 'rightness'. (p. 235)

Heath supports this claim with observations that in Roadville, "prayers are brief, simple, formulaic, and often said quietly.... A public prayer is not an occasion for performance." She quotes a resident as saying, "We learned at church and at home too that things were either right or wrong; you did things the right way and you were right, you did wrong or said wrong and everybody knew you were wrong" (p. 143).

Such assumptions permeate the way parents introduce their children to literacy activities. When showing their children picture books, they ask questions for which they consider there is a single "right" answer. "Parents ask simple questions and expect their children to be predictable information-givers, repeating the specific and discrete bits of information the adults have preformulated as the answer" (p. 227).

Heath explores many such patterns of social behaviour and documents recurring themes that run through a community's patterns of interaction and through their literacy use. Heath argues that in these communities, "The different ways children learned to use language were dependent on the ways in which each community structured their families, defined the roles that community members could assume, and played out their concepts of childhood that guided child socialization" (p. 11).

Each community, she claims, has "its own traditions for structuring, using, and assessing reading and writing" (p. 230). She argues further that literacy must be seen in the light of standard social patterns since literate traditions are, "…interwoven in different ways with oral uses of language, ways of negotiating meaning, deciding on action and achieving status. Patterns of using reading and writing are interdependent with ways of using space (having bookshelves, decorating walls, displaying telephone numbers), and using time (bedtime, meal hours and homework sessions)."

She then compares the patterns shown in both Roadville and Trackton with the patterns prevalent in the nearby town, where black and white "mainstreamers" control the work places and the schools. These mainstreamers have their own cultural practices, but their practices are the ones that are reflected in and demanded by the educational system. She describes how the townspeople develop their views of the world and how:

> When their children are born, they begin to play again the same script they have followed since childhood, secure in their own success with the necessary roles and lines. They believe their ways of talking about what is written and responding to the content of written materials will impart to their young the necessary skills for achieving school and job success. For them, these ways of thinking and behaving are natural and they expect others to share them. For the children of Trackton and Roadville, however, and for the majority of the millworkers and students in Piedmont schools, the townspeople's ways are far from natural and they seem strange indeed. (p. 262)

Heath's characterization of the commonplaces

Like Freire, Heath has very specific people in mind in her characterization of *User*, in contrast to Olson's shifting conception of those who interact with literacy. For her, *User* is the people of the Trackton and Roadville communities. She claims to focus particularly on the children, writing in the Prologue, "The descriptions here of the actual process, activities, and attitudes involved in the enculturation of children in Roadville and Trackton will allow readers to see these in comparison with those of mainstream homes and institutions" (p. 8).

Given her stress on the process of socialization, however, it is not surprising to find that the activities of the adult members of these mill communities are as thoroughly, if not more thoroughly, documented. Heath does discuss the teachers and other townspeople, whom she sees as representing a "mainstream" attitude to literacy, but their presence as *User* is of interest only for contrast. In many ways they are presented as the context against which to set the real *Users*, rather than being considered *Users* in their own right. In this, her pattern is similar to that shown by Freire, who also sets his specific notion of *User* against a backdrop of a larger, dominant *Society*.

As indicated earlier, Olson's approach is very different. His conception of *User* is more fluid, with any human of any age or historical period being included. An individual or community on which Olson focuses will usually be compared temporally rather than geographically or politically and the contrast will be served to illuminate both groups, rather than presenting one as the backdrop for the other.

Heath writes about specific real individuals, but from her viewpoint they are individuals who function as a group. She is interested in what they have in common rather than the ways in which they differ. In this sense, *User* is the community rather than the individual; and these communities can be seen as typical for many other communities. Heath states, "Throughout the Piedmont Carolinas there were many 'Roadvilles' and 'Tracktons'.... The youngsters in Roadville and Trackton had much in common with most of the children in the classrooms of the region"(p. 6).

Because of the stress that Heath lays on the role of the community in shaping literacy understanding, the community of people in Trackton and Roadville have a function in both the commonplaces of *User* and *Society*. In the characterization of *User*, the limits of the two communities form the outer boundary of the group. Here Heath's focus adjusts from close observation of individual members of those communities, to a more distanced look at entire communities and the cultural practices they display. In her understanding of the *Society* commonplace, however, we see this overall view of a community as a tight focus. Now a community such as Trackton is viewed as a single entity set in a larger context of other communities, each with their own social and historical patterns, interacting with current economic conditions. Playing a key role in this larger context are those social institutions such as the textile mills and the educational system with which the inhabitants of Trackton and Roadville are largely forced to interact. Heath presents these as embodying a "mainstream" attitude to knowledge and language use, a position that she documents in some detail.

In contrast to the other two writers considered, Heath has a relatively straightforward characterization of the commonplace of *Text*, using it to apply to any piece of written material that can yield meaning. She thus defines as a literacy event such encounters as children finding prices on merchandise, or reading brand names on cereal boxes, as well as interactions with longer texts such as letters or newspapers. Heath's own term for *Text* is usually "print," but she also refers to "reading materials," "texts," "a piece of writing," "message," "written material" and "the printed word."

Olson and Freire both extend the idea of *Text* to embrace the world in which the *User* lives, seeing interaction with *Text* as essentially being a way of thinking and of making meaning rather than a process of decoding the written word. By contrast, Heath's characterization is very concrete and tied to actual print.

Heath's conception of the *Process* of literacy is more complex, because the essence of her argument is not merely that the way in which literacy is viewed and used will vary from community to community, but that that variation is not random. Instead it is a reflection of the fact that literacy cannot be divorced from the basic social patterns that determine all aspects of life, so that a community develops its own form of literacy in correspondence with its norms, habits and values of all forms of human interaction.

The particular *Process* by which any *User* is socialized to the practice of literacy is therefore idiosyncratic to the community in which he or she lives. Heath thus gives us a range of different processes by which people both interact with text and develop those patterns of interaction. The general *Process* that underlies such particular manifestations, however, is clearly defined as one of socialization.

> This book argues that in Roadville and Trackton the different ways children learned to use language were dependent on the ways in which each community structured their families, defined the roles that community members could assume, and played out their concepts of childhood that guided child socialization. In addition, for each group, the place of religious activities was inextricably linked to the valuation of language in determining an individual's access to goods, services and estimations of position and power in the community. In communities throughout the world, these and other features of the cultural milieu affect the ways in which children learn to use language. The place of language in the cultural life of each social group is interdependent with the habits and values of behaving shared among members of that group. (p. 11)

Expressed in terms of the Commonplaces, Heath is thus suggesting that *Society* shapes the *Process* by which *Users* interact with *Text*. Implicit in this is the assumption that *Society* also affects *User* directly, since *Process* is not an external interaction between *User* and *Text*, but an internal set of assumptions about *Text*, habits of *Text* use and view of self in relation to *Text*. Thus she focuses on the relationship between *Society* and *Process*, exploring how the *Process* is affected by its societal context. *Society* is the starting point for Heath, and she essentially looks at how it affects and shapes the other commonplaces. For Olson, the line of interest travels in the other direction as he explores how the *Process* of interaction with *Text* will shape *Users* who in turn will shape *Society*.

We can thus sum up Heath's position as arguing strongly for the position that *Society* shapes both *Process* and *User*. She demonstrates minimal interest in *Text per se*, and despite the apparently people-centred ethnographic approach, she displays relatively little interest in the *Users* as individual people, seeing them instead as parts of the overall community or *Society*.

If Olson is interested in what effect literacy has on *Society*, and Freire is concerned with using literacy as a tool to shape that effect, where can we locate Heath in terms of the purpose of her writing? *Ways with Words* falls into two distinct sections, one of which seems closer to Olson's interest in understanding the *Process*; the other more nearly approaches Freire's practical desire to change mainstream *Society*.

The first part of the book is written by Heath, the ethnographer, who tries to understand and to document. The second part of the book is written by Heath, the educator, who wants to change educational methods to take account of the culturally specific concept of literacy practices documented in the first half of the book. By the end of the book, one has come to see Heath as having much in common with Freire, both in terms of the purpose of their writing and in terms of their understanding of literacy. Both stress the links between *Society* and *User*, but whereas both acknowledge that *Society* will shape the *User*, Freire sees the possibility of the *User* shaping *Society* in turn via literacy. For Heath, literacy is not so powerful. It is merely one of many patterns of interaction, all of which are shaped according to the norms of behaviour and understandings of the community in which *User* lives.

Summarizing the use of the commonplaces

The simplest statement that I believe one can make about literacy is that it involves someone interacting with a text within a certain context. If I am correct that this is the simplest possible statement, then the four elements within it—that is, a user, a text, an interaction (*Process*) and a context (*Society*)—must be the commonplaces on which any other more complex discussions of literacy are based. These four commonplaces, therefore, can be seen as defining the field because no adequate discussion of literacy can be held that does not take these into account. By providing a basic framework for the discussion, it is hoped that we can better understand individual writers by comparing their positions relative to the common framework.

When we recognize, for example, that both Heath and Freire characterize *User* as a non-mainstream community, we can not only see a similarity between these two writers but we also see relationships between these two writers and others. The Southam Report, for instance, also focuses on a *User* who is not in the mainstream but there is less sense of community about this notion of *User*, and more of a group of scattered individuals. This would suggest that to understand the relationship between Freire or Heath and Southam, it might be fruitful to consider the relationship between *User* and *Society*.

As I have tried to suggest above, each of the three writers whom I have examined focuses on a different aspect of literacy. Olson is intrigued by the effect of *Process* on the *User*, while Freire wants to see *Users* affecting *Society*. To complete this apparently neat circle of effect, Heath's interests lie in documenting the way *Society* shapes the *Process*. But the pattern of effect does not have to be uni-directional or circular. It is almost certain that every commonplace will play a part in shaping the interaction between itself and the other three. There are numerous relationships to be explored here and we should not be misled by my selection of three diverse positions into seeing literacy discussions as so neatly polarized.

Although none of the writers I have considered in depth is particularly interested in *Text*, there is of course a large literature that explores the ways in which changes in the nature of *Text* affect the development of literacy. Thus we have discussions of the impact of the length or complexity of text, the authorship, the interest level, the context in which the text is met and the familiarity of the schema that underlies it. The language in which the text is written is also considered to influence the *Process*, as is the script that that language uses. As is evident, many of these considerations of *Text* actually involve scrutiny of the interaction between *Text* and another Commonplace, assessing the impact of changes in *Text* on *User* or *Process*, for example.

The commonplace of *Society* seems to have attracted a considerable amount of attention in discussions of literacy. Some of the key questions relate to the role that literacy plays in particular societies, and the role that societies play in shaping literacy. The effects of literacy on society have been explored from economic, cognitive and historical perspectives, and the effects on specific institutions such as the legal system or religion have also been considered. The commonplace *Process* has not been neglected either. Considered mostly from the aspect of the development of literacy skills, there is a considerable literature from the fields of education, psychology and sociology that attempts to describe, chart, evaluate or enhance the *Process*.

The commonplace *User* has also received considerable attention, with a number of ethnographic studies and child observation studies. Cognitivists such as Olson look for cognitive change in the *User*, and critical theorists like Freire look for conscientization of the *User*. And yet, although literacy is essentially an individual attribute and performance, in all these studies, the individuality of *User* is obscured in favour of viewing *User* as part of a specified community.

When I look back to my pilot study, I can see many shortcomings in it, but one strength it does possess is its recognition that even though Fazli and Yusefi share much in common in terms of community background, they still approach literacy differently and exhibit different understandings and assumptions.

We have a number of studies discussing how the literacy *User* is affected by the *Process*. We have relatively little that suggests that the interaction is two-directional. For me as a second language teacher, the variety of background exhibited by my learners has always been a very significant factor in language learning situations. And yet, prior to the period of doctoral study, I had bought into the notion of literacy as a neutral technology that would operate the same way in all cultures and in all individuals. Heath and other ethnographers were soon able to convince me that the community in which one was raised would affect the literacy process but it was only the pilot study that drew my attention to the individual component.

As so often happens, when one comes to suddenly understand something in a different way, more than one influence was at work. While I was struggling with deciding how to write up my practical experience with the pilot study, I was also being challenged theoretically in full-time course work. One series of courses was to change my whole thinking, and would eventually lead to the autobiographical *User* study that this work primarily addresses.

In discussing the use of commonplaces to bring the literature to terms, I have obviously outpaced the narrative of my personal growth of understanding of literacy. In the next chapter I would like to explore how I came to see the *User* as the neglected commonplace in literacy discussions, and why I came to feel that an autobiographical study could be so informative.

Chapter Four

Coming to a personal view of literacy

My interest in the literacy *User* was evident at the time of my pilot study. However, while I held to a position that literacy was a neutral technology, my interest in *User* was restricted to seeing the *User* as a sample rather than as an individual who would shape the process. Not surprisingly, from this position I was not able to reconcile a technological view of literacy with my growing awareness of the importance of literacy's cultural and possibly individual base. As I carried out doctoral studies over the next couple of years I returned to this problem over and over again, scrutinizing it in the light of new approaches, information, and finally epistemologies.

When I began full-time doctoral study, my expectations of the learning process related to the acquisition of specific pieces of knowledge. I had been conscious for some time that my knowledge of applied linguistics and language pedagogy was not as complete as it might be. My previous graduate degree had been in the field of literature and did not seem to have much relevance to second language learning, and I had never had any formal teacher education. Although I had done a considerable amount of reading on my own and had attended conferences and workshops on second language pedagogy, I was very aware that there were gaps in my knowledge of the field. I hoped the course work for the Ph.D. would fill those gaps.

Despite this awareness of the limitations of my knowledge base, I do not remember ever feeling any dissatisfaction about my basic epistemology. On the contrary, I don't think I even entertained the possibility of an alternative. Because I never scrutinized my own epistemology, I cannot now claim to reconstruct it with total accuracy. However, evidence from various intellectual shocks I was shortly to receive suggest that I believed that education was essentially the transmission of a defined body of knowledge along with sufficient skills to be able to access, understand and use that knowledge. I believed that there was an absolute truth underlying the apparently confusing evidence of experience, or research data, even if we were not yet in a position to define what that truth might be. I assumed there was a split between practice and theory, and that one would consider theory out of the context of experience, then go back into practical work and try to change one's practice to accommodate theory. I don't think I even considered that theory might be shaped by practice, much less that one might be lived out in the other.

This kind of thinking had not been challenged by the education courses I had taken prior to doctoral work. Indeed it had perhaps been strengthened by them. I had made use of my practical experience to answer questions in classroom discussions but my assignments and the lectures had drawn entirely, it seemed, on a discussion of the theoretical literature. The courses had been designed to allow me to participate in a certain shared knowledge base and the grades I was assigned measured the amount of that knowledge that I had acquired.

In my first year of doctoral study, however, I was enrolled in a number of courses that addressed the process of education in a different way. One of the first courses I took involved a very close analysis of Dewey's *Experience and Education* (1938). We pored over the text, sometimes spending three hours discussing a single paragraph and thrashing out exactly what Dewey might have meant. We were rebuked for proceeding on to an attempt to relate Dewey's writings to our own experiences until we had first determined exactly what Dewey had said in his own terms.

I had been used to approaching texts rather more loosely, taking notice of what an author had to say that related directly to my own experience and shaping his or her suggestions or arguments to fit my own circumstances. I had never considered that I might gain a richer understanding of the text by holding back my own reactions until I had assured myself that I had thoroughly understood what the author was expressing. It was also frequently pointed out to me that in written assignments I had used terms loosely, perhaps using power and strength without distinguishing between them. I became very conscious of the significance of the words I and others chose to express my arguments. In the process I became aware that in my written work, I referred to literacy variously as a set of skills, a process, a behaviour, an ability, and a state. It did not seem that I was using these terms thoughtfully, since their use was almost random. Rather, they reflected a confusion in my thinking.

The other component of this course was a sequence of exercises and assignments designed to encourage us to relate our own personal experience to our studies. Working in small groups, we exchanged stories that in some way related to learning or teaching, and we reflected on why those particular stories had stayed in our memories, and how they might have shaped our perception of the learning process. We tried to formulate our own rules of practice, exploring the way we tended to react to classroom situations or the expectations we had for ourselves and our learners. We wrote narratives of our own lives, searching for rhythms, themes, or recurring motifs, and relating them to the way we taught. We read Clandinin (1986) and Elbaz (1983) on teacher's images of the classroom and we considered what our own images might be.

I found this course tremendously exciting. The work with Dewey was rigorous and challenging, so that I was engaged academically as I struggled to come to terms with a text in a way I had never done before. In the process I was forced to rethink the approaches to learning in which I had had such confidence before this. It was the personal work that really had an impact on me, however. In my work as a research officer, I had been largely apologetic about my years of practical experience, seeing them as somehow inferior to the years of theoretical study my colleagues had spent. I had obviously drawn on my practical experience when writing books for teachers or when doing workshops, but in academic discussion I had seen such input as inappropriate. I also had unconscious assumptions about the form that contributions to academic discussion should take.

I remember, for instance, attending a colloquium session where one of the audience had phrased her question in the form of a fairly lengthy story about one of her own children who had displayed a behaviour pattern in direct contradiction to the claims being made by the speaker. I remember my ambivalent attitude as I listened. I found the woman's story very interesting and relevant and yet I was uncomfortable listening to her. After the session two people commented separately to me on how inappropriate such anecdotal evidence was in such a forum and I realized that my unease during her recital had not been related to the length of time she was speaking but the strangeness of hearing that story in that setting. I would like to be able to say that I defended the woman's right to bring practical experience to bear on the problem, but I'm afraid my reaction was instead to mentally review my previous contributions to the colloquium series to make sure I had not committed such a solecism myself.

This course gave me a validation of my personal experience. As I struggled to determine the relationship between theory and practice, I finally questioned the validity of any theory that did not arise from and was not supported by practical experience. Reading Oakeshott (1962), I recognized that I had allowed the misguided certainty of "technique" to persuade me to undervalue practical knowledge.

I recognized too that stories of our personal experiences are powerful ways of allowing others to share those experiences with us and as such they are as critical in academic discourse as they are in any other form of communication. I felt there was a feminine element here too. It had always been my experience that women shared stories as ways of establishing trust and openness, as well as ways of communicating information. When we tell an event in the form of a story, we show ourselves in the way that story is crafted and interpreted, and we lay ourselves open to our hearers. Much academic discourse, it seemed to me, hid the speaker behind safe generalities and third party attributions. It was an exciting academic experience to be encouraged to draw on my personal background rather than to suppress it, and it allowed me to participate in an academic discourse in a way that was in harmony with my preferred communication patterns.

The reading for this course led me to considerable reflection and inevitably I began to think about literacy. I looked back on the pilot study and was confirmed in my feeling that a study that looked closely at the way in which individuals experienced literacy would be a valuable addition to the research. I was surprised in retrospect how little interest I had expressed in the learners themselves and the way in which they experienced the process. I had never really questioned why Yusefi's work looked so different from Fazli's, or considered what they might bring to the learning experience other than prior knowledge of the topic. Having become aware of the value of my own practical experience as a teacher, I realized too that I had missed a valuable resource by not making a serious effort to seek out the input that the regular class teacher could have given me.

A second course that I took at this time was one in the Adult Education department called *Facilitating Adult Learning*. The word "facilitating" in the course title did not come into focus for me for some weeks. I had not previously recognized a difference between facilitating and teaching, and this course forced me to think about what my image of learning was.

As early as 1978 when I took my first ESL training course, I had been told of the perils of the banking model of teaching. I had been able to apply this to my ESL classes, where the process of language use was clearly as valuable as the transmission of information about the language system. But somehow, I had never thought this idea through in my work in teacher education or in my own studies. My idea of a well-planned workshop was one where I was thoroughly well informed about the topic, and where I presented that information in an interesting, lively and relevant format. Yes, I included participant activities, but largely as a classroom management technique for maintaining interest and involvement, rather than because I really saw such activities as an important part of the learning process.

I was equally rigid in my own approach to study, coming to my courses with expectations of acquiring a certain number of facts and otherwise departing unchanged. The Foundations course described above had obviously begun to rock the mental assumptions on which these claims are based, but I think personal change is a slow gradual process so that the impact of an experience will take time to show itself fully.

When I attended the first class in Adult Education, the instructor asked us to write down what we hoped to get from the course. We worked in groups and I was uneasy to see that the contributions coming from other members of my group seemed disconcertingly airy-fairy. They wanted to become better facilitators or to understand their own learning styles. When it was time for my contribution I said that I wanted to learn the major tenets of Adult Education and become familiar with the literature, thus reverting firmly back to my information-based notion of knowledge. I never did get control of the Adult Education literature. However, one thing that this course did allow me to learn was the difference between my concept of teaching, (i.e. force-feeding information) and facilitating or helping learners to make their own discoveries.

The whole course was based on process rather than product, and once again I was encouraged to consider my own experiences, feelings and understandings as part of the learning process. When the professor asked us as part of the first-day evaluation, "How do you feel," I was embarrassed at what I saw as a totally inappropriate question. As I wrote in my journal (a course requirement), "I would rather she had grilled me on the basic tenets of Malcom Knowles than be asked such a question in such a forum."

It took some time before I was ready to recognize that my feelings, or the feelings of any learner, are a critical part of the learning process. Again I went back to the pilot study. How did Yusefi feel? How significant was it that the students who could not write were separated out from the others? How did their feelings affect their learning and how much could we as teachers affect those feelings? My embarrassment in the Adult Education class came partly from my British upbringing, which decrees that feelings are not a topic of general discussion. But it was also individual in reflecting a conflict between my very critical feelings and a desire to be truthful. How many of the students who came to my literacy sessions in the afternoons were torn between their feelings that they should go along with the teacher's suggestions and their own preference for staying with their classmates?

The third course I took that winter had, perhaps, the strongest impact of all, although again, the impact took some time to make itself felt and was initially something I resisted. The course was *Alternative Methods of Teacher and Student Thinking*. Like the first course on Foundations, it was taught by my future thesis supervisor, Mick Connelly, and combined intensive textual study with considerable personal reflection and interaction. This time the texts under particular scrutiny were Polanyi's *Personal Knowledge: Towards a Post-critical Philosophy* (1958, 1962) and Schutz and Luckman's *The Structures of the Life-World* (1973), both of which explore an understanding of knowledge that is personally constructed.

I remember an incident at the beginning of this course that casts some light on my understanding prior to working with these authors. We were discussing in class the difficulties of shaping a thesis out of the mass of apparently unconnected data that one might collect in a qualitative study. Mick told a story about another student of his who claimed that the data was like a beach full of pebbles. One had no alternative but to walk among them picking out the ones that caught the eye as particularly attractive or valuable. I was deeply troubled by this account and found it hard to believe that Mick was offering it seriously. I was convinced that there was a basic truth to be discovered in the data and that any other account had to be wrong. The notion of selecting only those pebbles that happened to fit a particular interpretation seemed dishonest. I was quite distressed as I argued against the researcher's right to construct his or her own interpretation.

Soon after this discussion, we began reading Polanyi's *Personal Knowledge*. Polanyi, of course, takes his reader by tiny logical steps to the position where one can no longer deny the personal involvement of the knower in any act of understanding. I was very excited by the book and could no longer argue against a constructivist position. However, I think my understanding was cognitive rather than visceral at this point. (Indeed I have to confess that there is still some trace of a belief in an underlying reality in my epistemology, in that I cannot account for my certainty of some things not being acceptable constructs, without some notion of possible truth for the other alternatives.)

Although the idea of personal knowledge took some time to become really part of my thinking, there were other aspects of Polanyi's writings that were immediately identifiable as being relevant to my interest in literacy. His chapter on skills is an example. He begins by pointing out how a skillful performance will involve the observance of a set of rules that we cannot necessarily articulate. This is obviously true of language use where we manipulate complex grammatical forms without in many cases being able to articulate the underlying rules.

I began to wonder whether this would also be true for literacy skills, and began thinking about the kind of rules that might underlie a fluent literacy performance, for example the sense of appropriateness of content and form. Polanyi goes on to suggest that "an art which cannot be specified in detail cannot be transmitted by prescription" (p. 53). Instead, such an art is taught by example. "By watching the master and emulating his efforts in the presence of his example, the apprentice unconsciously picks up the rules of the art, including those that are not explicitly known to the master himself" (p. 53).

Current literacy teaching seemed highly impoverished in the light of this view of learning. By focusing on those aspects of the literacy process that lent themselves to explicit rule formation, we are depriving our students of the opportunity to learn the knowledge we hold tacitly. Reading this in Polanyi made me aware that I had never had enough faith to build demonstration into my classes as an integral part of the teaching and learning process.

I found useful, too, Polanyi's distinction between subsidiary and focal awareness. When we write fluently, our awareness is focused on the content of what we are writing, and we have only subsidiary awareness of the pen or machine that is allowing us to write. If we switch our attention to the letter formation, we are no longer able to focus on the content. Similarly if we concentrate on the processes by which we are reading, we are unable to attend to the meaning of the text. I found this distinction gave me a vocabulary with which to describe the varying performance that literacy learners demonstrate as they attempt increasingly complex tasks, and shift back and forth from focal to subsidiary awareness of the decoding or encoding process.

As I suggested earlier, these insights from Polanyi were easy to recognize and they took their place in my mental framework without seriously dislodging the existing ways of viewing things. The concept of constructed knowledge required a much greater mental shift, however, and I was consequently much slower in coming to accept it.

Polanyi's logical step-by-step arguments received support from a number of other writers I was studying at that time. Chief among these was Schutz (1973), who demonstrated how our prior expectations shape the way we make sense of new events. As Schutz points out, in the natural attitude we do not question our knowledge or the world around us. We take it for granted. Only when a novel event occurs that does not fit our reference schema do we become aware of the deficiency of our understanding.

This was a pattern I had encountered many times in my own and my students' cross cultural experiences. Time after time it seemed I had made assumptions as to the interpretation of events or behaviour, only to be jarred into surprise when learners from another culture offered a different interpretation. With this sort of background, it was perhaps surprising that I had not previously recognized knowledge as being socially constructed. Or perhaps, as Schutz would say, it was inevitable for anyone operating in the natural attitude. Having once stepped out of the natural attitude and begun reflecting on the kinds of assumptions I had previously taken for granted, I was more open to suggestions that came from a number of sources.

Some months previously I had enjoyed a conference presentation on the role of cultural knowledge in reading comprehension. The speaker had argued that difficulties with language were only part of the challenge facing second language readers. Since no text could ever include all the related information, it was inevitable that the reader would be called upon to supply considerable background knowledge before a meaning could be constructed, so second language readers might well need considerable background knowledge about the target culture as well as linguistic knowledge. This was a familiar notion to me, but the speaker went further. Each culture, he claimed, had certain expectations about the organization of text types, which he referred to as story grammars. Story grammars determine such factors as the characters in a piece of text, the order in which events are described, the presence or absence of a climax, a surprise, a resolution or a moral, and so on.

The Western story grammar for a murder mystery would thus demand the characters of victim, detective, and suspects. The order of events would guarantee that the discovery of the body preceded the unmasking of the murderer and so on. The story grammar for a newspaper lead story would of course be very different from that of the murder mystery but would still be a shared expectation on the part of newspaper readers. In other cultures, the expectations of a particular text genre would not necessarily reflect our patterns, the speaker pointed out, which could make our texts baffling to foreign language speakers.

I was intrigued by this presentation, which seemed very relevant to my work with literacy students. I began reading writers such as Brewer and Lichtenstein (1981), Kintsch and Greene (1978) and Mandler and Johnson, 1977, who all suggested that we come to text with a specific set of cultural expectations regarding both the information we are likely to find there and the organization of that information.

One study, carried out with second language learners, helped me take this understanding a step further. Steffenson and Joag-Dev (1985) demonstrated that not only did readers have pre-set expectations of the text, but also pre-set expectations regarding particular events. They gave accounts of an Indian wedding and an American wedding to members of both groups, and tested them on comprehension and, some weeks later, on recall. They found, as expected, that each group showed better comprehension of the account of the wedding story from their own culture and were also able to recall this story quite accurately. What I found really interesting, however, was that when the American learners were asked to retell the story of the Indian wedding some weeks later, they told a story that had been reshaped into the familiar American style wedding. This article was my first introduction to schema theory and I can still remember my excitement at its implications. It seemed to explain such a lot about the difficulties I had had in cross-cultural encounters, and the difficulties my students had in making sense of unfamiliar texts.

Obviously my thinking in this area was affected by reading Schutz and I began to explore schema theory more seriously. I no longer saw knowledge as a series of discrete items, but as sets of related propositions that had developed as a result of societal conditioning and personal experience. For another course, I was reading Rumelhart (1980), Bransford, (1983) and Kintsch and van Dijk (1978), all of whom demonstrated the implications of this insight for the reading process. It appeared that there was already a considerable literature in the second language field of which I had not been aware, which discussed the use of schema activation in reading. (See for instance Carrell, 1983, 1985; Carrell and Eisterhold, 1983; Hudson, 1982; Johnson 1981, 1982).

I found the notion of schema theory enticing and I began self observation, trying to develop a sense of the form of my own schemata. Generally it was only when something would surprise me that I would become conscious of my own expectations. One text-related example I discovered concerned the magazine *New Yorker*, which I was first introduced to around this time. I found the magazine tremendously frustrating at first because part way through an article I would suddenly realize that I was reading fiction, not an editorial, and would have to readjust my response to what I had read. Frequently I would be forced to go back to the beginning of the piece and reread it with this new information in mind, before I could feel confident that I had understood it appropriately. The cause of my confusion was the magazine's layout, which gives an identical format to all the feature articles, and which scatters article illustrations, cartoons and random small pictures throughout the journal.

Struggling with these pieces, I realized that I expected editorial articles to look visually different from fiction pieces. I also expected illustrations to be directly related to the story or article appearing on the same page, unless the illustration took the form of a joke or cartoon. There was no particular logic to these expectations—they simply reflected my prior experiences with print. The point is that I had never consciously thought about these expectations until I found them violated. Now that I see the magazine more frequently and have a schema specifically for it, I find it as easy to read as any other. My problems with the *New Yorker* are very similar to the problem encountered by Yusefi, the learner in my pilot study, who did not recognize or did not know the specific layout conventions for completing a form.

Yusefi's and my expectations of print layout are obviously fairly easy to identify and describe. A much more complex and difficult to examine schema, which underlies my *New Yorker* story, relates to my feeling that a change in text genre made it necessary to reread the text activating different information and attitudes.

It is virtually impossible to identify exactly what knowledge, approaches, emotions, strategies, or degrees of belief may have been involved in the expectations that I brought to that article. What seems certain is that the words on the page and my fluent decoding skills were not sufficient alone for me to comprehend the text. The implications of this for my teaching were far-reaching, in that it suggested that a significant component of the literacy process was not being addressed by standard teaching methods. I had to assume that Yusefi, Fazli and my other literacy students brought comparable sets of assumptions to text based on their own experiences. I was interested to know to what extent these assumptions arose from individual experience and how important learners found them.

If my assumptions were so rigid that I could not make sense of an article in a magazine written in my own language, then the likelihood of them interfering with an attempt to read a document from another culture seemed inevitable. If, as I suspected, such expectations and assumptions had a culturally specific component to them, then it was naive to assume that those who were literate in one language could necessarily transfer all their literacy abilities over to the second language. Although there was research about schema activation and its effects, it did not come close to addressing my concerns with the ways in which individual experience shaped the expectations one brought to text. I became committed to the idea of an intensive learner study, which would attempt to identify a learner's expectations and the effect those expectations had on the process of acquiring literacy in a second language

After I had worked with the notion of schema theory for some time I began to question the relationships between the parts of the schema. It seemed to me that the various propositions did not exist independently of each other but were tied into complex structures. None of the material I was reading seemed to address this question of the relationship between the various components. The schema for a restaurant visit for instance was commonly described as including a waiter, a menu, some food, an act of payment, etc, as if a schema were nothing more than a shopping list of items to be expected for a specific occasion. I found the descriptions unsatisfactory and continued to think about what else might be involved, thinking back over my own cross cultural experiences and teasing at those occasions where it was obvious my schemata had not been appropriate.

This issue was a key one for me in that second year of doctoral study, when I was fortunate to have the opportunity to work closely with Mick Connelly in a relationship that he referred to as an apprenticeship. I participated in his courses and we met regularly after each session to talk about every aspect of the classes. In addition, all his students were writing journals, to which both he and I would add a written response. Mick never gave me explicit rules for how to respond to these journals, or for judging whether a class had been successful. Nor did he directly prescribe a particular epistemology. By working with him closely, however, attempting tasks in the light of his example, I came to absorb some of his thinking and some of his art in the way in which Polanyi (1958. 53) describes a successful apprenticeship. By the end of this period, I was a committed narrativist.

I do not remember ever discussing this explicitly. Nor do I recall being affected by reading any of the articles he has written in this area, excellent though they are. Only certain aspects of an understanding can be made explicit and shaped into the words and sentences of an article or book, and those understandings are a small part of what I learned in my apprenticeship.

My understanding of narrative

Raw experience comes to us in tiny isolated fragments and yet we talk about our experience in the form of stories. Just as we have a story grammar for a particular type of text genre, so we have a narrative structure underlying the way in which we try to make sense of experience and the way we choose to see and to tell our own lives.

Initially, we choose to acknowledge, or perhaps we are only capable of acknowledging, a tiny proportion of the experiences available to us. Walking down the street, we discard perhaps such experiences as the pressure of the street on the soles of our feet, the smell of gasoline in the air, the details of many of the storefronts, the clouds in the sky and the faces of passers-by and so on. We choose to pay attention only to a small portion of raw experience and, of course, the selection of the items that we choose to acknowledge is a personal decision affected by our narrative expectations.

We then impose relationships on those experiences that we have acknowledged, grouping certain items into stories. We acknowledge the temporal thread of experience but we choose an arbitrary point and designate it as the beginning of the story. Because we have grown up in a culture in which our stories must have closure, the very definition of a beginning immediately sets up the expectation of an ending. In between these we look for a climax and a resolution. We have a certain number of characters available and we tend to assign roles to ourselves and other people according to the sort of story that we are telling.

If we are telling a story of personal ambition, for instance, we may assign to another player a role such as "rival," not recognizing that the raw experience underlying this understanding may be interpreted in many different ways. Each of these impositions of relationships shapes the way in which we understand other parts of the story, just as notes in a melody are understood differently from the same notes struck at random. Thus the pieces of a story take on a different meaning when they are grouped in this way, and the stories themselves may be understood differently when they are set within the context of a larger story, or seen from a different temporal perspective. We develop our basic narrative patterns through social interaction and through individual experience. Hence the kind of stories we have heard and told in the past will shape the way in which we make sense of the future.

Not all of experience is structured according to the same story, and we may become conscious of this storied nature of experience when we try to come to terms with a complex sequence of events. I first became aware of this when I was attempting to write my personal narrative as a course assignment and found myself having great difficulty in storying an event that had happened to me in my twenties when I had been the victim of an attempted murder. I could tell that story as a tragedy, in which my confidence and spontaneity were permanently crippled. Or I could tell that story as one of triumph, in which I overcame an enormous personal trauma.

In the same way, if less dramatically, I can retell my experience as a mother, a student, or an employee as stories of warm success or frustrated failure. These varying stories are marked in part by the selection of different raw events, but also by the order in which the events are retold, the selection of one or another point as a climax, the mood and setting, which are incorporated into the story and the roles that are assigned to the people involved.

Stories are not self-contained units, which sit unchanging on the shelves of our memories. Each story is part of some larger story, and it will change according to the setting in which it is placed. As MacIntyre (1981. 206-9) points out, the story is shaped too by the intention attached to the actions recounted therein, so that each level of intention will set the story within a larger story. MacIntyre (1981), Carr (1986), Hardy (1968, 1977) and Mink (1978), among others, discuss at some length the question of whether narrative is taken from art and applied to life, or whether narrative is a primary act of mind transferred from life to art.

I have not yet convinced myself of the merits of either side of the question. However, the question does intrigue me, because it clearly relates to second language education. If narrative is a primary act of mind and we are incapable of processing experience in any other way than through narrative structures, one would expect that such preordained structures would appear in all cultures. However, evidence such as that cited above relating to story-grammars, suggests that even if it is a universal human characteristic to interpret experience narratively, the specific stories that we see people using to make sense of experience are often culturally specific.

Some years ago, I attended a conference at which Jerome Bruner spoke on, "Forms of Self Report: Autobiography and its Genres." He was discussing the way we present our personal histories as texts that are subject to revision and amenable to alternative interpretation. One claim I remember Bruner to have made at that conference was to have a significant effect on my thinking about the way in which narrative would affect learning a second language. Although I was later to find I had somewhat restoried Bruner's words[1], it was the restoried version that stayed in my mind and shaped the way I came to understand the role of narrative for literacy education. I, therefore, owe Bruner an apology, along with my thanks for setting me off on a new train of thought.

I remember his words as, "The events that happen to us are less significant than the stories that we have available to make sense of those events." I understood this to mean that any event that may happen to us, irrespective of the nature of that event, can be understood as a triumph, a disaster or a triviality according to the ways in which such things are viewed in the community in which we have been raised. Even such basic elementals as pain can potentially be restoried into positive events. An example might be an injury caused by a physical fight with an unknown assailant. It might be storied as a triumphant entry into maturity via battle; as a traumatic violation of personal space; or as one in an ongoing series of daily battles for survival.

However, we are not raised with all these possible stories available to us for adoption. Instead we accept the limited set of overarching stories that are endorsed by our community and we select and develop our personal stories within the confines of that set. Individuals and individual communities will have particular narrative structures through which they are prone to see the world and will also associate specific events with specific types of stories.

Members of a strongly religious community, for instance, might

---

1 When I was later able to get hold of a printed version of Bruner's speech, I found the actual remark to be, "Self report is framed by stylistic conventions and by rules of genre. From very early in life we are bound by strong conventions regarding not only what we say when we tell about outselves, but how we say it, to whom, etc.... The shape of a life is as much a function of the conventions of genre and style in which it is couched as it is, so to speak, of what 'happened' in the course of that life."

see the hand of God as shaping events and would thus tend to structure their entire view of the world in terms of divine retribution or reward. Specific events such as individual financial success might be placed within a story of divine reward or within one of secular temptation, according to the prevalent community story. Within that community, an individual would also have personal stories of his or her role within the world, so that personal events and interactions would be storied within but still shaped by the larger community story.

As a teacher of learners from other cultures, I had often been exposed to these different ways of understanding the world. I had had Libyan students who would always demur when asked if they would be coming to class next day, because to make such an assertion would be to set their plans in potential opposition to those of God. Eventually I learned to ask them if they would try their best to come to school next day, a question that they could more easily answer. I had had students who assumed I was useless as a teacher because I was a female, and others who assumed I was promiscuous because I was a female Westerner. These assumptions came from community stories, and they varied from community to community.

It seemed inevitable to me that such stories would play a part in the way in which literacy was understood and used in a community and by an individual, and it appeared to be an area that was not being well considered in the current research. Heath's work looked at the way in which a community's understanding of the world affected its use of language, but I felt that the literacy process would also be affected by the stories of the individual learner, and that this possibility had not been explored as yet.

Potentially there would be many stories playing a part in the way in which literacy was used and understood. Communities would have stories about the purposes of literacy and the ways in which literacy could best be used. People who use literacy would be assigned roles within that community story of literacy and would be expected to display or share their literacy expertise in accordance with that story. The relationship between the text and the real world would be understood narratively as would the nature of the process. Individuals would have expectations about the way in which literacy was learned, used and displayed. They would express these expectations through stories of their own abilities as learners, and their understandings of what constitutes good learning and teaching. Would these stories vary across cultures and across individuals? Were the stories easily adapted to new environments? These questions seemed very important for second language literacy but none of the familiar research methods seemed to offer any possibilities of answers.

What was needed, I felt, was an intensive learner study that would consider more than simply observable behaviour but would try to document the learner's story from the inside. I wanted to understand the kind of expectations that an adult attempting literacy in a new language might have and to look at how those expectations would be fulfilled or modified. I wanted to be open to the possibility of information on every aspect of the learning process, so that I could get a sense of the whole experience.

The more I considered the difficulties of asking another person to open his or her heart and mind to me like this, the more convinced I became that the kind of data I wanted could be best gathered through an autobiographical study. I knew I could not claim that the data would necessarily be more honestly portrayed simply because I was reporting on myself. My performance would be a text that I would be called upon to interpret, and as Bruner points out, such self-report texts are "subject to revision, exegesis and reinterpretation" (Bruner, 1987. 2). Crites, in his article on, "The Aesthetics of Self Deception," would go further, suggesting that experience itself is "an imaginative construction"(1979. 107):

> We have an extraordinary power to deceive ourselves...The human propensity for self-delusion is rooted not merely in the way we choose to interpret our experience, nor in occasional pathologies of experience but in the very formation of experience. An aesthetics of experience is also an aesthetics of self deception. (p. 108)

Pointing out that a key part of our self-deception lies in getting others to endorse our story, Crites focuses on the very act of narration as part of the self-deception, saying it consists "in shaping the way they [the facts] are narrated so as to make them add up to a story that is perhaps more favorable to the teller than some other story that might be constructed from the same facts" (p. 120).

I had originally written that I would pledge to make the story free from any conscious distortion, in that I would not intentionally attempt to impress the researcher or provide what appeared to be the required answers, but I was reminded of Crites' remark that, "Surely there are few moments more ripe for self-deception than those in which people are puffing and straining to be honest" (p. 111). I can only counter this by citing Crites once more on the value of the traditional contemplative disciplines, to the aim of clarifying experience. I would agree with him too that, "People do reveal themselves, but mostly indirectly," and trust that the story I would be telling would unfold in sufficient detail to allow the reader to see through whatever cover stories I might be imposing on the experience.

One area in which I was confident that an autobiographical account would be nearer to the "real story" related to its avoidance of the problem of communicating through a foreign tongue. There would be no failures of interpretation between researcher and learner based on simple misunderstanding or misuse of language—a common problem when working with second language learners, and one of which I had been very conscious in the pilot study. There were logistical advantages to an autobiographical study too, since I knew of no other learners who would be prepared to spend an unpaid year exclusively on literacy development.

The final advantage to an autobiographical study came inevitably out of my own personal story. I was raised in a community where personal questions are always asked indirectly, and I am not comfortable asking other people probing questions. When I tried to imagine the demands I would be making on another person, asking them to share memories, explore assumptions and expectations, and discuss feelings, I cringed. The role of researcher would not have been sufficient to let me rewrite my story of appropriate adult interaction.

There was only one way in which I, as the research agent, could come to understand the way in which literacy might be affected by personal and cultural narrative, and that was to become my own subject. I began making arrangements to learn to read and write Chinese.

PART TWO

STUDYING CHINESE

Chapter Five

The stories before the story

The selection of Chinese

In the previous chapters I have attempted to demonstrate how my experiences as an ESL literacy teacher led me to research in this area, and how my interest in the individual literacy user led me to an autobiographical study. What led to my choice of Chinese as the language in which I would try to become literate?

The first decision I made related to the script in which the language was written. It seemed I had essentially three choices available. I could learn an alphabetic language such as Arabic, where a limited number of letters are used to represent the sound of the words. I could learn a syllabic language such as Cree, where the transcription is still based on the sound of the words, but the number of signs to be learned is considerably higher as each combination of consonant and vowel has its own sign. Or I could learn an ideographic system such as Chinese, where the written signs correspond primarily to meanings, not sounds.

As Taylor and Taylor (1995), Tzeng and Hung (1980), Venezky (1973), and others have discussed, the different script systems affect the demands made on the beginning reader. In general, phonics-based systems such as English are considered to make minimal initial demands on the learner's memory, thus allowing a beginning reader to progress to decoding and encoding text fairly rapidly. By contrast, ideographic or logographic systems demand a large initial commitment of memory work before the learner can hope to express or understand much in the way of text.

It was obviously tempting to select an alphabetic system in which I could reasonably expect to become sufficiently literate that I would be able to read and write short pieces by the end of the year. However, my goal was less the development of a certain amount of skill, than it was to see how literacy was understood by different people, and what common ground might lie beneath all manifestations of it. If I chose a literacy system that shared the same basic orthographic structure as English, then any discovery of common ground might simply be a feature of that common alphabetic system. I decided that I needed to choose a literacy system that had as little in common with English as possible, which meant that I was looking for a system where the written symbols were based largely on meaning rather than on sound. Chinese is, of course, the most widely used of the various ideographic languages, which made it an obvious choice.

My decision was also affected by the significant number of Chinese immigrants in Canada, and the likelihood of increased immigration from Hong Kong as 1997 approached. If I were able to develop any real facility in the written language, it would potentially be useful to me in future encounters with Chinese students of all dialect groups. Although my study would be looking more generally at the role of the individual in literacy development rather than the specifics of Chinese literacy, it was likely that in the process I would come to a better understanding of the relationship between English and Chinese literacy, which was something that I would certainly be able to put to good use in future literacy classes.

The final reason that prompted me to choose Chinese was personal, however, and simply reflected an interest in and a fondness for the Chinese people. As I shall be discussing later in this chapter, I had a very positive attitude towards the Chinese culture and was enthusiastic about learning the language.

Having selected Chinese, the question arose as to which dialect I would learn. At that point, I had no real understanding of the implications of choosing one dialect over another, but essentially narrowed the choice to either Cantonese or Mandarin. I knew that Cantonese was the most common dialect spoken in Toronto, which suggested good opportunities for practicing oral language. However, Mandarin was the official dialect, which would be most useful if I were to go to China or back to Singapore, a country I had previously lived in. Both seemed to have advantages and I decided to make the decision based on the best available tutor rather than on the dialect itself.

Writing the preface to the story

My study would essentially be one of looking at the kind of expectations that an adult attempting literacy in a new language might have and exploring how those expectations would be fulfilled or modified. The experience would inevitably be shaped by my prior expectations and assumptions both about myself and about the Chinese language and culture. At the time, I felt it was thus important to document as fully as possible those assumptions and expectations that were held at the beginning of the study.

In retrospect, the material I documented then is of interest largely because of its total irrelevance to the issues that came out of the study. I obviously had little inkling that I would be faced by a challenge to my own sense of self, and to my sense of literacy. Instead, I carefully documented other language learning experiences, friendships with Chinese people, experiences working in Chinese communities such as Singapore, my very limited and often erroneous bits of knowledge about the Chinese language, and so on. The material does provide clues as to my subjectivity as a researcher, and the ways in which that subjectivity was constituted when I began this study. As Peshkin (1988) suggests, I was to find more than one "I" suggested in this material—a conflict that I shall be exploring in later chapters.

The final paragraph of this attempt to describe my preconceptions, reads as follows:

> My initial goal is to be able to stroll through Chinatown, looking at the posters pinned up in the shop windows, and be able to gather the gist of their meaning. Although there are many thousands of characters, I am told that knowing 2000 of the most common will allow one to understand most everyday texts. I would like to be able to walk into a shop, make myself understood to the shopkeeper and successfully complete a purchase without resorting to gesture. I shall aim to achieve this in six months, but I am prepared for it to take up to one year of full-time study.

As will be evident from the above to anyone who has studied Chinese, I had very little conception of the task that was facing me, as is evidenced by my off-hand reference to coming to know 2,000 of the most common characters. Not only is this a goal that I never came anywhere near achieving, but it is demonstrative of certain assumptions about how one might express progress in literacy. However, in this I was perhaps very close to the average ESL literacy learner who comes to the first class with similar misconceptions and a similar tendency to assess literacy according to easily measured criteria.

Finding a teacher

Around this time, I was very fortunate to be introduced to Cindy Lam by a mutual friend, who knew I was looking for a tutor. Cindy was working at that time as an ESL teacher and teacher educator and was studying part-time towards her Master's degree. She had taught ESL literacy to a number of Chinese students, and was interested in literacy as a research topic. I was delighted to hear of someone who was not only qualified to teach me Chinese literacy but who would share my interest in the project.

I have described my first meeting with Cindy in the Introduction to this book. At that time I asked her only enough personal questions to assure myself of her ability to teach me Chinese and of her interest and commitment to the project. As we got to know each other better we began to talk more about our own backgrounds, and I came to understand more of how Cindy thought about language and literacy. As I shall be discussing in later chapters, it became apparent that Cindy and I conceived of literacy differently, and that our different conceptions grew out of our personal and our cultural experiences. For this reason it is important that the reader have some understanding of Cindy's background.

While Cindy was working with me, she was simultaneously taking a Foundations of Curriculum course, for which she was asked to write her *Personal Narrative*. In the text that follows, I have extracted from that and another paper she wrote on *Linguistic and Cultural Identity*, as well as on our personal conversations.

Hayden White, in a discussion of history and narrative, makes a distinction among *annales, chroniques and histoires* (White, 1973a, 1973b), which reflects the degree of unity demonstrated between the events listed. Applying White's distinctions to personal narrative, I find it presumptuous for me to attempt to write Cindy's histoire, or narrative. Consequently, I am calling this Cindy's chronicle.

Cindy's chronicle

Cindy was born in Hong Kong, where she lived with her mother and father and eight siblings. Her father, a university educated man, had serious health problems, which limited his opportunities, and which kept him at home when Cindy was little. She describes him with great affection as "a scholar, a musician and an athlete," who would keep her "intrigued and occupied" when her mother was out, and who would give her unexpected treats of fruit and candy. Her father held education in high esteem and often described it as "the way out." He would not allow Cindy to play with the other neighbourhood children, whom she would watch at play "from the other side of the fence." She invented games for herself, with "playing teacher" being a favourite. When she was six years old, her father died, leaving her mother to raise the nine children alone.

Cindy had some serious health problems when she was little and missed the first year of school entirely. She attended a small, one-room, private school, which included children from kindergarten to grade six, so she was soon able to be working with her peers, although her health problems continued for a number of years.

Asked whether she liked school, she comments on the noise, confusion and activity of the multilevel classroom, but adds that the work was "so easy." She remembers how the students were always ranked when given their report cards, with the top three being given prizes. "I was always able to be in the top three. I remember it as a very proud moment, actually. Standing up to get the prize and the report card—and then coming home." In another context, though, she comments, "Good students are always left alone...apart from standing up to receive a prize at the end of a semester there weren't many chances for those of us at the top to be noticed."

Certainly the school seemed to stress conformity. Cindy comments, "So much of what we did as kids was for approval, and grades and stars...You didn't ask questions and teachers didn't tell you why they were doing it...Discipline is a big part of life."

Cindy kept a private diary, in which she wrote regularly, but she does not remember ever reading books outside of school. Instead she would come home from school and immediately begin her homework, which always included character practice. In particular, she remembers being asked to practice writing her name over and over on a daily basis.

When she was eleven, her mother brought the family to Toronto, where Cindy was placed in grade six. Cindy comments that she entered the Canadian school system with an English vocabulary of little more than "please" and "thank you." In her *Narrative* she writes:

> The first day of school in Canada was scary. Then it was humiliating. Everyone ducked when the teacher asked for a volunteer to be Cindy's 'big sister'. Then it was baffling, 'This is a teacher?' She was a woman with loosely braided hair, a squeaky voice, clad in a work shirt and corduroy skirt, flip-flopping across the room in open-toe clogs. (I had never seen a teacher's toes before).

Cindy speaks of the isolation she felt in school, and of the other children being "less than cordial to New Canadians." As she moved on to high school, she responded by focusing on her school work, which she found easy, developing her academic skills but building up little in the way of friendships. "Everything academic was easy. Everything social was traumatic."

> In retrospect, my acquisition of English was conscious and intense. Inhospitable treatment of New Canadians was probably largely responsible for my determination to learn the language.... I enjoyed tremendous success in both English and French and even in Latin. My diary progresses from all Chinese to English-Chinese to all English with the occasional (experimental) French essay. I was proud of my ever increasing linguistic abilities. Although I continued to speak Chinese at home (a regional dialect with my mother and Cantonese with my older siblings) I read and wrote in it very infrequently. I had stopped writing to my childhood friends in Hong Kong to mask the fact that I could no longer write Chinese coherently and without errors. I did not want to be compared to them; instead I staged a comparison between myself and my Toronto peers, many of whom came to me for help with their English essays and French assignments.

There were many other ethnic Chinese at the high school that Cindy attended. Most of the group were keen to stress their Canadian identity, and "many denied that they could speak their mother tongue...Inherent in an admission to speaking the mother tongue was a confession that one was less than 100% Canadian. Yet they continued to frequent the shops and restaurants in Chinatown and to enjoy the comfort of being with other Chinese. They wanted to be Chinese in English. It was an elusive identity."

Cindy writes that she "...did not share their ambivalence. While I had turned my attention away from Chinese I was never ashamed of it. I was confident that I could always return to it. It was like riding a bicycle, I thought to myself, incognizant of the inevitable."

In grade eleven, Cindy tested this theory by enrolling in a Mandarin course, which was attended primarily by more recent immigrants. She soon discovered that language learning is not like riding a bicycle and comments that her "ego took a thrashing." However, she adds that, "While my friends continued to deny having any knowledge of Chinese, I continued to deny that I was losing it," and reassured herself that she would come back to developing her written Chinese when she had more time. She continued to do well academically in school and in reaction to the school's stereotyping of all Chinese students as "math whizzes," she selected only arts courses, eventually going on to the University of Toronto to study English and French. At university, she was one of only a handful of visible minorities in her chosen departments.

> Nowhere had I felt to the same extent the isolation of being a minority as I did while I was in University. The combination of being Chinese and an English major was somewhat of a shock to many, students and professors alike. I was once asked in casual conversation what my course of study was. I replied 'English,' to which he enquired 'Why? You speak okay to me.'

> I had more than one confrontation with professors who attributed my difficulties with the subject to my being an immigrant...When I continued on to the Faculty of Education, I chose English to be my teaching subject and the isolation continued. When I stood in front of a class to teach mother tongue English during my practicum I felt an indescribable sense of displacement...I did not attempt to get a position as a mother tongue English teacher or as a French as a Second Language teacher (for which I later became certified) not because I doubted my abilities but because I no longer had the stamina to face career long isolation.

While studying for her B.A. and B.Ed., Cindy was also working as a bank teller in an area with many Chinese customers. It was a time when Chinatown was growing considerably, and the situation was ripe for her to rediscover her Chinese identity.

> Both my bank job and the Chinatown expansion were favourable factors, which initiated my rediscovery of Chinese. In the bank, I used Chinese as a public language for the first time. Against the isolation in school, I felt a renewed sense of intimacy with Chinatown, and with my Chinese colleagues who were wonderfully tolerant of my underdeveloped command of our language. I pursued every joke, every humorous remark and realized how invigorating it was to laugh again in Chinese. I immersed myself in videotapes, music, magazines and grammar books and thus began my re-acculturation. It was only after I had regained some Chinese that I realized or admitted to myself that I had lost much of what I came to Toronto with.

To supplement her income as a bank teller, she began teaching adult English as a Second Language at night. She says she took the job more out of need than desire, and indeed had to be talked into it by a friend. However, she soon became very involved with her students, taking a particular interest in their problems and lives outside of the classroom. She comments that, "My early teaching techniques stemmed from the Chinese tradition of the teacher as the authority figure. My involvement in my students' personal lives was very untraditional. I maintained the traditional image in front of the class and the other when the class was over. (Some of my students, in retrospect, must have suspected me of having schizophrenic tendencies.)"

Soon she was supporting herself by a variety of part-time ESL jobs, including bilingual ESL for Chinese learners. As her experience grew, so did her confidence in her abilities as a teacher. "For the first time I was totally at ease with my surroundings. I was among other minorities who needed me and who did not question why I was there."

Asked about her teaching philosophy, she recalls, "…the strong sense of routine in the classroom, the laboriously planned lessons and the need to know exactly where I was heading, or where I was leading the students at all times." Gradually as she built up confidence in her teaching, she began to resolve the split between the authoritative in-class teacher and the caring out-of-class facilitator. It began when she realized that a long series of lessons on bank language had been irrelevant to learners who avoided all-English banks.

> It was a jolting revelation, one that shook my self-credibility. Painstakingly I convinced myself to put my authority on the line and I asked them what they wanted and needed. When that was not met with disaster, other changes began to creep in. I made changes in routines, seating arrangements and most importantly, in the curriculum. There were unconscious changes too [including allowing] myself to be led off on tangents by my students. With an increased workload I was forced to spend less time and energy on personal favours. I economized by covering recurring issues in class and the students approached me less frequently after class. I did not know at the time that I had haphazardly improved my teaching. As I depolarized my two persona I became a much better, more effective teacher.

After some years as a teacher, Cindy was asked to take on the administration of the evening program and to become involved in teacher education. Eventually, she became a lead teacher in the adult ESL program for a large school board, a position that involved her in helping other teachers with their practice, on both a day-to-day basis and through teaching formal in-service courses. She enjoyed working with other teachers, and comments that she found it an eye opener because she "...had experienced teaching in total isolation up to that point." Observing in other classrooms helped her realize "how much one's teaching was reflective of oneself, that it is not just how one was trained, but how one processed the training."

In Cindy I had found what appeared to be the perfect Chinese literacy tutor: sufficiently Canadian for us to be able to communicate with little cultural interference; sufficiently Chinese to give me an authentic literacy experience. I looked forward to our classes with enthusiasm.

Chapter Six

The story of learning Chinese

In the later chapters of this manuscript I will discuss how my personal and social narrative had an impact on the way in which I learned literacy in Chinese and the impact that that experience had in turn on myself. To help the reader follow that discussion adequately, I would like first to describe the experience of the Chinese study. The focus of this study is, of course, on the experience of learning to read and write Chinese. However, my progress as a literacy student and my role as a researcher were inevitably affected by the classes in oral Cantonese that I was taking simultaneously. Consequently, I describe below how the entire experience unfolded, even though the data related to oral language learning is not fully explored in this study.

Planning for the study

Cindy and I agreed that we would begin Cantonese classes in the fall, with our initial plan being that we would meet twice weekly for approximately two hours per meeting. To supplement these classes, I decided to enroll in a course in spoken Cantonese offered at the local university. This course was not intended to teach any Chinese literacy, but I felt that Cindy and I would be able to make more rapid progress with the characters if I had a wider oral knowledge base on which to build. I hoped the course would also provide me with the opportunity to share experiences with other learners and to observe my progress under the stress of the formal classroom setting in which most second language literacy teaching takes place. The university lessons were scheduled to run through the academic year, which was approximately the duration that Cindy and I had mapped out for our tutorial classes.

One of my major concerns at this stage of preparing for the study was the actual methodology of data collection. One part of me wanted to organize the entire process, setting up categories and checklists to make sure that I didn't unwittingly omit critical areas of information. Another part recognized that once I set up such a system, I would inevitably start to shape my experiences and my observations to match whatever categories I had decided to observe.

Consequently I decided to use very global methods of data collection, which would aim to record all the information available to me without any attempt to pre-sift or categorize it. I planned to tape record each tutorial with Cindy and each class at the university. During the classes I would also make brief written notes as memory aids to information that would not be collected on the tape. Such notes would include visual material, emotional reactions, triggered memories, personal strategies, observations on other students, and so on. After the classes I would transcribe the complete tape recording, and then annotate the transcription, incorporating any notes that I had made at the time, and adding any other material that seemed relevant. In addition, I planned to keep a daily journal in which I would reflect on the course lessons, the tutorials and the assignments, and attempt to record on paper both a detailed record of my direct interactions with the new language and a sense of my attitudes and images towards the process as it [was] being undergone. I also planned to use recorded think-aloud protocols in an attempt to capture some of the ongoing thought patterns when I was actually attempting literacy and language-based homework tasks.

It is probably apparent from these plans that I did not understand the amount of time needed to transcribe tapes. I doubt if I could have fulfilled this schedule even if the tapes had been recorded entirely in English, and of course the time demands were aggravated because my tapes contained considerable amounts of Cantonese dialogue. I was setting myself up here for what was to be an ongoing stress throughout the project, as I constantly struggled to get caught up with my transcription, annotation and journalling. This was eventually to take shape as a pull between Jill-as-language-learner, who wanted to continue with as many classes as possible, and Jill-as-researcher, who wanted to restrict language learning input to an amount that could be adequately recorded.

The first classes: September and October

My first Cantonese class was a tutorial with Cindy, held in the rather cramped quarters of my shared student office. Cindy did not go straight into teaching, but began by asking me to tell her what I expected of her. I answered by talking about teaching methodology:

Jill I guess in some ways I expect you to orchestrate the lessons. That it would be your decision whether the most useful thing for me to start with is, maybe, a group of characters that sound the same or a group of characters that have meaning, or whether you decide that you would prefer to start with some oral language. To that extent I'm assuming that because you know the language, you're in a better position to point me in a particular direction. On the other hand, I would like to feel that when we get into the process enough I have some basis on which to base a judgment, that I can say to you, "I really have a hard time with this, could we spend some more time on it," or "I've been trying to decipher characters on the street and all the characters we covered so far are very literary, could we do some street characters so that I've got a chance of walking down the street and seeing if I can recognize something?" You know, that kind of thing.

You know, I'm starting from an absolute blank at the moment so I guess, because I'm an absolute blank, I'm sort of sitting here saying, in effect, "Okay Cindy, teach me." Teach me whatever you want, any way you want, but, if a month or so into the process I can say to you, "I wonder if such and such a method would be useful for the activity we tried together last week," that that would be something we could at least discuss. You know the language, and if you say, "No, it wouldn't work for Chinese because of so and so," then that's fine, but that I wouldn't be treading on your toes by making the suggestion.

I then went on to address what to me was a much more difficult area to raise—that was the question of how we might resolve and indeed exploit potential conflicts. It seemed likely that there would be occasions when teacher and learner saw things differently. The research process would force me to make such things explicit rather than following my normal social pattern of avoiding direct acknowledgment of any difference.

Jill ...every fourth lesson, or every two weeks depending on how we work our lessons out, I would write you a letter that said, "This is what I think has happened over the last two weeks." Inevitably, I think there are going to be places where I think,

"Oh, she's asking too much of me, I can't do this," and that I can say so in a letter without feeling that it is a criticism of you as a person—that those become learning situations we can explore—and that you would feel equally free in your response.

I would ask you to respond to the letters—you would write a response to my letter plus your own view of what's happening and you would feel free enough in that letter to say, "I am getting so exasperated by the fact that you're not doing this or that," you know, that you wouldn't feel you'd have to give the kind of encouragement you would offer to a student in normal circumstance, but that it could be a truer analysis. I'm sure that my responses to those would be to say, "I was deathly hurt when Cindy said I was being stupid about so and so," but I still think we have to have it, even if it does hurt my feelings! [laughing] I think we need a honest sense of when I fail to meet your expectations.

Cindy Okay. Well that's, er—some of this is new to me, I mean that's never been asked of me before. I've never taught in this context before, because what's at stake for you isn't the same as what's at stake for students—those are ESL students—it's not as important for you how much you learn as it is important for you to, I guess, document the process. That's why I think it is important for us to have these reports and I'll have to say again that I expect a lot of feedback from you, as I told you before this is very new for me.

Cindy went on,
The next question I was going to ask you was, "If you had a choice what would you do first?" For instance the thing you might think of is numbers. Or your name. If you wanted to find it somewhere, on a piece of paper or something...or whether you feel it is necessary for you to have a name in Chinese. Is it necessary for you to know what my name is in Chinese? Those are the questions I have. Some people, the first thing they ask is, "I want to know my English name."

Jill I hadn't thought of it but I think that would be nice...I would like, I think, to start with print that I might meet in the environment so that I can go out and look for it. So perhaps numbers—do they put prices up in Chinese or do they...?

Cindy Arabic. They use Arabic numbers

Jill   Well, then maybe the names of some of the vegetables, or things that they might actually label. Oh dear, I should have gone to look at the street signs, not so much the street signs but the store signs. Or a menu—how about some of the food items because I could look for them on a menu?

Cindy   I have something to say about that, because in terms of writing, you really do have to begin with the simplest characters.

Jill   Well then let's follow that pattern but if we are looking for an example and it can come from these environments, then fine. Let's start with the simplest characters and work on up. Because I think we can rely on the university course to take me through, "My name is…," and it might well be that if I can get oral control of, "My name is…." I can come to you and say I now have a piece of Cantonese that I want to learn. But let's do the print stuff in the way that it's logical to want to write it. Start with simple characters and work up.

Cindy   Well that's the logical—that's the way it's been logical for a lot of people to learn Chinese, but you may find your own way. You may find what I am going to give you too easy.

Jill   [laughter] I doubt it.

Cindy   That's also possible. I can't assume that everybody should start the same way.

Cindy had brought along an illustrated text book, which was developed for children learning Chinese in Heritage language classes. Each page provided a sample character done in brush strokes, and a chart of one-inch squares designed for character practice. Somewhat ominously, Cindy commented that she did not feel the forty-eight squares provided for each character would give me sufficient practice space, so she asked me to practice on photocopied charts rather than writing in the book.

Although teaching me numerals was obviously Cindy's primary agenda for the first lesson, she actually began her introduction to Chinese by talking about her own name. In what was to be a very typical pattern, she wrote the name in Chinese characters and discussed its meaning before she provided the sound of the new words.

Cindy   My Chinese name, my last name is first—Lam—and then the middle word—there are three words usually in a Chinese name—is small and the last word by itself would mean very spoiled or even barbaric—that's if you take it apart. But the reason why I was given that name is because of the two words in the middle, which follow my last name. If they were connected to something else it would mean a woman with a very slender figure, and it isn't really as crass sounding as that—it's supposed to be very nice. And that's what it means.

Having shown me her name in standard characters and in cursive, Cindy asked me to try writing. The way we worked with the characters was to be typical of many encounters to come over the next few weeks. First, Cindy commented on how rapidly I was writing the characters. I assumed this was praise and continued to work rapidly. A little later she commented on the stroke work again, in a way that made it clear that her earlier comment was not intended as a compliment.

Cindy   [It's interesting] that you should be doing the strokes so quickly. I expected—you know what I expected—I expected this [draws heavy slow strokes]. I expected—probably because I've seen kids and that's the way we started—everybody moving very slowly—and especially for someone who has never attempted it before. I find that very...[laughter]

Jill   Maybe because I like to sketch?

Cindy   Ah, yes that's true. You're very light handed as if you are sketching. But the thing to remember is you have to be more heavy handed than that if you want to get the strokes because it just doesn't have the same effect. If you want it to be sharp you can't do it like that. You have to press hard.

Although I increased the pressure, I still maintained my speed. Some minutes later she addressed the topic of pace directly.

Cindy   I think you have to...you're rushing through them. It doesn't matter how many you do. You just have to do them well.

Jill   Yeah, yeah, okay.

Cindy   So do them slowly.

Another pattern of the study demonstrated clearly in this first lesson was the difference in the ways we talked about the characters. I found it very difficult to work from a single handwritten model, and tended to ask for very specific rules.

Jill   Er…I don't know what the essentials are and I don't know whether what I produce is within the boundaries of tolerance of normal variation or whether I malign the basic character…I'm looking at the fact that you crossed the blue line there and I'm thinking, now is that critical?

Cindy's response to this particular question was, "Don't worry." In response to other similar queries, she responded, "Watch me do it again," "Watch me do this," or "That one is good." While I appeared to see the characters as so many intersecting lines drawn in relationship to each other, she saw them as whole units that could not be broken up in that way.

Because, at this stage, I saw the task of correctly producing a character as one of visual and small muscle coordination, I asked questions that focused towards the development of those skills. Cindy, however, responded from her own more holistic understanding. Discussing the implications of incorrect stroke order, for instance, she commented that it would be very difficult to produce a good character if she made the right hand stroke before the left. Thinking about physical production problems, I responded, "Your hand would be travelling the wrong way."

Cindy's point had been quite different, however. "Well, I wouldn't be able to create the same feeling of unity in the word."

The bulk of this first lesson was spent on the characters for 1, 2, 3 and 4. We followed a pattern here that was to become our standard way of working with new characters. Having demonstrated them for me, Cindy watched me as I did some initial practice attempts until I had the basic strokes and stroke order under control. The next step was the introduction of the sounds for the characters and some oral work with tone, and with matching characters to sounds.

Cindy then asked me to do some manipulations with the new characters, writing them to her dictation, combining them in sequences, and so on. She used the brush-drawn sample characters from the children's text to introduce these new words.

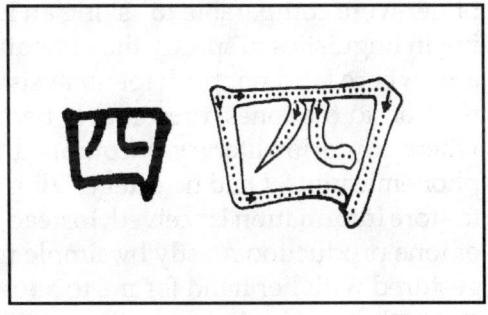

Figure 7

Inherent in the brush-work strokes were extra curves and end pieces that I found difficult to reconstruct with my felt tip pen. It was also difficult to determine whether such variations were a critical part of the character or merely an artifact of the brush. These did not seem to be issues that we could easily resolve, as in this example of miscommunication:

Jill   Is it a curved stroke, or is the ideal one a straight line?

Cindy   It's not straight like this because it was originally done with a brush; that's why it looks like a bone. The brush creates these thick little corners here. You can see it isn't really straight, sort of pointed up a bit.

When we moved on to the sounds of the characters, there were related problems. Once again I wanted to be able to break the unit into component pieces that I could label and identify. When Cindy first modelled the Cantonese sound for one, I did not fulfill her request to repeat it, but instead tried to identify the sounds I was hearing.

Jill   I'm really having to struggle to hear whether there is closure on that.

Cindy   You have to stop it. Okay? Instead of saying…you probably have a tendency to add a "t," like *yat*, or *yad* with a "d." There's nothing…well, there's a sort of a stop but there isn't any letter to it. *Ya*.

Cindy, of course, had never had any cause to break Cantonese down according to the English phonetic system, and consequently found such questions difficult to answer. The demands I was making of her were comparable to asking an English speaker with no training in linguistics to specify the intonation pattern in a sentence. One area where I did not push for analysis and rules of definition was in relation to the tones, presumably because in contrast to phonemes where my prior literacy encouraged me to break sounds up into phonemic units, I had no categorizing system at this stage by which to store information I received. Instead, I appear to approach the task of tone production mostly by simple mimicry. At one point she has gestured with her hand for me to allow the tone to fall on the word *yi*, and I comment in some exasperation:

Jill   Yi. Yii, Yiii. I know cognitively it goes down but I don't hear it as going down. I can't hold in my head the tone that is right.

After I had made some approximation of the sounds of the new words, Cindy moved on to various activities in which I read or wrote the characters. Again, in this first lesson, a warning note was struck that was to be heard in a number of future lessons. One of the tasks Cindy asked me to do was to write the characters in response to her dictation. She read out the Chinese versions of the string, 3241231432, and I attempted to write each character appropriately as she dictated. When Cindy looked at my work, she commented:

Cindy This one is—you're losing your concentration and going too quickly. You noticed your own mistake here, which is good but this one is...

Jill   Lousy? [laughter] Okay, let's try it again. Yeah, that's sort of a Western notion, almost, that, "Oh well, the current task is to show that I know what the number is and not to do the character properly."

Cindy Mmm, we have to concentrate on more than one thing at a time. [pause] Good.

Despite the apparently good humoured response, I have to confess that I was irritated by her reaction at the time, though I did not verbalize it either to her or even, at that point, to myself. In my notes on this lesson I wrote,

> I immediately did it like a vocabulary test. She would say it and I would write it down as fast as I could to be ready for the next one. And it was obvious that my letters [sic] were departing from what they should be quite radically in this hurry, that I was not thinking about character shape anymore and that this was not an appropriate way to do it.

Rather more honestly, I annotated these notes somewhat later to read, "I felt as if I had lost points in a multiple choice test for going out of the lines when ticking the correct boxes." There were to be many instances in the weeks to come where we would discover that we had differing assumptions as to the purpose of a task. I was already aware of this at a cognitive level by the end of the first class, as the following comment suggests.

Jill   I'm trying to say to myself, "Slow down, you don't get prizes for being quick." It's like all my learning is sort of, "The quick answer is better than the correct one five minutes late." [laughter]. That's a whole new thing.

However, acknowledging this was a very different thing from actually understanding it or changing my behaviour as a result of it. I was to find this issue to be one of the most challenging aspects of learning Chinese literacy in the weeks to come.

In the last part of the lesson, Cindy introduced a new activity. She had brought along a tape of a Cantonese singer, from which we listened to a song in which she thought the words were exceptionally clear and easy to hear. After she had played the song, she asked me if I had noticed anything.

As always, when faced by a musical task, I felt a sense of panic. I'm not exactly tone-deaf but I'm certainly below average in musical skills. I had not known why Cindy was playing the song, or what I should be listening for. I certainly had not noticed the repetition that was so evident to her. She assured me that the refrain included a word with which I was familiar. She asked me to listen to the tape before the next class and see if I could identify the word. After she left, I played the entire song nine times without recognizing anything.

Finally I gave up on my listening skills and fell back on a cognitive strategy. I listed the words that she had taught me, and played only the refrain, checking for one particular sound each time. Working in that way, I was soon confident that I had heard the number three—*sàam*. Unfortunately it later turned out that I was mistaken. I was hearing not *sàam* but *sâm*, which is the word for heart. Perhaps because my performance on this task was not too impressive, we did not work with music again.

A week after my first lesson with Cindy, I had my first class of the university course in oral Cantonese. The class was held in a fairly small, pleasant room in one of the newer university buildings. The twenty-eight people present at this first class were squeezed around a large rectangle of tables designed to seat a somewhat smaller class.

I was surprised by a number of things on this first night. For some reason I had anticipated a larger, darker more old-fashioned room with rows of desks all facing forward—the kind of room in which I had studied as a child. The presence of ten or twelve Chinese faces among the students was also unexpected in this beginners' course. In some ways, though, the biggest surprise was the lecturer's approach. He began by urging us to, "Speak up, don't be afraid. If you make any mistakes, it's okay—you are just starting to learn Cantonese."

Listening to these words, and hearing him describe the conversational approach to teaching the language he would use, I realized that I had assumed I would be taught by the traditional grammar-translation approach, which had been used in my French and Latin classes in high school. There was no rational reason for this assumption, of course. It is likely, I think, that some of my expectations were related specifically to the subject I was studying, and reflected my experience with Chinese learners who tended to expect traditional teaching methods. However, I suspect too that assuming the student role in this particular context had brought to the surface some of my high school memories and high school expectations.

I am at a loss to explain why my expectations of this course should have been so influenced by the study patterns of my youth, particularly when I had been in graduate school courses so much more recently. It is possible that these high school expectations had dogged all my graduate study, but because I have never had previous cause to make my expectations explicit I had not confronted them before. Certainly, later in this course I was to discover with embarrassment that it was not merely a matter of high school expectations, but also high school behaviours that were shaping my performance.

The teacher, whom I shall call David Lee, began by giving us a short introduction to the Cantonese dialect, explaining that Cantonese is closer to the classical Chinese language than is Mandarin.

> Cantonese is much closer to the language of ancient China than is Mandarin, so when you read classical Chinese—Tang poetry—it is much better to read it in Cantonese, because Cantonese still retains the tones of ancient Chinese...In modern Chinese, Mandarin, there are four tones, first, second, third and fourth tone. For instance, *mà, ma, mah, màh*. Whereas in Cantonese, it's much more complicated. We have nine tones, that's why native speakers of English find it much more difficult to pick up Cantonese.

This was not an auspicious beginning for someone who is not strong on aural activities, but I was reassured by Mr. Lee's systematic presentation of the material to be covered. He did not expect me to be capable of remembering and reproducing sounds after merely hearing them. Instead, we would be given a text (Chik, 1985), which used Yale Romanization—a system that breaks down the Cantonese oral language into sounds that can be transcribed in the Roman alphabet. Although many of the sounds were still extremely difficult to hear and to produce, I welcomed the charts showing the nineteen possible initial sounds, and the fifty-one potential finals. Large though the number of combinations could be, at least they gave me the sense of a limited number of possibilities to be learned. Prior to this point I think I had assumed an unlimited number of new sounds to be conquered, with each new word bringing a new challenge. I welcomed too the ability that Yale Romanization gave me to classify and record the new language I was learning. In our second lesson, for example, Cindy had taught me the character and sound for "seven." Transcribing that lesson I had variously recorded *tyat, tyut, chut, jut* and *cha* in an attempt to express the sound I was hearing. In the Yale text, I found the word transcribed *chât*, a transcription that encoded both the tone and the pronunciation of the word.

Given that the decision to assign particular letters to sounds that do not appear in English is essentially an arbitrary one, such a transcription does not help one to pronounce the word. Nonetheless, I was relieved to see that the sounds could be fixed into visual units so that the relationship could be seen between them, and I immediately felt better about my chances of learning the language.

> He has a systematic approach to represent both sound and the tone. Cindy and I spent a lot of time together this morning trying to decide on the sound for "I"—*ngor*, we called it. Lee transliterated it as *ngóh*. Similarly, *sei, chât, sàam and sahp* seem clearer when I see them written because I can recognize the relationship between them. Thinking back to my difficulty in transcribing the notes on my lesson with Cindy, a lot of the problem was with knowing how to record these sounds.

Our teacher worked his way through the various symbols used in the Yale system, asking the class to repeat the sounds and words after him, initially as a whole group, and later as individuals. In the process of doing this, he explained the meaning of all the Cantonese words used as examples, commonly putting them into the context of a Cantonese phrase or sentence. Intellectually I welcomed the fact that he was introducing us to so much language, but as a student I was distressed to hear phrases that I could not even hear as words, much less understand or remember. I seemed to feel that I should have control of everything the teacher said or did, and I found it difficult to move on to new material, when I was still struggling to sort out the previous sentence. I was grateful for the small head start that my work with Cindy had given me.

At the beginning of the class the group of students were very quiet, but as we answered our questions in turn, we began to relax a little with nervous laughter. My notes on the class read:

> The class seems to relax a bit during this practice, especially when some of the learners are prepared to admit their fears, confess they are stumped, etc, there are gales of laughter. A lot of time is spent on *ngoh*, which continues to give difficulty…I was quite happy to join in. I liked the fact that [the teacher] did a lot of repetitions as a whole class and I was able to speak up loud and clear. You didn't feel that you were putting your personality at risk.

Inevitably, however, the teacher moved on to individual work, and I became very aware of my personality being at risk. I didn't merely want to do it right. I wanted to do it better than anybody else. This was not the last time I was to become aware of my competitive classroom behaviour.

> Then he went around the entire class…I found I was hoping very much to be given one of the easy ones, wanting a chance to show off but dreading being the first to be asked to do something…I seemed to get a tough set of words to say and I was disappointed because I had hoped to be able to do better. And yet in fact the class as a whole did not do well. The only people who seemed to find it easy were those with Chinese faces who seemed to have some previous exposure…The tones are quite baffling. You really don't even feel confident that those differences exist much less that you can hear them.

Our teacher was unfailingly encouraging, on this first night, as he was to be for the entire course. He constantly reassured us that we would get used to the tones, and that by the time Easter came we would all be capable of holding a conversation in Cantonese. At that point it seemed unlikely to me, but I reserved judgment as I set off for home.

Getting used to the classes: October and November

Over the next four or five weeks the study began to settle into a more regular rhythm, with a clear pattern to each week's activity. The week for me began on Tuesday mornings when Cindy gave me my literacy tutorial. (Time pressures had changed our original intention of meeting twice weekly.) The rest of Tuesday and all of Wednesday would be spent transcribing and if possible beginning the annotation of the tape recording of the session. This was rarely finished before Wednesday evening when I attended the oral Cantonese class. Transcribing the two-and-a-half-hour tape of the university class took up the whole of Thursday and Friday and a chunk of the weekend too. Also on the weekend I would do my character practice and the homework for both classes. Mondays were scheduled for annotating the computer transcripts and writing lengthier, more reflective pieces in my journal to supplement the brief daily entries. Most Mondays, however, it seemed I would find myself with a backlog of transcription or homework, so that there was usually a real sense of pressure to get the various tasks completed before I began a new round of classes the next day.

Patterns were also becoming established in the classes themselves. As I got used to my new teachers and to their methods, I began to expect certain things to happen and to see the various classes in relation to each other. In the oral course I was taking at the university, one clear pattern was the ongoing reduction in class size. By the beginning of November there were only twelve of us who continued to attend my particular class with any regularity.

Most of the Westerners present were either married to Chinese spouses, or had business connections with Hong Kong. Two of the Chinese came from Cantonese homes but considered English their first language, and three more were fluent in another dialect of Chinese. Most people in the class had constant access, therefore, to speakers of Cantonese outside of the classroom, as was evidenced by the fact that a lot of the new language heard in the classroom was introduced by the students. My initial sense that perhaps I had an edge over the other students because of my tutorials with Cindy was fairly short lived, therefore.

The bulk of the first two oral classes was spent teaching us to be literate in the Yale system, so that we could recognize the conventions of sound and tone as indicated through letters and diacritical marks. Because Yale simplified my transcription problems, and I spent many hours per week transcribing my classes, I became familiar with the system fairly rapidly. However, it was noticeable that my visual memory was selective. Once I had seen a phrase written in Yale, I usually was able to remember it.

For instance the teacher regularly used a phrase that meant, "Do you have any more questions?" I began to recognize this in context but could not sort out the various sounds or repeat it until he wrote it on the board for us as, *"Yáuh mòuh mahn tàai a?"* When I came to rewrite it, however, I would find that I had learned it as if it were an English phrase, remembering the alphabetic letters but forgetting the diacritical marks. I would also occasionally forget the letter "h," which functions as a tone marker, not as a phoneme, or the double vowel, which indicates vowel length. Apparently my visual memory for word spelling was not simply capturing an image as I had imagined, but was considerably influenced by my first language literacy skills.

Once we had some understanding of the transcription and sound system, we began to work more systematically with the textbook *Every Day Cantonese* (Chik Hon Man, 1985). This text was designed for Hong Kong residents and followed a broadly situational approach with chapters on shopping, visiting a restaurant, bank and so on. For each situation, the text provided a dialogue, vocabulary list, grammatical features, question-and-answer exercises and drills. A cassette tape provided a recording of the dialogue and most of the oral exercises.

I found that I enjoyed having a textbook and being able to predict what would be coming up in a new class. I rarely found the time to read ahead as I intended to, but I frequently found it valuable to go through the textbook after class, matching a transcription to a sound, or clarifying a rule. Just as in my work with Cindy, I was constantly trying to classify and organize the material I was learning, so the explicit grammatical rules were very welcome. This tendency was one that was reinforced by Mr. Lee, who always presented the language as an organized system, stressing the relationships between three or four examples rather than presenting a word or phrase as an individual entity.

This led to a variety of digressions on the part of the teacher as he brought in other vocabulary items that perhaps shared the same tone or vowel sound as the word under discussion, or as he tried to explain the cultural background to a certain phrase. Mostly, I welcomed these digressions, but on occasion, in these early days, I found myself being very critical of his teaching methodology. Usually, my criticisms would come when he was working through a drill on sounds and became distracted by commenting on the meaning or transcription of the sample words. I found it hard enough to distinguish between two similar sounds presented consecutively, and it seemed an impossible task when two or three sentences of explanation intervened between the contrasted sounds. I wrote in my journal at the time:

> As an ESL teacher I am getting upset because the purpose of the exercise, which is tone recognition, is being lost to a vocabulary building exercise. If I am going to build vocabulary I want more useful words than 'perfume'. I cannot hear the distinction between different tones when they are separated from each other.
>
> He then calls on individuals to read out a pair [of words where the tone is significant] making the contrast evident. As the first person on the alphabetic list I get to go first, distinguishing *tóuhngoh* from *tóuhngò*, that is, *hunger* from *diarrhea*. I try them without ever having heard his model. Everyone roars with laughter—at my task, and with relief that it wasn't theirs.

Despite the disclaimer of speaking as an ESL teacher, I hear the high school student voice in that entry. One of the more positive patterns that seemed to have stayed with me from high school was that my urge to show off encouraged me to be a risk taker in the classroom, a feature that research suggests is an asset in language learning (Naiman et al. 1978; Rubin, 1975; Seliger, 1983a; Gillette,

1987). The degree to which people actively participated seemed in part to be a cultural pattern. My journal notes, "I seem to be a risk taker in this group. The Chinese don't answer questions unless asked directly—even though they know the answers better than we do!" In these first weeks of the course, nearly all the questions came from Westerners, though this was a pattern that was to change as the group got smaller.

Once the classes moved away from tone drills and onto phrases and sentences, I began to feel very positive about the course. I found the recorded dialogues understandable, and I enjoyed reading along from the transcript in the text book, trying to match my intonation to what I was hearing. I was usually able to perform well in class, no doubt aided by the fact that I had thoroughly revised the previous week's work in the process of transcribing it. I was building control of basic patterns and vocabulary so that I could make simple statements or questions, slotting new vocabulary into known patterns.

The textbook provided a short Cantonese-to-English glossary, which allowed me to look up new words I met in the text and build up my vocabulary. By November I was feeling very confident that I would indeed do well in this course, and fulfill the teacher's claim that I could hold a conversation with a native speaker by Easter.

I was not feeling so sanguine at this point about my progress in the literacy classes, however. When Cindy and I met, we would largely follow the pattern set up in the first class. After greetings and some social interaction, she would review my written homework, and check that I remembered the oral forms for the work I had written. Then she would introduce me to three to five new characters, which I would attempt under her supervision, and work on later at home.

I was very troubled by my slow progress during this period. I was concerned as both a researcher and as a learner. The researcher fretted because, if I learned only three or four characters a week, it seemed unlikely that I would be able to attempt meaningful text within the time frame of the study. When I verbalized my discontent it was usually in the voice of the researcher. The real distress was felt by the language learner, however, who saw the limited progress as personal failure.

I considered that I was working hard at learning the characters. Usually I knew the shapes within a few minutes of first being introduced to them. For homework I would practice characters literally hundreds of times, so I was quite confident that I had learned them well. And yet, Cindy would commonly ask me to practice them some more. Often I didn't understand what I was supposed to be practicing. I would spend long periods trying to recreate some feature that I had triumphantly "recognized" as significant in the model, only to discover that it was an insignificant variant.

The transcripts of this period show that Cindy praised my efforts in the tutorial classes. I discounted her praise as meaningless encouragement, however, because to me it seemed evident that if my work were really satisfactory, we would be progressing more rapidly.

In the next chapter I shall be considering this conflict in considerable detail, looking at the way in which it was played out, and the impact that the experience had on me. For this overview chapter, it is perhaps sufficient to say that I was unhappy and discouraged at this point, primarily because I didn't understand what Cindy was trying to teach me. My reaction was to fall back on patterns of learning that had proved successful for me in the past, searching for rules that I could apply and trying hard to link my new learning to existing pieces of knowledge.

As I shall be discussing in the next chapter, these strategies were of limited value in learning Chinese literacy, at least the Chinese literacy that Cindy was trying to teach. I found it very stressful to be making my best efforts as a learner and yet to be achieving what I saw as so little success. The problem was sometimes aggravated by well-meaning acquaintances who would ask questions about my progress. I remember the man with whom I shared my student office asking, around this time, whether I could write sentences yet. I shook my head in some embarrassment, and admitted that I only knew seventeen characters, ten of which were numbers. I made some remark to the effect that at that rate of progress, it would be years before I could write sentences. What was it that was so difficult with the characters, he wanted to know. Did I find them hard to remember? Oh no, I found myself assuring him. They weren't hard at all. It was my teacher, she wouldn't let me go on any faster.

I shocked myself a little with this remark. I think I had been trying to put some of the "blame" on Cindy for a while but my sense of obligation to her for giving up her time to teach me had prevented me from allowing it to surface. Certainly my sense of sociality prevented me from raising it with her except in the most oblique ways. I suggested, for example, that she might assign me characters for home study, and I worked ahead in the children's book practicing new characters without any sense of the sound or the meaning of the word I was writing. It was only later when I had begun to feel reassured about my progress that I was able to openly discuss this question with her.

In my concern that November over what I perceived as disappointing progress, I did not recognize the potential value for the inquiry of the conflict in which I was embroiled. I was working crazy hours trying to learn the language and get the data recorded, while still holding my family life together at the same time. In particular, the task of transcribing and annotating the tapes of the lessons took an alarming amount of time. The tapes of my classes with Cindy were fairly easy to transcribe since they were essentially a conversation. Cindy never used unknown language, so that the Cantonese that appeared on the tape was language with which I was familiar.

The tapes of the university course were very different, however. There were numerous speakers, many of whom were not close enough to the microphone to be easily heard. Often more than one voice would be heard at a time, or the activity would demand complicated patterns of choral response and sentence build-up that were difficult to transcribe. Most significant of all, however, was the high proportion of Cantonese on the tapes, a problem that increased with every lesson as the teacher became more confident of our ability to understand him. Often I would have to play a piece of tape seven or eight times just to decide which sounds I was hearing before I could begin to attempt the recording. It was not uncommon for me to spend forty hours transcribing and annotating the two-and-a-half-hour tape. In addition I was trying to do my homework for the oral course, and my character practice for Cindy, and maintain a journal, and perhaps fit in a few think-aloud protocols too.

Another commitment was providing me with the opportunity for native speaker interaction. Once a week I would go down to Chinatown for a *dim sum* lunch (or rather *tihm sâm* as I had now learned to call it). I had found a restaurant where the various *dim sum* were brought around by elderly ladies who spoke no English. As they pushed their trolleys around the restaurant, they would call out the names of their wares, and the constant repetition gave me a wonderful listening opportunity. A similar opportunity arose when the hostess would assign numbers to waiting patrons, to be called out as their tables came ready.

On the literacy side, I could search the menu for a familiar character, or more likely work with the simpler text on the chopstick wrapper or the small chit on which the selected dishes would be recorded. From this I was delighted one day to recognize the character for *small*, which I had met in Cindy's name, next to the character for *middle*, which I knew from the phrase "Middle Kingdom," that is, China. It did not take much deductive ability to realize that the first symbol of the three was probably the character for *large*.

These were relatively passive interactions. When I tried to take a more active role, I was not always so successful. On one memorable occasion I took a friend along for lunch, and trying vainly to use my spoken Cantonese to ask what things were, somehow ended up with enough food on the table for ten people, most of which seemed to be various versions of *siu maai*. I soon realized that I did not know how to say, "No thank you!"

In these early weeks I was totally committed to maintaining the language learning opportunities and the data recording schedule I had originally outlined. I was so busy doing the work that I did not perhaps take enough time out to consider whether my time was being spent in the most useful way. Journal entries in late October document this sense of pressure very clearly.

> I am concerned that the reflective process is getting neglected at the moment. The pressure is always on to get the next set of notes transcribed before the class, and as always the deadline material takes precedence over the more nebulous sitting down and thinking about the data. And yet I seem to be living this data at the moment. It's always in my thoughts, so the reflective process is in fact ongoing. What is missing—because so much of this is done in the shower, in bed, while peeling potatoes, etc.—is the recording. I still jot in my black journal book, but the very pervasiveness of the data in my thoughts means that a lot of thought occurs at times when the black book is not to hand.

> I had a dream last night in which I was painstakingly copying over information from one sheet to another. It wasn't in Chinese but I was struggling to get the placement right on the paper in exactly

the same way as I had struggled to put my characters in the right position in the square during my assignments. I woke to find myself in the middle of an asthma attack—bad asthma like I haven't had in years. I eventually used Karen's inhaler, which helped. In the morning I was clear as a bell. I don't understand this!

Some of this sense of pressure that I expressed in relation to the demands of data collection was probably related to my distress over my difficulties with literacy, as the journal entry about the dream would suggest. However, I did not acknowledge this at the time and saw it simply as a reaction to the long hours I was working and the correspondingly limited amount of time I was able to spend with my family. Only my sense of satisfaction at my progress in the oral Cantonese class helped to lighten the load. However, while the sense of pressure from data collection was never to abate, my reactions to the oral classes and literacy classes was shortly to be reversed.

Sudden reversals: November to December

My disenchantment with the oral classes came fairly abruptly. It seemed that one week I was rolling along full of confidence, and the next I was struggling. As people dropped out of the course the teacher expected more input from those who were present, so one was called on more frequently in class with less opportunity to learn from the mistakes or questions of others.

For the most part the drop-outs were those who had found the course difficult, either for lack of ability or preparation time. The average standard of the class, therefore, rose and Mr. Lee taught to this improved standard, using considerably more of the target language in class and increasing his speed of speech.

As an ESL teacher I had often spoken in favour of providing students with the experience of dealing with speech at normal speed. I soon changed my mind. An annotation on the lesson notes for October 26, reads, "When he speaks at real speed I am horrified and feel like I've made no progress. Never again will I ask for native speaker speed."

Mr. Lee seemed to be reflecting the pattern demonstrated in the cassettes that supported the text book. The dialogues for the first few lessons were recorded at a slow, clear pace, which most students were able to follow fairly well. By Lesson Five, however, the dialogues were being presented at what seemed to me to be native speaker speed. At that pace I found it difficult even to distinguish which dialogue I was hearing. On one occasion, trying to review the tape while walking over to my class, I came to the conclusion that I had brought the wrong cassette, since I was unable to find anything that I could identify as the passage we had studied the previous week and that I had spent hours transcribing. It was not encouraging to discover that I did indeed have the correct tape, and I realized that the artificially slow pace of the first lessons had misled me about my progress.

The amount of material covered in each lesson also seemed to increase considerably so that I was often struggling in class. By early November I was writing comments on the transcript such as:

> I feel a little panicked at the start of this exercise. I want him to slow down; I want time to stop and make a note. He seems to be rattling off more language this week. Has the pace picked up or have I been too busy transcribing to spend the necessary amount of time on homework? I notice that B., who is normally fairly confident, is having a very difficult time this week after being absent last week. People like M., whose job makes her miss class occasionally, must find it very hard.

I was not alone in this sense of panic. When I arrived at class the next week, the other students were discussing exactly this topic.

> M. comments on how difficult she is finding it since she has had to miss two classes. This produces a flood of comments on how the course suddenly seems to have got more difficult, on how much faster the taped conversation is in Lesson 5 than in previous lessons, on how much Lee pushed the pace last week, etc. It seems we are all out of the euphoria stage and into the panic.

The panic was also self-defeating. I found that once I was flustered, I didn't seem to hear the help and advice being offered to me, even though the teacher was, as always, supportive and encouraging. That same evening, he called on me for a substitution drill.

Lee   Substitution drills, do it one by one now. First one is, *M'goi neih beileuhngda ngoh la.* Er, I would like Jill to say this.

The story of learning Chinese

Jill   Can I just work out what it means?

Lee   Sure.

Jill   Er, please you give…couple…dollars?

Lee   Could you give me two dozens.

Jill   Ah, two dozens,

Lee   *M'goi neih beileuhngda ngoh la.* Have we learned this before? *M'goi neih beileuhngda ngoh la.* I explain the sentence first then. *M'goi* is please, please. *Neih,* you all know, I think, you. *Beileuhngda ngoh la.* Give me two dozens, literally, give two dozens to me. *M'goi neih beileuhngda ngoh la.*

Jill   *M'goi neih beileuhngda ngoh la.*

Lee   *Saam da.*

Jill   Er, er, *M'goi neih beileuhngda saam da,* er *M'goi neih beisaamda.*

Lee   *M'goi neih beisaamda ngoh la.* Good, good. *Seida?*

The trial continued for what seemed an interminable period. My notes on this part of the transcript read:

> I am to substitute these various number phrases for *leuhngda.* I never feel I have got the grasp of this sentence so that I am trying to reproduce a stream of sounds rather than a pattern I understand. It seems like every time I clear out some short term memory to take in the new number he is giving me, I lose the sentence again and have to look down at the book to reload. There is never the 20 seconds I would have needed to process this and I go blank half the time. I never realized what a strain it was to go first on material you haven't had a chance to think through.

I reacted to this and similar situations by trying to protect myself. Whenever we began an exercise where I was likely to be called upon individually, I began surreptitiously working ahead to prepare answers for the upcoming questions. Even discounting the fact that it prevented me from participating in the lesson, it was not always a successful strategy, as in this interchange. (Annotations to the transcript are indicated by square brackets).

Lee   Okay, good, right. The next question, er, Jill, can I ask you a question too. Again you are buying fruit from me. All right?

Jill Mhmm.
[Actually I don't take this in at all, I am so busy trying to find the place in the book. The last question was #3, so I am sure I will get #4, and am busy reading it over and mentally preparing an answer.]

Lee *Juhng yiu m'yiu daihyihdi yêh a?*
[Panic. This isn't question 4. Where has this question come from and what on earth is it all about? I eventually find it as question 5.]

Lee *Juhng yiu m'yiu daihyihdi yêh a?*

Jill Do you want any more fruit or not? No?

Lee *Daihyihdi yêh a? Juhng, juhng*—still.
[I swear I never heard him say this.]

Jill More of this?

Lee *Daihyidih—Daihyidih*, meaning other, okay?
Yeh—things.
[I don't think I heard this either.]

Juhng yiu m'yiu daihyihdi yêh a?

Jill So, Er, *m'haih. Ngoh m'yiu, ngoh juhng m'yiu saangwo la.*

Lee *M'yiu la, m'yiu daihyihdi la.* Okay, good.

For the rest of the fall term I never felt that I had caught up with the material that the teacher was covering, and the sense of calm confidence never returned. This is not to suggest that I wasn't making progress. As the term moved on we took on a number of individual assignments such as making five-minute speeches in Cantonese, which were obvious indications of our growing competence, but my emotional reaction to the classes remained one of unease.

In the same period, however, my attitude towards the literacy study also changed completely. At the beginning of November I was frustrated and unhappy with my progress but couldn't seem to find a way to improve things to my satisfaction.

One issue that I did not recognize was that I was resisting Cindy's teaching. She was teaching me in a holistic, experiential fashion, which stressed discipline and concentration, balance and harmony. I was responding from a position of analysis, hypothesis, and rule testing. As I will discuss later, when I finally started to listen to Cindy and let go of some of my preconceptions, I found a dramatic change in the way I was working and feeling.

Before I could make this shift, however, I needed to feel some sign of success, so that I could feel sufficiently better about myself to have some faith in my learning ability, my teacher and my task. This indication of progress came in a lesson we held on November 1st. Cindy had taught me the character for woman, *néui*, a couple of weeks earlier. In this lesson, working on the large one-inch squares that I disliked so much, she began by teaching me *jí*, a child. Then she demonstrated that when the two characters for *néui*, and *jí* were written together in a single square they formed the character, *hóu*, meaning good. As the transcript shows, I found this very exciting.

Jill   They go together? And that goes in one square?

Cindy   *Hóu.*

Jill   [excited] Oh, it changes the sound? Oh!

Cindy   It's the concept that when you put the two words for a girl together you get good. Like sugar and spice.

Jill   And it's *hóu*! [incredulous] Oh, that opens a whole new door. I thought when you put things together you got —*neui ji* !! [laughter]

The annotation on this page reads:

This was a real surprise to me, I'm not sure why. I had been told that characters incorporated other 'pieces' or radicals. I think I assumed they changed or joined, i.e. you can see *yahn* and *siu* in *neih*. To see two entire familiar characters simply sitting next to each other but forming a new word was an eye opener. Until this point I hadn't realized the significance of the square. The charts which I disliked so much make sense now.

We worked on a number of such combinations in this class and I realized that my limited number of characters were actually some of the basic building blocks for a number of other characters. At the end of my transcript of this lesson, I wrote, "This seemed to be a particularly positive lesson—it opened up a lot of possibilities so that it seemed as if I had crossed a threshold onto a new level of writing with the characters."

Things began to improve considerably after this lesson, and I found it easier to work in the way in which Cindy had wanted me to all along. At the time I did not reflect unduly on the changes that were occurring. I was aware that I felt much better emotionally but I was still too preoccupied with my commitments as learner and researcher to sit back and reflect on the way in which I was changing my learning style. The Christmas holiday, however, brought me a three-week vacation from classes and an opportunity to look at the larger picture of the study rather than being obsessed with the small details. A number of entries written over the Christmas period demonstrate that by that point I had come to view my progress in the literacy classes as being much more complex than a simple character count would indicate.

> I am very encouraged by the learning of characters which I have done. Although this has seemed to be slow progress in some ways, in others I feel very confident that what I can do, I can do well. I do not have the same confidence with my spoken Cantonese.

> Perhaps this is a direct result of the way in which I have been taught. It is interesting that I kicked against the tight control which Cindy imposed, and yet I must say that what she has taught me seems well learned and well within my ability to produce. I wonder what would have been the result had Lee taught me my tones with the same patience and structure. Would I be confident that I could say phrases in an intelligible manner?

> Somewhere around week five or six, things began to improve. One of the most noticeable breakthroughs was the realization that the various parts I had learned would also function as 'parts' of other characters...I recognized that these 17 characters I had learned, could be manipulated to make more characters without more 'study' so the character count was higher. But also, I had been learning the basic strokes which I would use in all the other characters—the down slope, the left curve, etc. They function almost like alphabetic letters in that they combine in different ways to make new characters.

> When I thought about this I realized that I had had to put in a lot

of time learning basic handwriting, but that other characters should come more quickly...I had also developed a sense of what kind of strokes the Chinese language was likely to use. I haven't met all the strokes at all yet but I have developed a sense of the way in which strokes modify according to their placement in the square, the kind of strokes which would be unlikely to occur—e.g. circles like we use for a, b, or c in English, or straight angular junctions like we have in v and w. I can recognize when writers have 'scribbled' and joined two strokes together so I have developed a lot of subknowledge—more than I have made explicit and thus more than I can spell out here.

Another area of learning was the concept of the square which I have spelled out elsewhere...The final area was in relation to attitude. It is hard for me now to recapture how strange it seemed when Cindy talked about balance and concentration at first...When Cindy first made her comment about not writing on the subway, I was really surprised. When she first pointed out a poor character with the phrase, 'You lost your concentration,' it seemed very strange...She would say, 'You have to have balance,' and I wouldn't be sure whether that meant in my head or in my characters... it does seem that one switches off the outside and goes into a purely visual mode if one is to produce not just good characters but *'felt'* characters. There is perhaps a second element here which is that if you have written a character many many times, it must get so automatized that you can produce it beautifully without needing to 'trance.' Characters which I have now used for some months I can produce fairly rapidly to order—for instance when Cindy gave me her little test I rewrote a sentence with a correction and she commented, 'I can't believe the way you can do that—you'd think you had been writing Chinese all your life.'

The effect of all this is that I am converted to Cindy's view of the necessity for concentration, mental discipline and balance if one is to produce good characters. I have lost my impatience with the process, mostly because I have recognized that what I am learning is every bit as vital for the study as doubling the character count would be. Cindy is apparently impressed by my progress and has used phrases like, 'I can't believe you are writing sentences already.'

Somewhat in contradiction to this endorsement of a more holistic learning style was an attempt I made at this time to describe my own learning patterns. In the early part of the study I had found myself using a metaphor of a network of pathways and bridges gradually being constructed over a lake. I explored this metaphor in my journal, without any apparent sense of the contradiction involved between this synthesis of explicit fragments and the kind of learning I was claiming to have developed from Cindy's experiential methods.

> When I struggle to learn something, I feel as if I am reaching out into a void—there is a risk involved. When something 'clicks' it is as if I had thrown out a life line which has connected. I am aware of constantly trying to push the boundaries of what is known to see how much language activity my existing knowledge can support and how universal the generalizations will be which I deduce from them. I find a standard pattern is to try to attach new learning to old knowledge—to find a cognate, to pair what my two teachers say on the same subject, to find common ground between two apparently disparate pieces of information. It seems that whenever a new piece of knowledge turns out to tie in with previous knowledge in some way, that the link is strengthened, as if a strand of the web had gained its strength by resting on other strands. I rarely forget knowledge anchored in this way. By contrast bits of knowledge which stand alone are like floating islands—potentially they may come to be useful but at present they do not provide any route across the surface—the chances are high they will sink back below the surface before they ever mesh into the active web which reaches the shore.
>
> I am constantly trying out routes over this surface, as I try to predict rules, and develop hypotheses. If my hypotheses are correct, a strong strand will join the main growth to one or more of the islands, allowing for more adventurous journeying over the surface or more direct routes to my goal. When such ventures fail, I retire to the margins and set out more hesitantly thereafter.

Significantly this synthesizing metaphor does not appear again in my notes or journals after this point. Instead, there are numerous references to a gradually clarifying understanding of a whole unit, as in the following examples.

The image of that comic strip and its language sort of coming into focus.

It's like watching a photograph develop. You have a hazy understanding of what it's about and imperceptibly you find it's clearer.

I can hear the intonation for this [phrase] in my head very clearly. Presumably because I have heard it a number of times. Maybe this is part of how one learns tones—you learn the melody of specific patterns and phrases and unconsciously later abstract from them.

Settling into a pattern: January to May

After the Christmas vacation I began to feel at ease in both the literacy and the oral classes. I was able to predict the kind of events that would occur and I was relaxed with my teachers and my fellow students. In the oral classes the numbers continued to dwindle until by February there were only four men and myself who continued to attend regularly. As the numbers of students dropped, the growing friendship among class members became apparent. If we arrived early, we chatted happily until class started. At the end of class, we waited for each other and walked out to the subway en masse. My notes describe a class towards the end of January at which I had arrived late:

> As we leave, the others comment on the small group and how hard they have had to work, especially B. and R. who were there the previous week. R. and D. comment that they knew I would turn up as I never miss class. We all walk out together, laughing as a group and there is a good sense of friendship. Lee has mentioned the possibility of a class over the summer. I am quite interested until he tells me he will not be teaching it. I would carry on with this group but am reluctant to re-establish myself in a new class with a new teacher. B. says she feels the same.

In the smaller group there was increased relaxation and trust among class members. Before Christmas, it seemed that people were nervous that they would fail to do as well as the rest of the class. People tended to stress their limited opportunities to study or their lack of prior exposure to tonal languages. Only one of the regular students had admitted to prior knowledge of any Chinese dialect. In the New Year we had all come back a little nervously, having forgotten much of what we had covered earlier. Gradually, we confessed our difficulties and our fears and it became easier to admit to assets such as prior exposure. I belatedly admitted that I was writing a thesis and thus spent much of the week working with the class tapes; the others admitted that they had various dialects of Chinese as a first language (in one case Cantonese itself). One student confessed that he was taking the course for the second time.

In this smaller group we were more prepared to take risks, so that there was more student talk in the classroom in both English and Cantonese. We seemed to do less work from the textbook and more work on spontaneous oral language production with activities such as describing the route by which we travelled to work.

The teacher often commented that the two-and-a-half-hour class was too long for us to spend simply on the text, so he supplemented the exercises with a variety of activities, including vocabulary lists, taped dialogues, and cartoon strip stories. One activity that I found interesting was the use of songs. Mr. Lee chose song as a way of helping us understand the tone system, which he often compared to music. He selected songs that had familiar Western tunes but that had been recorded in Cantonese. One example was the Disney song, "It's a Small World," which we met as *"Saigaai jàn sai síu."* My minimal musical abilities were demonstrated when I did not recognize that this was a melody to which I had ever been exposed before, and initially congratulated myself on the speed with which I picked up this "Chinese" tune.

Equally daunting was the translation of the Cantonese lyrics. All the other language to which we were exposed was either transcribed oral language, or was designed specially for learners. These songs, however, demonstrated the complexity of the literate language, and indicated clearly that one needed more than vocabulary and character knowledge to be able to express oneself appropriately in writing. The phrase, "Don't be afraid," for example, was expressed by *"bât bit sàm léuih tiu"*—literally translated as, "Not need heart inside jump." As it happened, I knew the words in this phrase, but it would certainly not have occurred to me to use them when writing, "Don't be afraid."

We were quite often asked to make short speeches in Cantonese, perhaps describing our activities over the weekend. It was noticeable that the other students had control of vocabulary items that I had never been taught in the classroom setting, so their difficulties with extemporaneous oral production focused on tone and syntax rather than vocabulary. To some extent the problems of tone and syntax were also key for me, but I commonly found myself stranded for lack of a key vocabulary item.

Some of the vocabulary I did have at my command turned out to have an inappropriate literary tone to it, culled as it was from my literacy classes. Many common Cantonese words such as pronouns, negatives, and particles have a different form for writing than they do for speech. The English word "he" would thus be translated as *keuih* in conversation but *ta* in reading. I only learned the character for the literary forms, of course, but it was necessary for me to know both oral forms. I found fairly often that I was mistakenly using the literary forms rather than the colloquial ones, an error that happened in reverse in the literacy classes, when I would write *ta* but verbalize it as *keuih*.

Our teacher put a strong emphasis on our learning colloquial Cantonese as it would be heard on the streets of Hong Kong. He tried hard, therefore, to accustom us to the natural speech speeds and rhythms of everyday conversation. The tapes he worked with were recorded at close to natural speed and he urged us to speed up when reading aloud. This was in direct opposition to the patterns and convictions of my literacy teacher, and I found myself feeling somewhat pulled in opposite directions.

As a learner, I found my attitude was a little different on passive versus active language. When listening to spoken Cantonese, what I wanted was to be allowed to work with an item at an increasing speed. Frequent repetitions of a fast paced item were not enough, it seemed, to improve my understanding. First the item had to become comprehensible, then the speeding up could take place. When I was producing the language, however, reading it aloud, for example, I was fairly happy to be encouraged to rattle it off. I found it much easier to speedily decode the Yale Romanization than to have to worry about my inaccuracies over the fine points of tone, which it seemed, at least to me, were more evident when I spoke slowly. Whether a native speaker would have found my "fluent" speech a sufficient compensation for my poor tones I do not know.

The tones continued to be a problem for me throughout the course, especially when words were heard or produced in isolation, as in a minimal pair drill where my performance was noticeably below par. However, I did have some sense of progress, which focused on the discovery that certain well known phrases—those that I had heard many, many times—were retained in my head with the tonal pattern complete. I was not able to say what tones I was hearing, nor comment on their relationship with each other, but I was able to "hum their tune." In this sense, my awareness of tone paralleled my ability to learn musical tune, which exists (if at a rather slower rate than that of most of my acquaintances), but is similarly not open to analysis. I got the sense from this that if I were to have ongoing extensive exposure to Cantonese, I would eventually build up a series of tonal patterns onto which I would slot the words I wanted to say. Towards the end of the course, I was becoming quite confident about my progress.

> As far as the university course goes, there has also been quite a leap forward. There are certain key phrases that Lee has used throughout the course, e.g. to watch TV, listen to music, etc. I never knew them but find suddenly all these taking shape for me. I do know them. I can string sentences together. My vocabulary seems to have leapt forward. I feel as if I can do a lot on my own now.

In April, I asked the professor if he would give me an evaluation of my language proficiency. In what demonstrated a fairly typical student-teacher miscommunication (many examples of which appear in the transcripts), he gave me something more resembling a report card, which commented favourably on my industry rather than my competence. This highlighted the distinction for me between material that is learned and material that is usable. I was aware during this course that I had control of a lot of material at the cognitive level that I could not spontaneously call on. I had learned but not acquired it, to use Krashen's terms (Krashen, 1981). This seemed to be less of a problem for the Chinese course members.

When the course finished, I attempted a self-evaluation of the kind that I had originally hoped for from my professor. In sum, my assessment was that I had learned enough oral language to be understandable to my teacher or another native speaker experienced with second language learners, to greet someone, introduce myself, talk about my family, my job and my interests. I had the language to purchase items in a store or market, discuss prices, count to 999, order simple food in a restaurant, and ask for directions. I could manipulate simple statements into negatives or questions, and I could mark for past tense, possession or adjectival status.

I had had relatively little success, however, in native speaker contact, except for such high context situations as ordering food in a restaurant, so I was forced to conclude that my accent or tone was not good enough to make me comprehensible to a native speaker who was not experienced with foreigners or who was not able to predict what I was likely to be attempting to say. In a similar fashion, I was able to understand my teacher and most of my fellow students when they performed the above functions, but I had great difficulty in understanding other speakers on first hearing, though constant replays, as when the teacher provided a tape of native speakers did prove helpful eventually.

Although the oral Cantonese classes finished in April, Cindy and I continued working together until June. Like the oral classes, the literacy classes were affected in the new year by a change in emotional climate. As Cindy and I got to know each other better, the relationship developed from that of tutor-tutee into that of friends. We would often go out for a meal after class where the conversation would focus on the personal rather than the academic. In class we were both more relaxed and it became easier for us to make suggestions, ask for changes, or offer criticism. The kind of teasing exchange shown in this example from a January lesson became common in the transcripts.

Jill   Mmm. You've made that [model character] very nice.

Cindy   Thank you. I thought so too! [both laugh]

Jill   Aren't you thrilled, getting praise from someone who has been doing it a whole four months! [laughs] Sorry about that!

Cindy   I'm glad you can recognize it You know good stuff when you see it! [pause] Yes that's better, that's good. It looks a lot like mine! [more laughter]

Jill   I wouldn't go that far but we are getting there.

As I settled into a relaxed routine of classes and homework, I found that I was coming to enjoy the character practice and as my characters improved, eventually I came to recognize the need for it. By this point I was surprised at the poor quality of characters I had written in the early days of the study and wondered how I could have failed to see their imperfections some weeks earlier. Right from the beginning of the study the transcripts show that I commonly referred to drawing characters, not writing them, and this habit continued. It may be that the experiential methodology exaggerated this tendency. The constant copying meant that I looked at each character produced as a visual object. I was some six months into the study before I really used the characters to convey meaning, and began to think of them as words rather than shapes.

Perhaps related to this tendency to see characters as drawings was the slow development of the ability to recognize a character in slightly different manifestations. I became aware that one could "see" a combination of strokes in different ways, in much the same fashion as one can see candlesticks or facial profiles in the classic perception-test picture. Once I had imposed a particular template on an image, it took considerable effort to see it differently.

Developing a sense of which features were critical for the templates of each character was a long slow process. One example was when Cindy showed me a cursive version of a familiar character, showing me how the basic strokes were all present even though the finished appearance was very different. I annotated the transcript of this part of the lesson,

> This gets at something very important for literacy, which is the minimal amount of information we need once the template is in existence. This creation of the template is one of the breakthrough points, I think.

As I made progress, Cindy began suggesting that I had reached the point where I could relax some of the external conditions originally imposed on me but I continued to embrace the discipline, taking pride in achieving a balance within and between characters. I continued for some weeks to practice heavily in this area where I was already fairly strong, ignoring in the process my need for work on tone, for instance. We were working now on increasingly difficult characters, with more component parts, more strokes, more pieces to balance, both laterally and vertically. Eventually I reached the point where new characters were rarely totally new. Sometimes they would include familiar radicals that were not only known in a visual sense but that even had a semantic component I could remember and recognize. Others were less simple but still familiar—in a ten-stroke character perhaps four of the strokes would form a component familiar from another character. Obviously, the more characters I learned, the more common this became. Eventually I did begin to move away from simple copying practice:

> I did a line or so of each character, then a day later, did a whole page. They didn't show much improvement it seems. In fact the focus seems to have shifted away from pages and pages of pure copying. We both seem to feel that (at this stage?) it is less productive. Is this because I don't work so hard at the copying or because I have conquered the first preliminary stage of muscle control and the next stage will take years of style practice rather than hours of stroke practice?

As indicated above, Cindy also felt that I had reached the point where such calligraphy practice was less necessary and so characters learned during this time generally received no more than twenty or thirty repetitions. However, I think we both underestimated the memory bonus that came from those endless repetitions. Whether the early characters that I copied literally hundreds of times are burned into my visual memory, or whether, as I suspect, they reside in muscle memory, I don't know. However, without those hours of fixing the character visually I was to find that later it was difficult to instantly recognize or recall such half-learned characters.

As the learning of new characters became easier, the amount of data being generated for the research was reduced and I found myself getting impatient with the process once more. My original goal of learning a specific number of characters seemed less important and I decided I would like to focus on some of the other aspects of learning to read and write. Accordingly, I changed the focus of my home assignments from simple copying of individual characters to attempts to produce sentences and more complex pieces. In late February, I wrote:

I have had time to do a fair amount of homework. Rather than practicing the same character over and over I have tried to write some sentences and even produced a small piece of semi-continuous text by searching the Cantonese text for the necessary characters.

This move to creating text affected the way in which Cindy judged my characters because the shift to meaningful units meant that the characters now had to be seen in relation to each other, not assessed individually. More significantly, though, this new material obviously changed the focus of the class, because Cindy now had to comment on my syntax and vocabulary, as well as handwriting.

As I became more proficient, my written work eventually developed into journal-type pieces in which I would tell Cindy about topics such as my family, my activities over the weekend, an upcoming vacation, etc. Many topics that I would have liked to have written about were impossible with the limited vocabulary I had, and even with careful selection of topics that called predominantly on familiar vocabulary, I frequently found myself lacking necessary characters. If I knew the spoken word, I was sometimes able to find the character from the pinyin to characters listing at the back of my textbook for the oral Cantonese class. Copying a character from a textbook, however, is not a simple matter.

As I have often discovered in ESL classes, one's definition of legibility is determined less by the calibre of one's eyesight than by the degree of familiarity with what is being read. Peering at ten or fifteen stroke characters printed within a three millimetre square made me very aware of the difference between the pieces with which I was familiar, which seemed very clear, and new groups of strokes that seemed impossible to sort out. Printed characters are also stylized in ways that are not appropriate for handwritten characters, so that sometimes my most careful copies would turn out to be least satisfactory as far as Cindy was concerned.

These journal pieces soon came to provide a major component of the tutorial sessions. I would read them aloud, translate them and work through them with Cindy for corrections to characters, lexis and syntax. An example of one of the more complex pieces is shown in Figures 8 and 9 on pages 139 and 140, which describe an upcoming trip to England for a reunion with some old high school friends. Of such pieces, I wrote:

I want to try to write something that carries some meaning. This is quite a challenge—I seem to begin each 'text' by writing in characters, then after I have had to abandon half a dozen sentences for lack of the appropriate characters, I settle on doing a rough version in half Yale, half characters, first to ensure that I will know the required words once I have led myself up the path. The Yale also gives me a chance to try out the syntax and head off some of the

Figure 8: Chinese journal, Week 29 (reduced).

most elementary errors such as including *sih* with a stative verb, or putting the time phrase at the end. I often write words such as *keui* and *ngohdeih* [oral forms] in the Yale, and don't really notice the difference when I transcribe into characters.

	和							
和	鴨	鵝	。	我	們	鍾	意	那
	校	。	二	十	五	年	我	沼
有	見	過	我	的	朋	友	。	我
高	興	見	她	們	。			
	五	月	二	十	日	我	們	去
酒	店	。	我	們	談	話	，	我
們	飲	酒	、	我	們	有	講	有
笑	。							
	一	個	朋	友	寫	信	給	我
她	說	「很	多	妳	的	相	片	來
我		過	一	本	相	部	。	

Figure 9: Chinese journal, Week 29, Part 2 (reduced).

This week I have written a short piece about eating out at the Jade Lotus on Monday. I am not sure whether I am pleased that I have constructed a more or less true piece of information, or self conscious and irritated that I can only express my self so meagerly...It makes me very aware how frustrating it must be for my students and others in monolingual classes, who can only display their personalities through limited English. If I got this Jade Lotus piece from an ESL student, would I see through the language limitations? I have heard ESL teachers say so often, 'If I get another journal which says, *Today I got up and I cleaned my teeth and I went to work etc.*, I'll scream.' But even to get that right is quite an effort when you are just beginning—it represents more achievement than I think I ever gave credit for. Most of my pieces begin with the date and the weather [always cold or not cold—I don't know how to write warm or wet!]. They still take effort and concentration. And I still make mistakes in them.

Another activity in the literacy tutorials was working with real life texts, such as the text on a take-out food carrier bag, a note from Cindy to her mother, or a poster advertising a church fete. Of these, the note turned out to be so simple that I suspect it was specially manufactured, and the others turned out to be so complex that they were rather daunting.

There was no question of my being able to "read" most of them, in the sense of understanding total sentences. Rather, I would search for familiar characters or familiar radicals and try to use global knowledge to make sensible guesses as to the likely context. Frequently I would fail to recognize a character I knew quite well because it had been written with a slight deviance from my inner template. Other times I would recognize and even name the character but be discouraged to find that it carried a totally different meaning in the context in which it was being used. This made any kind of prediction very difficult.

Often I would find while working this way that I knew the meaning of a character but had forgotten its sound. The transcripts show that I tend to verbalize directly into English rather than read aloud the Cantonese and then translate.

By the end of the sessions with Cindy, I had worked with some two hundred and twenty characters and knew a further fifty collocations, where two or more characters are used together to make a new meaning. It is striking looking back, though, that the characters learned through repetition are much more firmly known than those that I discovered for myself and used in the journals.

Although my literacy skills are obviously restricted, I feel more confident that what I produce in writing is comprehensible to a native speaker than what I produce orally. I am not sure how much of a "foreigner" stamp my writing would have—whether it would look like a second language learner's or merely look childish. However I have exchanged notes with a non-English speaking Chinese student of my sister's and found that I was able to convey the requisite information—though I found his responses difficult, of course, since he called on a wide range of characters I have not yet met.

I was very sorry to end my literacy tutorials. In the last couple of months of the study I had been engaged by the language learning and was beginning to feel confidence in my ability to make progress. This reflected itself in a growing sense of independence as a learner.

> I haven't written a lot about the learning so recently. In part I think I have been enjoying the challenge and got absorbed in it. I think I have made considerable progress of late—the tones are beginning to take shape for me—not so much as individual words but as 'whole chunks' of language which are learned with tone intact. The characters are much easier now. Almost anything which I can track down a printed text for I can work out the component parts and produce appropriately. I have changed my homework away from mere repetitions of a character towards trying to write a connected piece of prose. I search the course text for the characters I need or I rephrase my own text. Often I have to discard my plan but I am still finding for myself and using six or seven new characters in each lesson—in addition to the ones that Cindy teaches me. This involves me in syntax decisions and moves me to another level of writing. C is becoming more of a resource and less of a teacher as I set my own directions and shape the classes myself with increasing confidence.

By early spring, I was also beginning to resent the time that the demands of a research study were making. In March I wrote,

> I am aware lately of a split between the learner and the researcher. I would love to sign up for more classes, to get on with the Chinese

and to focus on making language progress but I keep getting distracted because the thesis demands come up first.

This thought was still with me in late April. My journal for April 27th comments:

I am in love with the Chinese learning—I wish I could forget the study temporarily and focus on the language.

Despite these comments, the language learner lost out to the researcher and in June I finished my tutorials and began the process of looking at my data.

Chapter Seven

Other versions of the story

Before I started the preceding chapter, which tells the story of my study of Chinese, I expected it would be a fairly easy chapter to write since the content seemed very clear to me. I had already crafted the story of this period, of course. I had been dining out for the previous twelve months on tales of my struggle with Chinese literacy. I had constantly discussed the experience with my study group and I had summarized my progress in regular letters to a friend working out of province. I had written up progress reports and I had made seminar presentations to my peers.

The story then had been rehearsed before a variety of audiences and in various genres, both oral and written. I believed it was already well polished and ready to be written down. As far as I could see, the challenges that remained in writing this chapter were basically literary ones, such as whether the major themes for later analysis should be discussed in the chapter or merely presaged.

Some part of me was aware that, when telling the more informal versions of the story, some account had been taken of the demands of the audience. If pressed, I would have admitted to a little conscious shaping of the story to make it more interesting to the listeners. The numbers were perhaps exaggerated a little, and the emotions intensified. It was possible that those incidents with a potential for humour or drama were given more attention than they merited in terms of the role they were likely to play in shaping later events. But with the exception of these minor reservations, I believed implicitly that the tale I was telling was true to the experience, and I approached the task of writing it up with confidence and enthusiasm.

I prepared for the writing by returning to the original data: the tapes of the Chinese lessons, the annotated transcripts of those tapes and the ongoing journal I wrote during the study. As I went through the material looking for illustrative quotes and incidents to support my story, I discovered, initially to my horror, that the story I had been telling was not always supported by the data. Indeed in a few places it was flatly contradicted by it. I suppose I should not have been surprised by this. A major thrust of this study is to demonstrate how we structure experience through story, and how the stories we tell shape the way we interact with experience and understand it. Why should the experience of a research study be any different? Despite my nod to Crites and his notion of self deception (see Chapter 4), I had obviously somehow assumed I would be immune.

My first reaction was shock and embarrassment at my failings as a researcher. It took some talking through with my colleagues before I was able to let go of the emotional response and recognize that the very restorying was part of the story, and an integral part of this study.

In the previous chapter, I have told the story as it is manifested in the transcripts and journals. I would like now to present some of the restoried versions of part of the experience, and consider why the experience might have been restoried in these ways. Many of the restoried versions that I told went unrecorded, since they were produced in the context of casual conversations. I can remember many of them, but I cannot judge how much I may have restoried my memories subsequent to the telling. Consequently I shall be drawing only on versions of the story that were recorded either on tape, or in writing.

The first version comes from a progress report written three months into the data collection phase, when a large part of the story still lay in the future.

> Although at the start of this study I paid lip service to the idea of different educational goals and methods, I did not allow sufficiently for the stress of learning according to a set of rules with which one is not familiar. I had deliberately tried to avoid preset notions of what would be involved in the learning but I still had, I think, assumptions that, for example, I would probably have a wider reading vocabulary than written vocabulary; that I would measure progress by the complexity of the text I could read, and hence by extension, by the number of words I could read, and so on.

> Although we did not make this explicit, it is clear in retrospect that Cindy considers literacy to be the ability to write Chinese. In her eyes, to 'know' a character was not to be able to recognize it but to

be able to produce it, and to produce it to a high calligraphic standard. My mood in the first five or six weeks was consequently one of impatience. I never felt I was being given enough to learn and I always felt I had learned it ahead of the point where Cindy considered I was ready to progress. My workload for week one for instance consisted of the numbers 1, 2, 3, and 4. As the first three numbers are made up of one, two and three parallel lines respectively, I saw my learning task as being simply the character for 4, which I had learned to my satisfaction within perhaps five minutes. A similar pattern was in evidence for the next four or five weeks, with my impatience appeased only a little as the characters became more complicated. I counted my progress in terms of "only 17 characters" and did gloomy arithmetic regarding my likely total by the end of April. During this period Cindy talked to me of "the square", of "balance" and of "concentration", insisting that I could not produce good characters without perfect conditions and total concentration. These concepts seemed strange and I was somewhat skeptical. I see myself as fairly artistic and I assumed I would have no difficulty reproducing the shapes.

This version, which was written while the data collection was ongoing, already incorporates some divergence from the data. It is true that I was assigned the characters for 1, 2, 3 and 4 as homework for my first lesson, but the transcripts demonstrate that I was also assigned the more complex characters, *siu* and *lahm*, which are found in Cindy's name. Perhaps because we did not continue to work with these characters, I forgot they had been introduced. In addition Cindy had brought in a tape of Chinese songs for me to listen to at home, and had assigned me a specific listening task based on one of the songs.

The next recorded version of the story elaborates this claim of being assigned minimal homework and extends it to strengthen the story of baffled frustration that I am trying to tell. This second version is a transcript of an impromptu speech I made in July at the end of the data collection phase when I was first beginning to look back over the experience as a whole. In the course of this meeting I described the experience as "startling," and was asked to elaborate that statement.

Well, er…I went into this with a fair amount of success as a learner and I don't normally have difficulty in learning new stuff. I also, I see myself as an artistic person so I was fairly confident that the literacy side of this would be something I would find relatively easy. And a number of people commented to me—'Oh Chinese literacy, that's really hard,' and I felt kind of smug inside that this wouldn't really be hard for me. But I was very worried about the tones—I have always presented myself as someone who was almost musically tone-deaf. I expected to have trouble there, and I was scared I wouldn't be able to do it but I thought the literacy would be easy.

So, I started these classes with Cindy and she gave me very very simple tasks to do—quite literally my first week's course of study—and this was before the oral classes even began, so I had a whole week to work on this, was the numbers 1, 2, 3 and 4 [writes the characters on chalkboard]. As far as I was concerned, I'd learned those within five minutes, just as you could shut your eyes now and do a fairly good representation of this. So, I had a week to work on this and I couldn't quite believe that was all she was going to assign me for a week. So I dutifully went and practiced it and—er, how many times can you practice two parallel straight lines?

I did about 300 of each of them because I was practicing quite faithfully but of course I didn't know what I was practicing for. So I came back with all these pages and she was totally unimpressed, and I thought, 'How can you be unimpressed with a straight line—I know them, now we'll learn 6, 7, 8 and will you please give me a few more next week?'

And Cindy was really unhappy with what I had done, and that made me feel pretty bad because it had been such a simple task and I hadn't done it to her satisfaction. So I learned 5, 6, 7 and 8 the next week and she wasn't pleased with those either, and this is Jill who can sketch a picture that people can recognize and she can't draw a shape the right way! So I started to fight Cindy. I started to think that, well she's being silly, she's not teaching them properly. She insisted that I drew on squared paper with each square about that big [one inch], and of course we do very little of that size in English so that although most of us can draw a straight line of say half an inch long quite smoothly, if you try to draw one that is 3/4" long that's absolutely straight, your hand starts to wobble because you're not used to it. So then I would get frustrated because these shapes were getting more and more unsatisfactory the more I made my hand rigid to try to get them right. And I wanted to work on straight line paper because this seemed to me to be more adult—these great big squares were for kids, they came from a kid's text book and I was fighting the whole system.

Cindy had told me I must not practice anywhere except at a table, in silence with no distractions and I don't have much of that kind of time free in my life, but I had all these other times when I wanted to practice. Maybe I'd finally got the kids watching television and I'd be sitting down next to the coffee table—if I could just lean over and practice a few, that would have helped. That would have helped me fix it in my head because I was sure that what I was trying to learn, see, was to get it in my head, but she wouldn't let me. So I would practice on the quiet and not show her those pages, and then I would copy them onto squared charts because I couldn't believe she was right.

Anyway we went on like this and it was like hitting my head against a brick wall. She kept giving me less and less to learn because what I was producing was less and less satisfactory. And I don't know what happened but somewhere along the line I began to see that I was going to have to do it her way and I even accepted these damn squares, and I realized that I had locked my head in by taking for granted a number of things. [...]

One of the big dangers, one of the things that gave me a great deal of trouble was that I had years of memories. For instance, I'd say, 'Oh, that's a cross, I'll be able to remember that one, that's a cross,' but it was very dangerous to say, 'That's a cross,' because that gave you a different type of proportion and once I had made those kind of connections, somewhere in the back of my brain I was imposing the other image on the character. Then I'd never get it right because you have to learn it as a shape in its own space, in its own right. Somehow once I had learned that, once I had made that transition it was very easy, it all went ahead smoothly and it was very successful but I don't know why I fought it so hard. I was frustrated and cross and I was turning it against Cindy—I wanted to blame Cindy because I was doing so badly.

This version absorbs the story that my first week's homework was only the four numerals and elaborates it with the claim that, "Cindy was really unhappy with what I had done." There is no evidence in the data to support this claim. Instead the transcript shows that I was the one who verbalized discontent with my performance. I had produced my many copies of each assigned character, which I gave to Cindy with comments such as, "I just got frustrated with myself," "I didn't know what I was going for," "I kept thinking, I'm sure this is wrong," and so on. It is true that the signs of enthusiasm or praise in Cindy's responses are somewhat limited but there is nothing to justify the phrase "really unhappy."

In this second version, my inaccurate claim about the homework assignment for the first week is elaborated to suggest that the pattern continued. Again the details are inaccurate. The assignment for the second week was not four more numerals but the six characters for 5-10, and once again the unhappiness with the characters was verbalized by me not her.

More significant is the fact that as far as Cindy was concerned, I did not even complete my assigned homework. I had practiced the characters at least one hundred times each, but I had done so on lined paper rather than the charts that Cindy had prescribed. I had meant to produce a final "neat copy" chart for each character but had never finished the last couple of charts. It is thus hardly surprising that she did not increase my homework assignments dramatically.

In this version of the story, I have also begun to impose patterns of cause and effect, as in the claim that, "She kept giving me less and less to learn because what I was producing was less and less satisfactory." This draws on the fact that I was given six new characters to learn for week two, four characters for week three and only two characters on week four. It ignores the fact that I was always asked to review and practice previously introduced material, producing combinations of new and old characters. Cindy herself said nothing to suggest that she was consciously reducing the amount of homework assigned, nor did she tie the reduced number of characters to my performance. As the characters themselves were becoming increasingly complex, it is possible that she considered all these assignments to be of comparable difficulty.

Another issue that is first addressed in this version, was the strain that this struggle with literacy put upon the relationship between

Cindy and me. "I started to fight Cindy. I started to think, well she's being silly, she's not teaching them properly." "I was frustrated and cross and I was turning it against Cindy—I wanted to blame Cindy because I was doing so badly."

A strained relationship with my tutor was not something that I would have talked about explicitly in class so I cannot go back to a transcript here to contrast it with the storied version. Nor would my sense of sociality have allowed me to criticize Cindy to friends or colleagues, so that source of immediate data is not available either. My best attempt at an unbiased recollection of this time does not recall the kind of animosity that this transcript might suggest. However, I do remember some stresses.

One stressful area concerned the kind of feedback Cindy gave me. As documented earlier, I initially found some of her feedback difficult to follow. There were many occasions in these early weeks when I wanted very specific instructions to help me improve my characters, but instead I was given general advice to slow down, to practice and to concentrate. Because these remarks were not what I expected, they were very noticeable to me, and they became part of the story I was telling, whereas I barely noticed the occasions when Cindy answered my questions in the more expected fashion.

Another stress in the personal relationship came quite early in the study when it became evident that Cindy was not likely to collect academic credit for her contribution. As a social person, I thus felt very much indebted to her for essentially donating her time, and consequently reluctant to press her for any greater commitment. As a researcher, however, I wanted to press her for longer and more frequent lessons, more written responses, and generally for more demonstration of commitment to the study. This conflict between two sides of myself may well have been projected in part onto Cindy. When she forgot, for instance, to bring a promised resource to class, I interpreted it as a sign of her loss of interest in the project. A journal entry I wrote in October suggests both this unease, and my reluctance to write explicitly about it.

> My progress in literacy is not so satisfactory—Cindy and I have never met the twice a week that we originally agreed. Last week she was sick so we never met at all. This week she was partially recovered but still not up to much, so we went out for lunch and

had a bare one hour session in Cultures [Restaurant]. The result is that after five weeks I still know very few characters. [Then follows a list of the characters]. That's barely three characters a week—oh one more I sort of know is her name, *lahm*.

I'm not sure what the problem is. Perhaps I do not do the characters well enough for her to feel that she can allow me to move on. Perhaps we just chat through the class and the extra material she had planned to cover gets left undone. I'm concerned though about this slow rate of progress.

This piece nicely embodies the contrast between my "official" version of the story and my personally held version. In the last paragraph, I am carefully putting myself on record as being "not sure what the problem is," with an apparent openness to the idea that the slow progress may be related to my performance. However, I have already ascribed cause and effect in the first paragraph where I document Cindy's absence and claim my poor performance as the result.

Neither my concern over Cindy's interest in the project nor my problems with her feedback would justify portraying us as being in conflict, however. And yet, on an occasion some nine months after the study finished, the tape demonstrates that I have begun to make the supposed conflict into the climax of the story. This version comes from an informal, off-the-cuff presentation I made at a seminar series on narrative. Having told the now firmly believed tale of the first week's assignment being the characters for 1, 2, 3, and 4, I went on:

I did my 200 copies and at the end of it, my teacher said, 'Oh yes, you've worked hard. Practice them a bit more for next week.' I didn't know what I'd done wrong, I didn't know where I was going wrong and I didn't know why I was practicing them again. So I was asking questions like, 'Should this line be longer?' and I would look at her model. Her model might have a longer line in one example but a shorter line in the next. So I would say. 'Oh, it's because I didn't cross the,' and she would say, 'Oh, no no, that's not important. Just practice.'

Now, I don't want to make this sound like I was the innocent victim because it's not as simple as that by any means. But this pattern

Other versions of the story

continued and it continued for some weeks, where I did get more characters assigned as I went along, but I always felt I was ready for much, much more before my teacher felt I was ready to go on…

What I failed to recognize was happening was that my story of what literacy was about, my story of the role of the teacher, my story of how a good learner operates, were in complete opposition to my teacher's story. Because we both held these stories unconsciously, it took a long, long time before we could make explicit our different expectations of what we were trying to do. I think, had I done something like tear my paper up and say, 'This is ridiculous! I can't do it!' it would have shocked a confrontation out of us. But I couldn't. My story of a good learner is, 'You do what the teacher tells you. You do it as quickly as you can. You do it, and perhaps you throw in a question to show that you're alert and you're thinking ahead a step!' The more she baffled me, the more I fell back on my own patterns; the more obviously I failed to give her what she was looking for, the more she fell back on her traditional patterns of, 'Don't rush. Practice will bring it. Don't hassle the student. Encourage the student.'

We were locking horns and yet we both had the best intentions in the world. Then I started to 'story' the process at another step. I couldn't imagine why I was making such slow progress. People would ask me,
'Can you write sentences yet?'
'Well, not exactly, no.'
'What can you do?'
'Well, I hmm, um…'

Inevitably…I didn't just have a set of assumptions here. I started to story it, I started to make heroes and villains, I started to imply cause and effect, I started to look for patterns—not exactly look for patterns—impose patterns. I wasn't conscious of it but I started to tell the story as, 'Well even though I work hard, she won't let me go on.' I never went so far as to say, 'She's out to sabotage me,' but there was this sense in which she was getting cast in at least an 'opponent role,' if not in a villain role.

My first and last tutorial sessions in Chinese were in some ways arbitrary points in the tale of my Chinese learning. My experiences prior to beginning Chinese study obviously affected the way in which the experience took shape. My understanding of Chinese was not frozen at the point of the last lesson. Some of the knowledge faded, while other insights were not recognized until months later. But I chose to tell this story as having been framed by my first and last lesson. Consequently the versions of the story that I spun were affected by their temporal relation to that span of time.

Carr's (1986) terms, *retention, intention,* and *protention* helped me understand why this story would be seen and told differently at different times. Carr uses these terms in relation to the immediate present, but I found them more helpful to me when applied to a longer time period. When I began the study, I had a story of literacy drawn from my experiences as a learner and teacher of ESL literacy. I had a story of myself as a learner that incorporated expectations of how one learned successfully. Although the experiences from which I had developed these stories had taken place over many years, my new exposure to literacy learning brought these stories to mind. They formed the retention, or the "held-in-mind" past against which the current moment was understood. The immediately anticipated future, the protention, was inevitably shaped by this retention. We can only predict based on our stories of what is possible. As I came to understand literacy in new ways, the retention changed and with it the understanding of the current moment and the possibilities for the future.

When I was both telling this story and still trying to live it, I saw events and interactions differently from the way I would see them once the study was over. Thus, stories I told in the first three or four months were not merely a history of the past, but narratives that looked towards the future. We do not merely story our pasts, we live stories and shape our futures according to the stories we tell. At the beginning of the study, I saw the impending experience in terms of a source for a published study and I was concerned with data collection schemes and logistics. Events that seemed to diverge from the patterns agreed on in the dissertation proposal threatened the future I was trying to write for myself. My stories varied between those that were designed to reassure me that a good study could come from this inquiry, and those that explored the possibilities of total failure. As I became more involved in the study, this *telos* became less in doubt and the language learning began to become an intention in itself. Once again, the future was uncertain; my apparently minimal progress in literacy was seriously threatening when I had no way of knowing whether I would ever fulfill my preconceived notions of success as a literacy learner. My relationship with my tutor was also developing during this period, shifting from a tenuous link that needed protective storying to a stronger relationship that could survive a more honest and critical exploration.

In telling stories about my Chinese study, I wanted to shape the future to include my achieving sufficient proficiency in Chinese literacy to be able to write a dissertation on the process. I wanted that future to include the stabilizing of the relationship with Cindy so that she would continue to be interested in the project. These shaping intentions (MacIntyre, 1981) affected both the way I saw the experience and the way I chose to write about it.

When I look at the same interactions and events from a different temporal vantage point, I see different patterns in the same raw experience. By the time I told the last quoted version of the story, I had achieved a proficiency in literacy that satisfied my need for success as a learner. I had come to recognize that the kind of data I was gathering would have been adequate for my research purposes even if I had never been able to reach my preconceived literacy goals.

I had developed a good friendship with Cindy, and we had laughed together over my fears of her lack of interest, and my attempts to story her as an opponent. It was no longer threatening to describe these problems because their power to shape my future was lessened. Thus, the shift in the protention changes both the intention and the retention. In hindsight, I am able to see these concerns about progress and relationship as incidents within larger stories that have successful endings. They become the conflicts without which there can be no resolution to the story and they become part of narrative unities (Connelly and Clandinin, 1988b), which were not apparent at the time. My developing friendship with Cindy was one such unity. My growth of confidence with Chinese characters was another. A third, which I shall be exploring in a later chapter, related to my emotional reaction to the process of the study.

PART THREE

THE EXPERIENCE OF LEARNING CHINESE

Chapter Eight

Stories shaping the literacy experience: Cindy's story

In Chapter 3, I postulate four commonplaces for discussions of literacy, that is, *User, Text, Society and Process*. I suggest that the use of these commonplaces enables us to see the relationships among the wide variety of models of literacy that the literature demonstrates.

If I consider my own study through these four commonplaces, I see *Society* as the starting point. In the terms of this inquiry, *Society*, the contextual commonplace, is understood as the cultural and personal community in which the literacy is developed. It is assumed that the cultural context will shape the understanding of literacy that is developed in the individual and that we thus learn a literacy that is culturally specific. This position has been well demonstrated for first language literacy by writers such as Heath (1983), Street (1984), and Fishman (1991).

My inquiry looks at the acquisition of literacy in a second language, however, where the intention is to learn a literacy that is located in a different cultural context from that in which the first language was developed. This is not simply a matter of learning new coding systems, but of coming to understand literacy in a new way—of rewriting our individual story of literacy. Society is thus conceptualized as both the cultural and personal context in which the first language literacy was developed, and the context in which the target literacy will be learned and used.

The commonplace, *User*, is obviously at the heart of this inquiry. As would be expected in a narrative study, the *User* is an individual rather than a group. In this, as a discussion of literacy, the study is somewhat unusual. The contrast is clear between this understanding and that shown in the writings of, for example, Olson or Freire, for whom *User* is normally conceptualized as an entire community or section of society. However, this notion of *User* as individual is also different from the notion of *User* that we see in Heath and other ethnographers. Heath does describe individual people in *Ways with*

Words, but she considers them as part of a group and focuses her discussion on the features that are shared by the group.

My study attempts to demonstrate the intensely personal nature of a literacy learning experience, and the ways in which the individuality of the *User* shapes and is shaped by the experience. Thus, the notion of individuality is critical to my conception of literacy. In this study, we see two manifestations of *User*, that is, the learner and the teacher, both of whom bring their personal narrative history to bear on the experience.

The major focus of this inquiry is the relationship between *User* and *Process*. I have earlier described the commonplace, *Process*, as referring to the temporal interaction between *User* and *Text*, suggesting that various writers see this interaction differently, or focus on different aspects of the interaction. For example, Heath discusses how the interaction is shaped by *Society*, while Olson focuses on how the interaction will cognitively affect the *User*.

When I began this study, I expected to find that the *User* would affect the *Process*, and indeed I found many instances to support this position. During the study, I also became aware that the *Process* was affecting the *User*, in ways that I had not imagined and had never seen described in other literature on literacy. Although at the beginning of this inquiry, I cognitively espoused the position that the commonplaces had to be seen as dialectically linked, I had not anticipated the emotional implications of that claim. I explore these implications in Chapter 10, where I reconstruct and reflect on the challenges to my self-image.

In the next two chapters I will be considering the ways in which the *User* affects the *Process*, exploring how the stories that Cindy and I held about literacy shaped the teaching and learning experience, and consequently the ways we interacted with text.

Cindy's story of literacy in English

When Cindy and I first discussed literacy we were, of course, speaking in English. Later remarks Cindy made suggested that the context in which she would consider the word literacy was affected by the language she was speaking as, for example, in these comments:

Cindy   Maybe we should have talked about what [process and progress] meant and whether this is different in the Chinese language. We were both thinking English, I think, until we got into it.

We were talking in English but we were probably thinking in English too. Since you and I have both taught English literacy we were [thinking English too] Somewhere along the lines I made the switch.

Because the only language in which we could communicate was English, in our early discussions of literacy, Cindy's contributions were shaped by her experiences and her training in English language literacy. Although she developed much of her competence in English through exposure to the other children at school, she was also taught English via a structured syllabus, and went on to study linguistics. Consequently, she had a considerable amount of metalinguistic knowledge of the language, and saw it as a system that could, if necessary, be broken down and analyzed. In addition, her work with ESL literacy students and teachers in Toronto had developed a very conscious awareness of the variety of ways in which literacy can be taught in English, the advantages of different methods and so on. She thus had a fairly explicit story about English language literacy, in contrast to her story of Chinese literacy, which had been experienced but only minimally verbalized.

In our discussions prior to beginning tutorials, and in the planning for the first class, Cindy suggested or openly espoused certain attitudes to literacy that I largely shared, and that consequently passed virtually unnoticed at the time. I will be exploring these assumptions later in detail from my own standpoint, but the most significant assumption we both appeared to share was that literacy in the two languages was essentially similar and could be taught and learned in similar ways. Although we were soon to be disabused of this notion, neither of us found it strange, in these pre-tutorial days, that we should be pulling on our ESL expertise in discussing the upcoming study.

The first indication that Cindy was thinking in terms of English language literacy was that she illustrated her points by reference to her ESL experiences rather than her own Chinese literacy learning. Thus in discussing my role as a learner, she commented:

Cindy   As I told you before, this is very new for me. I never taught someone before who wasn't at some kind of disadvantage. By disadvantage, I mean maybe someone who is illiterate in his or her own language, or someone who needs this stuff by tomorrow.

Similarly, when we first discussed methodology, we considered the variety of techniques such as *Total Physical Response, Language Experience Approach* and so on, which are popular for teaching ESL, but are not commonly used to teach Chinese literacy. In these early days, Cindy was apparently open to some choice in methodology, and asked me if I wanted her to follow any specific approaches. We agreed that since she was the expert on Chinese, she would decide on the most appropriate methodology, which gave her the freedom to duplicate either her ESL classrooms or her own childhood learning, or indeed to create some third image of her own.

In Cindy's planning for the first tutorial, the pattern is suggestive of the ESL literacy teacher whose prime concern is less the subject matter than the comfort of the learner. She planned a variety of activities to maintain my interest, including some Cantonese popular songs for me to listen to. Her first instruction to me was also reminiscent of current ESL methodology, in its stress on student comfort over accuracy.

Cindy   Pick any one of them [the characters of her name]. Don't worry about the strokes, don't worry about the order. Just see how you feel with the pen.

I think that was the first and last time that I was allowed to approach characters in such an unstructured way. Most striking of all in this first lesson, however, were Cindy's efforts to create a learner-centred lesson. She began by asking me not simply what I wanted as a researcher, but what I wanted as a learner, particularly providing me with the option of such individualized activities as working with my name.

Cindy   And the next question I was going to ask you was, "If you had a choice what would you do first?" For instance the thing you might think of is numbers. Or your name. Or whether you feel it is necessary for you to have a name in Chinese? Is it necessary for you to know what my name is in Chinese? Those are the questions I have. Some people, the first thing they ask is, "I want to know my English name."

Conceivably then, with this beginning, Cindy and I could have settled down to a working pattern that would closely mimic many ESL literacy lessons I have observed. Such a pattern might have incorporated the learner selecting the content for each lesson, perhaps by dictating an oral phrase or narrative for the teacher to transcribe, as in a language experience story. We could have worked from a global understanding of a whole story down to recognition of reappearing characters, gradual distinguishing of frequently used characters, ability to recognize them out of context and so on.

In the event, we worked quite differently. Once Cindy began to teach me Chinese, she began to think in Chinese about literacy. Eventually it became apparent, although it took us both some time before we realized this explicitly, that her story of literacy in Chinese was different from her story of literacy in English. Not surprisingly, Cindy's understanding of Chinese literacy reflected the way she had learned to read and write as a child.

Cindy's experience of learning Chinese

Talking about her early school days, Cindy comments that in the one-room school, she remembers relatively little explicit instruction from the teacher, except in mathematics. She learned to read and write essentially by copying from a primer—first individual characters and later model sentences. The characters were presented in order of their complexity, with the simple strokes of the numerals providing the first introduction. The focus was on writing:

Cindy   When I think of literacy in English, I think of it as teaching... but literacy in Chinese to me still has to do with learning to read and write, because I had so much of it as a kid, it was all so—a lot of it was writing. You really didn't get into much reading, first you had to learn every single character you read.

Jill   Learn in the sense of writing?

Cindy   Writing, yes, and remembering it. I associate literacy in Chinese so much with writing, and less with reading.

During one of our lessons, she described the endless hours of practice aimed at achieving attractive characters:

Cindy   When I think of Chinese I think of it as a student and I remember sitting all those hours doing homework, just working on the one character because—not that you don't know what it means or that you can't read it when you see it, but that you have to be able to write it in a way that satisfies the teacher, I guess. It's not that you don't know your own name but you really have to practice it a lot in terms of writing, because that would have implications for future new words that you might come upon. I mentioned earlier that—I don't even know if you should call it calligraphy or penmanship—isn't important in English. It's not the writing, it's the knowing and the recognizing that's important. But in Chinese it's the writing art that is as much a part of literacy as the reading and reproducing.

Underlying these comments is the belief that the form of a text is inextricably linked to the content. "Ideas are important but ideas have to be shaped in such a way—it's the presentation, not just the idea."

She explained that her teachers felt it was not acceptable to develop the ideas and then try to work on the form. The form and the concepts had to take shape simultaneously. She commented that one of the differences between Hong Kong and Canadian schools was "the lack of attention to form." For her teachers, "The flow of ideas and the development of form should be concurrent. It's too late by the time you have got the ideas out, to go back and look at form."

It has been suggested to me by other people of Chinese origin that the handwriting practice, which is such a hallmark of traditional Chinese literacy approaches, is directed less towards the actual character production, than towards the development of mental discipline and inner harmony. This view certainly seemed to be supported by the kind of feedback that Cindy gave me as a learner in which she stressed balance and concentration. When I suggested this to Cindy, however, she had some reservations and pointed out how all-pervasive the concept of discipline had been in her life as a young child and how the literacy training was merely one exemplification of it.

Cindy Well, discipline was such a big part of life—discipline in actually producing a character. I suppose in a general way it applied but discipline was so important in every other way that I didn't see it as just something that was particular to learning to read and write.

Cindy was raised to believe that, regardless of any mental improvement that might come about from character practice, there would certainly be a visible improvement in one's handwriting, which played an important part in the kind of respect one was accorded in the community. "If you've only had a grade six education then the chances are that you won't have a very nice handwriting, and people will judge you according to that."

She often mentioned in passing that even now as an adult, her mother would comment on the calibre of her writing, urging her, for instance, to avoid using ballpoint pens, or to work on a particular character to improve it. Similarly, Cindy herself commented on a written notice we were studying, "It's amateurish. It's these kids in high school who came over before they got to be any good."

Cindy also felt that one's writing style directly affected the story one told about oneself. "The way you produce the character says a lot about your self," she stated explicitly when we were discussing this—a remark that suggested to me that the characters might be seen as a reflection of the mind, not merely as an indication of years of schooling.

Just as discipline in literacy was inseparable for Cindy from the discipline expected in all aspects of life, so she saw the relationship with the teacher as part of a much wider story. When I asked her about the extent to which as a child she might have questioned or challenged her teachers, she commented:

Cindy   I think that you are less encouraged to challenge authority and older people, but it's not just school. I think it's an entire system—if you buy into the system, you probably will not challenge the teacher. It really isn't a teacher-student thing, in that it doesn't have anything really to do with that individual who's standing there at the front of the classroom. You have no more or less good or bad feelings about him than you may have for any other person. But first of all, if instructions are explicitly given, there really isn't any need to ask. And secondly, by high school where you are in position to challenge people, because you get into more conceptual things, you've already bought into that system. The way you are supposed to learn is to receive—and that's in the teachings! You do a lot of observing and then you think about it. You may not feel it's necessary to challenge the teacher but there are always people who will, and in any system there will be people who see something wrong. But I think you have to remember that the others, the ones who don't challenge, may not be doing any less well than the people who did challenge.

Cindy's and my relationship never reflected this pattern, but it was noticeable that the indications of our development of a personal relationship were mostly manifested outside of the classroom rather than within it. Cindy rarely made any remarks of a personal nature during class time, in contrast to frequent irrelevancies introduced by me. Instead our classroom relationship became almost a humorous take-off of the traditional Chinese teacher-student pattern, with a series of ongoing jokes related to the way traditional Chinese classrooms were run. Praise for a character would often take the form, "This one deserves a shiny red star," while for poor performance, she would jokingly threaten, "If there was a back of the room in this room, I'd send you there!"

The educational system in which Cindy developed her initial literacy was not one that focused on the individual interests of the students. In a discussion of some of the differences between the uses of literacy skills in Hong Kong and Canadian schools, Cindy commented:

Cindy   Another difference would be that Canadian children are encouraged to write about their feelings. As I remember it, the stuff I wrote had a lot to do with facts. Happy was the only state that I think anyone of us would have described. I don't think the children in Hong Kong would be open to discussing negative feelings—you don't have a relationship with the teacher where you would talk about those things. The children here are encouraged to write journals, but this would have been very private in Hong Kong... we were encouraged to keep diaries—it goes back to more practice, more discipline, but we were never asked to show them.

In ESL literacy teaching in Canada, there tend to be two major foci of attention. The first addresses the learner's presumed wish to write personal material, while the second attempts to meet the learner's immediate functional needs. The first written texts are thus often about the self, while the first reading texts are pieces of print found in the environment, such as traffic signs, or medicine labels. Sampson (1990) has argued that, for the Chinese, literacy is seen as a means of improving the self, so that texts are carefully chosen for their content, which must serve a moral purpose.

The focus in classrooms is thus on material that represents the traditional philosophy and moral thinking, rather than on the students' individual interests or needs. In many cases, the text is in the form of a *koan*, a short aphorism or tale that incorporates a moral point. Cindy's memories of classroom texts supports this notion. She does not remember doing any reading for pleasure in the classroom, or indeed out of it, and her private journal provided the only opportunity for a use of literacy that had a personal base.

How the stories shaped Cindy's teaching

It is fairly evident that the way in which Cindy learned Chinese literacy was different from the way in which she has been teaching ESL literacy. At the beginning of the study, she planned teaching activities that reflected her English language assumptions. As we became more involved in the study, the ideas from English literacy became less and less frequent and we began to recreate something much closer to the kind of literacy experience that Cindy had had herself. After the study was over, I asked her about this, and it became apparent that she had not consciously chosen to shape the experience in this way.

Jill   At one point in the transcripts, you look back and you say, "Oh I think I was thinking in English then." Were you surprised by the way our study turned out?

Cindy   I didn't have very high expectations because I knew we only had a few months—the only thing I could compare it to is how long it took me to master those characters, if I ever did. I really was thinking,—I wasn't expecting much—Jill is doing this for her studies. She can probably handle a small digestible chunk of information and she can probably even produce the characters but I really—I think the amount of characters that you did manage to learn and use, that you were able to manipulate—you demonstrated that toward the end—surprised me.

Jill   Were you surprised at the way you found yourself teaching?

Cindy   Er, yes, because—at the beginning I was asking for suggestions because this was something I hadn't done before, and I...was thinking that certain things would be expected of me because of my ESL experience. I'd never taught Chinese before and I was thinking, maybe she can give me some suggestions. But you weren't—I don't remember you being very specific, and er, you fall back, I guess, on what you know best and that's your own experience. And in this case, not as a teacher but as a learner, so there were times I think in our sessions when I was surprised by how—I actually was insisting on certain things—and I trusted you understood why I was insisting. I experimented less than I thought I would. In retrospect I thought I would be more adventurous than I really was.

Jill Do you think that relates to something—er, is it simply a matter of falling back on your own experience in Chinese, or do you think its something that's fundamental to Chinese?

Cindy I don't know which it is, to tell you the truth. It was something new to me too, and I always approach anything new with caution. When in doubt, you tend to use what you think will work. I really believe that it had to be done that way. That might surprise you now.

Jill Oh no, on the contrary—tell me more

Cindy I thought even if you were doing it for your thesis, you should be—I mean you don't want to be doing it just for the thesis—so I felt you should go through the same thing I went through, you ought to be proud of your characters.... Maybe there was something that I had—something within me but never articulated—something never even actually told to me. But I think I did know deep down what the definition of literacy was in Chinese, and it had a lot to do with how you produced the characters. Now what you learned was enough to allow you to communicate. You may have made mistakes, minor mistakes with individual characters or grammar mistakes, syntax mistakes, but I think that a person reading that would have been able to understand you. It goes back to what the definition is, what do you expect of yourself?

Cindy, it appears, was as surprised as I was at the way in which we both shaped the study, and as unconscious of the process while it was ongoing. As I have indicated, she planned my first lesson largely in accordance with popular ESL methodology, that is, the learner-needs enquiry, the use of music, the attempt to personalize content and the flexible approach to writing a meaningful unit of language. She suggested the use of lined paper and dismissed my questions about the best writing implement as unimportant. However, in the event, nearly all these things changed, and we developed a pattern of working that was much closer to Cindy's personal experiences as a learner than it was to her teaching experiences.

One part of the story that seemed to play a large role in affecting how this turned out, was the way in which Cindy knew Chinese literacy. She had learned to be literate largely through a pattern of imitation of provided samples. There had been little analysis of the component parts of the characters, or discussions of the relationship between one character and another. Perhaps because she had learned the characters as a small child who was simultaneously developing small muscle control, the characters had developed their accuracy and their shape simultaneously. With a few exceptions, Cindy had never had any call to analyze the relationship of the various strokes in a character, any more than she had needed to know whether the *ma* sound for mother was higher or lower than the *ma* sound for horse, in order to produce it properly.

The result was that she knew the characters as whole units, rather than as sets of lines joined at specified points, and she taught them accordingly. The characters were analyzed according to the sequence of strokes, but the stress was on simple repetition of the specified order, not on the implications of order for shape or meaning.

A typical introduction would be for her to present a model character in a book, demonstrate the stroke order for me, then ask me to try to reproduce it myself. The transcripts are full of incidents where I try to get Cindy to specify such rules as, "Line x crosses line y at point z," and she responds with comments such as, "The character needs practice." At one point she commented:

> You are asking questions, the answers to which I have never thought about. You mentioned something about implicit and explicit knowledge and I guess that's true because it's all that I know. I had never really even studied the teaching and learning of Chinese. I don't even know how much I remember in terms of the process itself—being in school in Chinese and what was done for me and to me.

Later she wrote in regard to a query of mine, "I don't know the rule or reasons. It was never explained to me in Hong Kong. We just kept following models."

In our preliminary discussion, Cindy asked me what I would like to learn, and, in line with my expectations of a functionally based literacy, I suggested the vocabulary of the market and the restaurant, which would give me the chance of real-life encounters with the characters I was learning. Almost immediately, however, she made it clear that this was not really an area that was open to discussion.

"Oh," she commented, "Well, I have something to say about that, because in terms of writing, you do have to begin with the simplest characters." Earlier, she had suggested that I might like to begin with the Chinese numerals, which had formed her own introduction to literacy, and essentially we settled down to working with these characters.

Cindy understood Chinese literacy in ways that she had never had any occasion to explicitly formulate and consequently did not think to share with me. She knew that the simple strokes demonstrated in the numerals and other elementary characters would reappear in more complex characters, independently, and in various combinations. She understood how the characters needed to be seen in relation to a square, not to a line.

Once she moved away from the notion of English language literacy and began instead recreating her own learning experience, she taught in accordance with these understandings. She recognized, for instance, that once these early characters were well learned, the later characters could be learned more swiftly. Consequently she moved very slowly through the first lessons. She was dissatisfied with the results on the lined paper and asked me to work with squared charts, although she was not able to make explicit the purpose behind them in a way that I could initially understand.

Cindy's expectations of what would constitute acceptable progress were affected by these understandings. She saw progress as being subsumed in process, and was very encouraged by signs of emerging harmony and balance in my work, which were imperceptible to me.

Cindy   I certainly have noticed that with your sense of balance, and I haven't really—I've only been showing you what that means, I haven't really been describing it to you, that much, but I guess you've got that sense and you can tell when you didn't make a good character...

I wondered had you realized that progress wasn't how many words you could string together...progress is actually subsumed in process the way we have been working on these characters. And I noticed you—the self awareness, you would know something or you would notice something—you were right at least fifty percent of the time about what was off-balance.

Your awareness of the concept of balance has impressed me tremendously. As a teacher whose philosophy is to promote independence, I'm delighted by your self-criticisms and self-correction.

Another indication of progress that impressed Cindy was when I was able to recreate for her some approximation of a character I had met elsewhere. On one occasion I mentioned that I had triumphantly pointed out to a friend what I thought was the familiar character, *ngoh*, (meaning I). Later I had looked more closely at the poster on which it was displayed and realized that I had confused it with another similar character. I told this tale somewhat ruefully, but to Cindy the ability to recognize the slight differences between the two characters was a sign of considerable progress. "When I first noticed you coming back with something and you could reproduce it, that told me you actually could put together an image in your mind."

Similarly, later in the study, I attempted a new character without bothering to check stroke order with her first.

Jill   Does it taper in towards the bottom like a *yaht* would?

Cindy   It would look nicer. [pause] So how many strokes?

Jill   Oh, now I'm doing it like *yaht* on the assumption that that's right. Er, 1, 2, 3, 4, 5—is that correct?

Cindy   Yes, you don't even have to think about it anymore.

In the margin of this transcript, Cindy wrote, "You've come a long way!" She was right, but because these signs of progress were not ones I expected, I did not always recognize them myself. Where I was constantly comparing my progress to those of English literacy learners, Cindy drew her standards from initial Chinese literacy. This was well illustrated on one occasion when she discussed the reaction that other Chinese speakers might have to my progress.

Cindy	Could you do me a favour—could you copy these two [class worksheets] for me, because I want to take them home?
Jill	Give your mother a good laugh, huh?
Cindy	I might show it to her too. She doesn't believe me.
Jill	What, that you are teaching it, or that I can do it?
Cindy	That you can actually write in Chinese. [laughter]
Jill	That's interesting, isn't it? No, I mean it's interesting in terms of what people expect about language. Because she doesn't think I've done it long enough, or because I'm not Chinese by birth and I don't speak it, therefore—or what?
Cindy	Well, she asked me how old you were and I said, "She's about 40." Hope I'm right?
Jill	42 , no, yes 42.
Cindy	And she says, "Well how often do you see her?" and I said, "Once a week," and I told her you were writing sentences, and I said that some characters you were doing better than I was—she would expect you to be doing it like baby scribble.
Jill	You see, I can't tell whether I am or not.
Cindy	I'll show you. I'll show you how a kid does it.
Jill	Oh yes, that would be fascinating if you have access to any kid writing.
Cindy	Because they don't have the motor skills you have and can't control it. You can't talk to them and say, "You have to control this stroke a little more." It only comes from practice with them.
Jill	Yes. Yet when I look back—you look at this day one stuff of mine and you really think, well the motor skills aren't as self evident as you think. I was looking at these *seis*—all over the page. There is some motor skill development going on as well—look at those—they're awful!
Cindy	It's better. Look at the ones you did today.
Jill	Something that—obviously if you've got thirty years of motor skills they've got to help but some of it I have to learn the particular skills for this language as well as…
Cindy	Yes, but I really don't think that—when I show this to her she's going to freak out. [laughter]

Cindy commented more than once that when she was a child in school, the good students were given relatively little feedback. In her *Narrative*, she wrote, "Good students are always left alone." To some extent this pattern was also repeated in our tutorials, with her comments tending to focus more on areas of work that required improvement.

Cindy   I guess I was struck—actually I tend to speak a lot more—if I were in an ESL class and somebody gave me a comment I would speak to that comment a lot more and I guess I am finding it—that it's a surprise to me that I somehow teach you very differently from other people I have taught in the same situation.

When she read the transcripts, she was very struck by the fact that her remarks sometimes sounded abrupt or critical. In many cases this was an artifact of the transcript that captured the words but not the gentle tone in which they were uttered. Her annotations often included comments such as, "You were probably somewhat threatened by that comment. Comments such as these seem very harsh in print. I can't remember how I sounded but they are meant only to convey my message directly." or "Seems abrupt. I don't know why I do things with you that I wouldn't do in an ESL class."

In a letter discussing my progress, Cindy raised this issue again, suggesting that she saw the cause in our relationship as peers rather than as student and teacher. "Lastly, I would like to say again that I tend to treat you differently from my ESL students. I have told you before that I had not taught students who were not considered disadvantaged in one way or another." While I would agree with Cindy that this inevitably had its effect, I suspect that her own experiences in learning Chinese had also played a part.

The nature of our joint literacy experience was, of course, shaped in many ways by features other than those derived solely from our prior experiences with literacy, and I am not trying to suggest that Cindy's educational experiences in Hong Kong were the only significant part of the story. Nor am I suggesting that she began exclusively with a story drawn from ESL literacy and then totally rejected it in favour of one drawn from Chinese literacy.

There were many occasions throughout the study where she continued to refer to her experiences as an ESL teacher. For instance, on one occasion she suggested we adjourn to a restaurant for the class. When I noted on the transcript my surprise, because, "She is the one who refuses to consider me working on the subway," she answered, "Somehow it didn't occur to me that this would be inconsistent with my insistence on ideal working conditions. My Canadian training tells me that I should try to break the monotony of the classroom once in a while."

A similar pattern was demonstrated in the kind of activities that Cindy prepared for our classes. Although after the first week, we settled into a pattern that was largely the one by which Cindy had learned herself, she remained open to other possibilities.

On one occasion, she brought in a photocopy of a notice that she had found posted in a Chinese Community Centre where she was working. We worked very differently with this piece of text, searching it for familiar characters and using prediction strategies to guess at unknown characters. On later occasions she brought in other pieces of real-life text, including a shopping bag from a take-out restaurant, and a note she had written to her mother. She was also amenable to my suggestions of other activities and welcomed my attempts to use familiar characters to cover personal material.

After my first journal attempt, she wrote, "Did I tell you? I was impressed. I was proud of you. I'm glad you took the initiative. I was getting so used to our meetings that I kept thinking we had all the time in the world to get to compositions,"—a warm response, which obviously contrasted with her own experience that, "Good students are always left alone."

There were thus indications that Cindy's experiences with Chinese literacy were not the only influence on her teaching but that her more recent experiences as a teacher in Canada had also shaped the process. Nonetheless, as I have outlined, there were many areas in which Cindy did repeat patterns that could be identified in her own early learning experiences. And further, she surprised herself by the way in which she taught me differently from the way she teaches ESL students.

It seemed that her entire life story played a part in the way in which she understood literacy and in the way in which she tried to share that understanding with me. Of course, as the learner I played an equally important part in shaping the interaction, as I will discuss in the next chapter.

Chapter Nine

Stories shaping the literacy experience: Jill's story

In the previous chapter, I explored how Cindy had a different story of literacy in Chinese and in English. This was not something that I was able to recognize at first. Indeed, in retrospect, it seems that one of my biggest assumptions was that because we both began the discussion with reference to ESL literacy classes we were thinking of literacy in the same way and would continue to see it in the same way.

Despite my attempts to explore my preconceptions before I began this study, it became evident that I had omitted some of the most significant preconceptions of all. I was claiming, at least at a cognitive level, that cultural and personal experiences shape the way we understand and make sense of every aspect of our lives, and yet I had not thought through the implications of this claim for literacy.

Instead, I began with an assumption that because Cindy and I shared a background in ESL we shared an understanding of literacy. Embedded within this assumption was the belief that this story of literacy was transferable to Chinese literacy. This story had obviously been at least partially shaped by the popular discourse that literacy is a neutral technology—that the difference between English and Chinese literacy is the way in which they are recorded. I recognized that different cultures used literacy in different ways but, judging by the way I responded to Cindy's attempts to teach me a different literacy, I think I must have understood this as different ways of working with the same tool, much as a musical instrument can be used to play jazz or classics. I didn't understand that literacy is more like making music with one's own voice—it will be shaped into the kind of tunes that society prefers, and used at the times that society approves, but the voice is a part of the human being and is shaped by the person's life. I saw literacy as a record of thinking rather than a shaping of thinking, and I failed to understand that the literacy cannot be removed from the individual for inspection.

The story of literacy and literacy learning with which I began this inquiry was drawn from many sources. One was undoubtedly the popular presentation of literacy that we see in the media, which I have described in Chapter 2.

My personal experiences learning to be literate as a child in England were no doubt also influential, as were my experiences teaching ESL students to read and write. The story I held of literacy learning determined my expectations regarding every aspect of literacy development, including the language itself, the role of the learner, the strategies for learning, the behaviour of the teacher, and the measures of progress. Essentially, I assumed that I could learn Chinese literacy in the same ways that I had learned and taught English literacy, and that the strategies that were successful for one would be successful for the other.

My English language literacy had given me a considerable amount of metalinguistic knowledge, which let me understand some of the system underlying English language and English literacy. I began with the assumption that there would be a similar systematicity underlying Chinese literacy. I was also aware of the systems that had been overlaid on English language literacy—the rules of spelling, which had been invented relatively recently, the specifications about letter shapes, which vary from country to country, and from period to period. Transient though these rules were, I had absorbed them as a child as the "right" way to do things and I expected to find their equivalent in Chinese.

I did not consider fully that in attempting a new literacy, I might be entering a new way of looking at education. Hence I assumed that a good learner would be the same in all systems, and that the kind of performance that had previously won me praise as a student would also gain Cindy's approval. Similarly, I eschewed certain habits that had never been well regarded in my earlier educational exploits. I also took for granted that my teacher's behaviour would be relatively predictable and that I would be able to interpret her actions and reactions according to my prior experience with teachers in Britain and Canada.

Some of my expectations were fulfilled when I began to learn Chinese, and I was certainly able to draw on my previous experience with literacy in English to help me with the learning. However, I also found that some of my prior learning was actually dysfunctional, in that my English-based literacy story was so firmly held that I interpreted new experiences in the light of the old story, manipulating events to fit a preconceived pattern, rather than being open to the possibility of a different way of understanding.

Linguistic assumptions

One area where my prior assumptions led me astray concerned the language itself. Essentially I looked to find the same underlying system in Chinese that I was used to in English and I initially interpreted what I met in Cantonese according to an English system. Interference in the second language from the patterns of the first language is a concept that has been well documented in the literature on second language acquisition (see for example, Lado, 1957; James, 1980; Fisiak, 1981), so that my experiences in this area were not surprising, and indeed many of them could have been predicted by contrastive analysis.

There are many demonstrations in the transcripts of my attempts to formulate Chinese sentences in accordance with the patterns of English. A frequent and ongoing syntax error, for example, was my tendency to write phrases such as, "He is happy" rather than, "He happy," which would be the correct Chinese form.

A rather more complex indication of my English-based assumptions related to the use of particles, which are common in Chinese. I first met the particle, *dik*, in the phrase for "my mother"—*ngòhdik mahma*—literally, "I, particle, mother." I assumed that *dik* represented a possessive particle and used it with some success in that form. I was baffled, therefore, when my oral language teacher used the oral equivalent particle, *ge*, in the phrase, *Sìnggabôge pàhngyàuh*, [Singapore, particle, friend], to mean a Singaporean friend, rather than a friend of Singapore.

As far as I ever sorted out this particular particle, I think it functions more as an adjectival marker than a possessive one, but it is possible that I am still demonstrating English language patterns by trying to classify it specifically as one or the other. My point here is not merely that the two languages have different underlying systems, but that my expectation of certain categories and classifications led me to a number of false conclusions, which retarded my progress.

Other areas of linguistic interference from English related to pronunciation. Obviously I found those sounds that do not appear in English harder to produce than those that were more familiar. Hence, I had trouble with the initial sound in words like *chât*, where the *ch* is representative of a sound that falls somewhere among English *j*, *ch*, and *ty*. I found too that I did not hear differences that were not significant in English, hence it was a struggle to even recognize differences in tone, much less to reproduce them.

There were also emotional barriers to be overcome. One of the first words I learned, *ngòh*, or "I," gave me (and the other students in my oral class) great difficulty, not merely because the nasal sound was unfamiliar in initial position, but because it was not what we considered to be an appropriate sound for us to make. After the first class at which it was introduced, I wrote on my transcript:

> This is one of those classic sounds that seem embarrassing to L2 speakers. Nice people don't make noises like this. All the words I would use to describe it are from animals; it honks or brays. I am 'surprised' that Cindy is so at ease with it—she's even prepared to lean forward into the tape recorder and say it loud! One part of my brain knows this is stupid. The other reacts.

There was a somewhat similar sense of embarrassment at making a real attempt to incorporate Chinese tone into my speech patterns. In many cases I simply did not know the required tone, but sometimes I thought I could hear the tonal pattern in my head, yet could not overcome a feeling that it was inappropriate for me to reproduce these sounds. Occasionally this was because the tonal pattern seemed in English to express an attitude with which I was uneasy. On one occasion, I noted that the woman speaker on the tape sounded petulant. It was a label that allowed me to recall clearly within my head the tonal pattern of the interchange. However, it was also a label that made me uneasy at making a serious attempt to reproduce it. Given a choice between sounding childishly petulant and having an English accent, I opted for the English accent.

In general, I found a reluctance in myself to really attempt to reproduce Chinese tonal patterns because they seemed to strip away the voice contours that express my personality. It felt as if I had spent years learning an appropriate use of intonation to indicate my emotional relationship to my utterances, including varying degrees of warmth, humour, decisiveness, authority, relationship with speaker, and commitment among other elements. When I communicated in totally different tonal patterns from those I was used to, my speech seemed to have been stripped of my personality and I became uneasy.

Assumptions about print

As I have suggested, the above examples would largely have been predicted by the literature on contrastive analysis. Less well documented in the literature is the suggestion that similar patterns of assumption will affect second language learners' understanding of the system of coding and decoding. In English language literacy, pronunciation of words is only minimally affected by context or meaning. We use context to distinguish between "lead," the verb, and "lead," the metal, for instance, but we do not expect to pronounce l-e-a-d as something totally different, such as "boat" or "fish," when it appears in different contexts. The link between sound and symbol is thus relatively rigid.

Although I knew that the phonetic link was minimal in Chinese characters, I still assumed that a given shape would provide a consistent pronunciation, and that once I had learned the sound for a particular character I would not need to relearn it for different contexts. I have cited in a previous chapter my surprise at discovering that the two characters, *neui* and *ji*, would be pronounced *hou* when they are written in a single square.

Later I came to work with collocations—two or more characters that are written in separate squares but that are understood together to make a different meaning. For example, when *bei* [secret] and *syù* [book] appear adjacent to each other, they mean "secretary." Sometimes in such collocations I would find that a character was verbalized in a completely different way, according to the collocation in which it was used, without even the clue of placement within the square to suggest that a different pronunciation would be required.

I was also baffled on occasion to realize that Cindy and I had a somewhat different understanding of what a word was. Some characters are pronounced with the same phonemes but in different tones according to their placement in a phrase. For "younger sister" one writes the character, *mui*, twice without any change in appearance. When it is said aloud, however, the tone is different for the two syllables, *muihmúi*. To me this was the same word repeated but apparently not for Cindy.

Cindy   And that one's ji. [and this is] mui. So ji mui means? If you put them together? Did I ever tell you? Sisters. Ji is older sisters and mui is younger sisters, and you put them together. Do you remember a word that also means older sister?

Jill   *Je?*

Cindy   Yes. Do you know another word for younger sister?

Jill   No.

Cindy   It's *mui*, same thing.

Jill   Oh? Yes—that's what we say in the oral.

Cindy   In where?

Jill   We have met *mui mui* in the oral class but I thought you meant another word.

Cindy   You see it sounds a little different because, er, when you speak it's *muih múi*.

Jill   Ah, the tone changes.

Cindy   Yes, but reading the word, it's *mui*.

Jill   Yes, okay.

We encountered somewhat similar confusions with regard to whether words rhymed. I was always struggling to pin down the sounds I was hearing and would often ask Cindy whether a new word had the vowel sound of a familiar one I knew. It soon became apparent that, for her, only words pronounced in the same tone could be said to rhyme, thus she did not consider *ha* [shrimp] and *ga* [family] to rhyme, because *ha* is said in high level tone while *ga* is high falling tone. Similarly, because I was very aware of the similarity between pairs of words such as *yât* [one] and *yaht* [day], based on their related Yale orthography, I was surprised that she did not also recognize the relationship.

One basic assumption about literacy, which it took me a long time to discard, related to the pattern by which symbols are arranged. In English, of course, we arrange our letters in relation to a horizontal line, or rather in relation to four horizontal lines, marking the upper and lower boundaries for various letters. Letters are formed in relation to the line, not to the size or shape of the word they are forming. Letters can also occupy different widths of page space, so that a four-letter word such as "till" will be narrower than a word such as "mown."

When I began the study, I was aware that many languages relate their letters to the line in ways different from the English style. For example, Arabic is written through the line, while Hebrew hangs below it. I knew that Chinese was traditionally written in vertical columns, and I appear to have unconsciously storied this as meaning that the characters should be written in relation to a vertical line. Within this story, I was also maintaining my assumptions drawn from English about the relationship among the various symbols. I assigned less space to simple characters than to complex ones, and I assumed that characters could come in different sizes.

Just as English includes some long thin letters such as "l," and some wide short letters such as "w," I produced characters that were long or short, thin or thick according to the number of strokes in a given direction. When Cindy asked me to work on a chart of one inch squares, I was frustrated because it seemed to give me neither horizontal nor vertical lines against which to align my characters. I expected to see each character sitting perhaps one-eighth of an inch up from the base wall of the square and was surprised when some of Cindy's samples varied widely from this expectation.

My eventual understanding of why Cindy wanted me to work with squares did not come from her feedback. I was so sure of my story that I interpreted her comments according to my prior assumptions or simply tuned them out. One day doing my homework, I got exasperated with my poor performance in the large squares assigned to me, and did a set of nine smaller characters nested into one large square. Cindy's feedback was quite explicit on this.

> When someone gives you a space to do a character, they usually expect you to put it in the middle and it should take up approximately half the square. Okay, this is for practice purposes, so if you did that [small character], I would say that is not good. I mean the character is fine but you didn't go according to the space you were given.

Although this guidance seems very clear in retrospect, I only took in part of it at the time. I never tried to fit nine characters into a single square again, but I obviously didn't listen to her guidance about centering the character. Some weeks later, I was once again frustrated with the large squares and decided to try some smaller characters. This time I did restrict myself to one character per square, but I tucked each reduced character neatly into the corner of the square rather than centering it.

The understanding of what Cindy was trying to tell me, came largely as a result of exposure to a variety of formats of print. In particular, one day I was sitting alone in my favourite *dim sum* restaurant, free of any classroom pressures to perform, and perhaps consequently more open to new understandings. I was passing the time by looking at a painting on the nearby wall, where the artist's signature block was a large square quartered into four smaller squares, each of which contained a character. The curves of the characters were stylized into straight lines, so that each character completely filled its square. Looking at this block to see if I could recognize any of the characters, I realized that the essential template for each character was a square, so that placement was not made in relation to the outside edges of a character at all, but to the midpoint.

Once I had recognized this, I found numerous examples of printed text that demonstrated this relationship very clearly, but the conventions of handwriting and the power of my own story had not allowed me to see this initially. This new way of looking at characters helped me understand, too, why the component parts of a character should change their overall shape when they were incorporated into more complex characters. Prior to this I had often failed to recognize known components in characters that I saw around Chinatown. The familiar character, *yuht* (moon or month), appears as a part of many other characters but because it is modified according to the rest of the character I had not recognized it previously.

moon   leisure   invite   bright

Figure 9: Examples of *yuht* in various forms.

Later as my story of literacy changed, the notion of the square became integral to my reading, so that I "saw" the square even when it was not present. At one point I commented to Cindy that I had recognized the character, *gwok* [kingdom], in my text book, because it "filled the square." In response to her query on this, I answered:

> I used to really resent squares, I used to fight squares and go and practice on a piece of paper, then come back and write it in the squares to satisfy you. I would still, given my preference, opt for a smaller square but somewhere along the line the realization has come that the square is a very useful part of the placement and that although when I get a piece of text it doesn't have squares in, the square is there. When I said to you about 'oh well *gwok* fills the whole square,' you put a note on it and said, 'Are there squares in the text?' and of course there aren't. I'm imposing my own grid on the text, but it's a way of looking at text I never saw before.

Another area of difficulty was in discovering which aspects of a character were critical to its production. At the beginning, even when Cindy pointed out distinctions to me, I did not seem to see them. She demonstrated two different versions of the character for four:

Jill   I'm sorry, I don't appreciate the distinction you're making.... Do yours again for me. I don't see the difference. Yours aren't joined? Is that...

Cindy   The difference is in these two strokes. In this one...

Jill   Oh, I see. You're doing two straight lines and they're doing a...

Cindy   In this one, it goes this way. In the one I did they just come...

Jill   Straight down?

Cindy   Sort of. Like, er, it's a little bit slanted. I use this one and everybody else I know uses this one too.

I tended not to notice features that would not be significant in English literacy. Some of these, such as the difference between a slight tail to a character versus a dead stop, were fairly easy to become aware of, perhaps because in English we use a similar feature to distinguish "g" from "q." Other distinctions, such as the need for the pen to trail off to a fine point on the end of certain strokes, took longer to notice and remember as significant. While blithely ignoring these important features, I would be struggling to reproduce other features, such as specially shaped corners, which it turned out were merely an artifact of the brushwork example. I was reminded here of students of mine in ESL classes who painstakingly copy the serif corners from text book typefaces.

In some areas it appeared that prior cultural experiences played a part in the way I saw and remembered certain characters. In the beginning, I was inclined to remember characters by noting their resemblance to familiar shapes or alphabetic letters. A character we studied in the early days before I understood the significance of the square was *sahp*, the number ten. The essential *sahp* that one will find in typeset is an evenly balanced cross like a large addition sign. In the handwritten version, which I met first, the horizontal is sometimes placed above the midpoint of the vertical. Having mentally identified this new shape as a cross, I produced rows of elongated crosses in which the horizontal stroke became shorter and shorter and its placement became higher and higher on the vertical. When Cindy tried to draw my attention to the necessary point on the end of the vertical stroke I visualized a palm cross I had been given as a small child at Sunday school, and realized that I had been drawing Christian crosses rather than writing *sahp*.

Sometimes it was noticeable that Cindy's images and mine were pulled from our different backgrounds. The character, *go*, a classifier that cannot really be translated into English looks like this:

Working on it alone while doing a think-aloud, I began to associate it with a particular image.

> This character makes me think of a gravestone with that little cross on it. Disconcerting. Okay, let's calm down and look at my characters and at Cindy's. Cindy's box is fatter than mine and going with the gravestones, I'm getting longer and thinner so that's one thing to stop…. You tend to put shapes in your head for some reason. This gravestone with a cross on it is getting to be past a joke.

Later when I described this to Cindy, she expressed surprise and said, "I thought you were going to say it looks like a semi-detached house." I annotated this comment with, "The curve of *yahn* [the side piece] would block me from seeing it as a roof. But of course Chinese roofs do curve, and Chinese gravestones don't look like this!"

Notions of literacy

As I discussed earlier, Cindy understood literacy in Chinese as being demonstrated in the ability to produce attractive characters, which evidenced the user's mental discipline and sense of balance. I began the study with a very different understanding of what I was aiming for. Primarily I think I was trying to read, rather than to write. My first discussion with Cindy, when I mentioned that I could learn characters on the subway train certainly suggested this view of literacy. Similarly, when she asked me what I wanted her to teach me, I selected words that I might usefully read but would have no cause to write. "Could we do some street characters so that I've got a chance of walking down the street and seeing if I can recognize something?"

As I document in Chapter 6, when Cindy began to teach me with a methodology that worked largely towards improving my writing of the characters, I was baffled and frustrated because I had learned to read the characters to my own satisfaction and I did not understand why she was not proceeding to new material more rapidly. Essentially I considered the message as more important than the form. This is a belief that is firmly storied in my English language literacy skills. So long as my students' or my children's work is legible, I respond to it based on the content rather than the format of the letters.

This preference for content over form is not a simple either/or situation, since I do give appearance some importance in my written communication. My handwriting in English includes both a fairly neat sloping hand for formal writing and a fast upright widely spaced scrawl for my own use. However, I fairly often sacrifice my neat writing to time pressures, and I do not expect people to judge me harshly for that choice.

When I began work with Cindy, I assumed that I could work in the same way with Chinese characters, producing more or less neat versions according to the context. On occasions when I was concerned primarily with content, I would use a scribble version of the characters. For instance, if I was recording homework or, later in the study trying to do a first draft for a journal, I would produce rapid versions of the characters, which had all the strokes intact and properly sequenced but which were perhaps lopsided or distorted in some other way. Cindy tried to point out to me that I could not afford to let the form slip or I would never find myself able to produce attractive characters, but I found it difficult to understand her point, when the scrawled character served its semantic function for me.

Because my story of literacy did not include a relationship between form and discipline, initially I showed a similar lack of concern with form when I was doing character practice for homework. I knew that Cindy wanted me to work in ideal conditions, which would allow me to concentrate, but I was so sure that I knew what I was trying to learn that I discounted this advice. Instead I decided that some prior practice in spare moments would help me learn the component parts of the assigned characters. One day, when she asked me about the conditions under which I had done my homework, I confessed that I had done my "real" practice on lined paper, before I came to do the charts for her.

Cindy   In fact your practice sessions are probably more important than the stuff you are showing me. It seems like you did the charts for me and did the practice sessions for yourself. That's why I think you should keep them, because I'd like to see them. If you could write I would make you write lines saying you would never do your homework in front of the television again! [laughs]

Jill   Yes, okay, that's fine. I guess I am splitting this task. I feel that one part of me is learning stroke order and prototypical character, and that I figure I can do in front of a television, in a car or wherever and the other part is training my hand to produce a graceful stroke and that part I am prepared to go to the desk for. I—I know in my head I shouldn't split it that way, but I also know my own patterns and that if I don't put in the hours when I've got the hours...[trails off]

My lack of understanding of what Cindy is trying to teach me here is demonstrated in my description of the split as lying between training the memory and training the hand. The concept of training the personality is not even considered. I elaborate on this assumption that what she is talking about is physical muscle training in my journal of the same week.

> The tails of the strokes, Cindy was also pointing out to me, should tail off to a point—they shouldn't stop dead. That's not so easy to achieve when you write with a pen. It means you have to determine your amount of push right when you start off. You can't just draw to the right spot and then stop, you have to launch yourself into it with exactly the right amount of impetus. I guess these are the reasons that she says you have to be concentrating when you practice, that you don't practice just for yourself.

There is nothing in the transcript to indicate that Cindy ever talked about small muscle training. I assigned this concern to her, because the only way I could make sense of her requests for homework practice according to my story of what literacy was all about, was by putting her requests in this physical skill context.

Expectations

Because I assumed Chinese and English literacy were essentially similar, I assigned myself goals based on the kind of progress I had seen my ESL students demonstrate, and I measured my progress according to a set of expectations developed from the same context. Obviously I was aware that there were differences between alphabetic languages and those written in characters, but I recognized only the surface differences and assumed that one could be seen in terms of the other. Thus I tried to understand characters in the familiar terms of words, syllables or letters.

My pre-study notes indicate that I began this study with some confusion as to whether symbols represented concepts or words. The characters that I was first taught were all equal to words, with the result that I promptly concluded that this would be true for all other characters I would meet. Having made this somewhat inaccurate assumption, I began to consider characters as analogous to English words in terms of how they might be learned and taught.

Initial English literacy teaching tends to make use of two major methods: one based on phonics, and one based on sight word recognition. The phonics-based method focuses on the link between sound and symbol and introduces words as sets of sounds to be combined. The sight word method focuses on the link between meaning and symbol and teaches the word as a whole unit to be recognized on sight, rather than decoded according to its sounds. Obviously I could not attempt to decode Chinese characters by a phonics methodology. However, it was very easy to see characters as sight words to be learned as whole units and recognized. This is indicated by the description I gave three months into the study of what I had seen myself trying to do.

> To me a character was something that was very intricate to learn and you had a sense of complexity and appearance being important, but I was seeing it, I think, as something that I would master to recognize, so writing them on the subway—even if what I produced was very scruffy—didn't really matter. What I was thinking I was going to be doing when I wrote them was engraving the pattern in my head so that when I saw them again I would recognize them.

Although sight word learning in English does make some use of phonic skills, in that, for instance, ESL students will often sound out the first letter of the word to guess at which sight word they are seeing, essentially each new sight word is learned as an individual visual entity. There is little carry-over between words, so that one basically takes as long to learn one's fiftieth sight word as one does for the tenth. Seeing characters as sight words meant that I made related assumptions about the time required to learn new characters. I felt that each new character would take the same amount of time to learn as the early ones did, thus if I learned only four characters in the first week, I expected to learn forty characters in ten weeks and so on. My journals in the early weeks of the study are full of entries where I count up how many characters I have done, and predict my likely progress based on such simple arithmetic.

As I developed a little more competence in the language, I was forced to question my assumption that one word equalled one character. In a journal entry in early November, I describe my attempts to decipher the character version of a dialogue I had met in Yale transcription in one of my oral classes.

> I looked for other words I knew and saw *siu*, which puzzled me. Little? What was "little" doing in this dialogue? I cross referenced

it with the English text and found it was part of *siuje* [Miss]. I hadn't realized that *siuje* was a collocation and had assumed that it would be written as either one character all of its own, or else it would have *siu* squeezed in as half a character with some other radical. Does this mean that any multisyllabic word is a collocation?...Somehow I was surprised to discover that it really was one square per syllable. One word does not equal one character, necessarily. One syllable equals one square. When two characters go into one square, as with *neui* and *ji*, you get a new syllable, *ho*. Theoretically *ho* could pair with something else to make a collocation like *siuje*, I suppose.

If anything, this discovery depressed me further, because it meant that my word count would be even lower than I had anticipated. Somehow, I did not see that I was developing a considerable amount of implicit knowledge that could not be represented in this simple character or word counting measure of progress. Some of this knowledge concerned developing a sense of the basic parameters underlying the shapes or the sounds of the language. I found, for instance, that I could recognize stylized versions of a character on a restaurant menu. I did not know which character I was seeing, but I knew that the combination of strokes was not normally one that would be permissible.

Similarly, in oral class, I was surprised when another student misread the teacher's handwriting to produce a sound combination that I knew was not permissible in Cantonese. I had not realized that I had developed a sense of the limits of the sound or visual system, but I found I was correct when I queried these things.

I was also learning more easily measured skills, such as the basic strokes from which many characters are made, some notion of basic syntax and so on. Obviously in the early stages of the learning, one is being heavily challenged by all these demands, and yet I was taken by surprise and failed to recognize what was happening. Obviously, those learning English for the first time have to make similar progress in terms of learning letter shapes, print conventions, and basic syntax, so that their progress would also be slow initially. However, I did not allow for this in my own study. I can only assume that my basic belief was that all my English language and literacy knowledge could be transferred, so that I saw the entire learning task as conquering these particular visual shapes.

My assumptions as to what constituted acceptable progress were so powerful that they shaped the way I heard Cindy's feedback. There were a number of occasions when she commented favourably on my progress in those first weeks, but I completely discounted her remarks.

I always praise all my students, if they are making a serious effort, regardless of final result. I simply assumed she was doing same to me, and saw her remarks as well meant encouragement that bore no relation to my progress. Some of the ease with which I could discount her praise is perhaps due to different expectations as to the kind of feedback a teacher gives. As I have suggested earlier, Cindy's own schooling made her less prone to profuse praise than I might have expected. Consequently, what she saw as explicit, obvious praise, I saw as a meaningless routine courtesy. I took it for granted, therefore, that she was as dissatisfied with my progress as I was.

The first suspicion that I might have misread her position, came in late October, when I wrote:

> I think it is possible that Cindy is content with the schedule—that it is part of the control/discipline approach to the language. You do not progress until you have thoroughly mastered previous material.

It was some weeks more, before I was able to recognize that she was not merely content with the schedule, but that she was actually quite pleased with the kind of progress I was making. It was even longer before I could recognize the progress for myself. Before I could do that, I had to rewrite my story of literacy and learning, which as I will discuss in the next section was not a simple matter.

My story of learning

As well as having expectations of literacy, I had a set of stories about myself as a learner. These included my strengths and weaknesses, my notions of successful strategies, and my ideas of appropriate learner behaviour. At the beginning of the study, I wrote a scenario of success in Chinese based on these assumptions. One aspect of my personal story that played a significant role related directly to my expectations of success. As I had predicted, I eventually did fairly well at learning the characters, while I never achieved more than minimal success with the nine tones of Cantonese.

It is possible that my prediction represented accurate self-knowledge of my potential abilities, but there are also indications that this prediction became a self-fulfilling prophecy. My success with the characters represented many hours of concentrated work, because I was not prepared to tolerate failure in this area, which I had designated as one of my strengths. By contrast, I tended to avoid tone work, finding it frustrating and embarrassing to fail repeatedly. To reduce the embarrassment, I tried working privately but I was incapable of judging my own progress and consequently would decide that I was wasting my time. I hated being asked to read aloud to Cindy, because she would not tolerate errors of tone. If I had to read something aloud, I was prone to gabble it off, in hopes that the tones would not be distinguishable. On one occasion, when she commented on my tendency to avoid opportunities to improve my tones, I answered:

Jill   I think you are right, [pause] I'm tending to work on the stuff I can do well, and block out the stuff I don't do well. Instead of saying, "Tones are really hard for me," I should be focusing on tones really hard—instead I'm saying, "Oh I can't do those so there's no point in bothering."

Cindy   I think you still feel inhibited—I don't know if it's because I told you it's important for me?

Jill   I think it's just because I don't feel confident I can do it right—so that inhibits me.

It is possible that if I had been confident enough with tone to practice regularly, and had devoted as many hours to improving my tones as I did to improving my characters that I would have surprised myself by making progress in an area that I had always assumed was beyond me. Unfortunately, my very conviction of failure was powerful enough to guarantee that end.

Not all my assumptions about myself as a learner were made so explicitly as this sense of my own strengths, however. As the inquiry progressed, I became aware of other assumptions that I had not thought to mention in my attempt to describe my preconceptions prior to the study. Some of them I had never consciously acknowledged as being part of my belief system. One assumption I discovered I held about being a good learner related to the speed with which one processed information. In my memories of learning as a child, it seemed that speed was always praised. I can hear my father's voice describing me with pride as being "quick on the uptake."

I remember an incident in high school with a fierce math teacher for whom I had immense, if knee-quaking respect. I enjoyed math and would often ask questions about the effect of changing the parameters in some way. This teacher never gave explicit praise, but one day she had taught us some geometrical item relating to a point within a circle. She paused after the presentation, and said, "And now I'm sure Jill is already leaping ahead and wants to know what happens if the point is outside the circle." It was the nearest to praise she ever gave any of us, and I treasured those words—and tried very hard from then on to continue to be the first to grasp the new material and push it a stage further. Not all my teachers were so enthusiastic about speed, when I think back more carefully. There are a number of comments on my report cards talking about my carelessness, but I never took such teachers, or such remarks very seriously.

I began Chinese then, with the assumption that speed was one of the strengths I had to bring to the study, and that the demonstration of such speed was one of the ways I could please my teacher. Unfortunately, Cindy did not see speed as being relevant or even helpful to the development of literacy in Chinese. She would frequently make remarks such as, "You're rushing through them. It doesn't matter how many you do. You just have to do them well." Or, "I'd rather you did three sentences well, than seven sentences badly."

Obviously I heard what Cindy was saying to me, but initially I reacted in much the same way as I did to those high school teachers who urged a more careful approach. I slowed down when attempting very specific tasks, especially while she was watching me, but mentally I continued without any change at all. When she introduced me to the character for my first classifier, I immediately besieged her with questions about the system of classifiers, and how they were used, grouped and organized. When she taught me the character for birth, I tried to relate it to the word for Christmas, which I had met in the oral class. The similarity turned out to be purely oral, rather than semantic, which involved us both in a lengthy digression.

I never really rejected this story, in that I continued to try to write rapidly and smoothly, and I continued to rush over my tones and other pronunciation difficulties. As I shall discuss in the next chapter, I did come to realize some of the benefits of concentration, and a more receptive learning style, but there continued to be many occasions on which my instinctive reaction was to leap into speech.

Related to my story about the speedy good learner, was my sense that learning consisted largely of analysis and synthesis. Much of my rushing into verbalization was an attempt to think out the relationships between new information and prior knowledge, or an attempt to break down an incomprehensible unit into pieces that I could classify and manipulate.

In our first lessons, Cindy tried to teach me the sounds by simple imitation. This led us into great difficulties, as in this example from an early class transcribed before I had met the Yale system. As this transcript demonstrates, my immediate reaction is not to repeat the word but to push Cindy to be more specific about it.

Cindy   *Chut, chut , chut.*

Jill   There's something I can hear there apart from the "t" and the vowel what is it? *Tsc? ts ? ch?* Is it like aspirated "t?"

Cindy   No it's like "hut," and it's not "h"—it's almost like a "ts" [repeats].

Jill   Is there a consonant at the end?

Cindy   It's almost like ut without the "t." *Chut* [repeats]. Try it again. Say it from 5.

Jill   *Ng lohk chut.*

Cindy   Longer, *chut.* The initial sound ends very quickly, so it's the vowel part that you have to carry over.

Jill   *Tsut. Thut.* I guess it's because I'm having a hard time getting that first consonantal sound and I'm swallowing it because I can't get it right.

Cindy   Try *ch, ch.*

Jill   *Tch, Tch.*

Cindy   Okay, *Chut*

Jill   *Chut.*

Cindy   Oh I don't need that t at the end [laughter] Now longer.

Jill   *Tchut, tchut.* How can you hold aspiration? It's over before you know it.

Cindy   That's better.

Jill   Give me a sequence like 6-7-8 or something so I can hear it.

Cindy   Okay. From 5. *Ng loh chut baat gau.*

Jill   *Chut , chut, chut, chut, chut, chut,* [laughs]

Cindy   Good that's better. Actually you've got the initial consonant.

Jill   I have? [laughter]

Cindy   You need to work on the vowel now.

Jill   I seem to need to close my throat off to get that initial consonant and I can't get it back into action to get the vowel out. *Chut, chut.*

Cindy   Better. *Chut.*

Jill   Okay. Let's try this. How would you write it? Would you use "ts?"

Cindy   Then you have the vowel as in "hut" but without the "h," so its *tsut*.

Jill   *Tsut? chut?*

Cindy   Okay, it's almost—there's a tiny space in there between that and the vowel. *Chut* [laugh] Oh, we'll come back to that one.

Jill   Yes. That one's impossible.

A week or two after this incident, I brought in to Cindy a chart that I had been given in the oral class, which classified all the possible sounds in Cantonese. Strangely, we both assumed that the chart was reliable, and gave it a higher credibility than Cindy's own native speaker knowledge. On one occasion we were struggling to identify the initial sound at the beginning of *jong,* and I asked her if it was the same sound as that at the beginning of *chat*. She experimented somewhat hesitantly and eventually agreed that it was. Later, I saw the word on the chart as *jong,* and found my immediate reaction was that Cindy had been mistaken. An equally valid reaction would have been that the chart was inaccurate, or that the similarity between the two sounds is so close that in certain cases one cannot clearly distinguish. But I was keen to believe in a system, and I did not want to have to tolerate fuzzy boundaries.

This search for system was by no means restricted to the pronunciation. I have mentioned earlier how I pushed Cindy for tight specifications on character production. Following a discussion of one character that seemed to break the rules of stroke order, I commented to Cindy on my assumptions about Chinese.

> I had this image of the Chinese language as being very rule governed and I'm kind of amused to discover some surprise in myself every time I find an inconsistency, as if I'm not prepared to allow Chinese to be inconsistent even though my own language is totally inconsistent...I tend to be very conscious of variations. I'm interested mostly because I wonder where I ever got the idea that it wasn't allowed to be an inconsistent language like every other language.

I showed a similar assumption of underlying system in my attempts to find syntax rules, and to manipulate language in small pieces rather than learning entire utterances. When I learned my first nouns that could be used as adjectives, I immediately said:

Jill   Yeah, I can make things with that.

Cindy Pardon?

Jill   Well I can kind of play around with that and string things together for myself. I like the way the pieces come together.

My annotation on this piece reads:

> This applies to far more than just these characters. I like combining initials and finals. I like combining strokes. I have confidence I can master a system in a way that I don't have confidence about an uncharted language.

A journal entry makes a similar point:

> I feel that I am getting control of the shapes of the characters quite easily. I still feel a lot of trouble with those sounds, although the

chart is useful. I like the sense of systematicity that came with it.

In this early part of the learning experience, I was still seeing my learning task as being one of gathering pieces of objective knowledge. I was very conscious of searching for a web of connections between apparently unconnected scraps of information. If the knowledge could be reduced to a rule-based system, I felt confident of my ability to get control of it.

I took pride in my ability to analyze and synthesize, to look for patterns and to find connections between apparently discrete pieces of knowledge. Such an attitude inevitably affected the process of my literacy development, just as had my assumptions about print, and language systems. But as I found out, this is not the only way to approach literacy. As Erbaugh (1990) claims, for the Chinese, "Learning means copying models." By focusing my attention on the figure rather than the ground I was learning a different kind of literacy. Before I could make the kind of progress that Cindy wanted for me, I had to change my assumptions about what learning consisted of. As I describe in the next chapter, this was a stressful experience.

Chapter Ten

The impact of the experience on the learner

In the previous two chapters I discussed how the personal understandings and assumptions that Cindy and I held affected the way in which literacy was both taught and learned. In terms of the commonplaces, these chapters show how the *User* affected the *Process*. I was to find however that the relationship between the commonplaces is a dialectical one, and that the *Process* of attempting literacy in a second language would also affect me as *User*.

Other writers have, of course, discussed the impact on the *User* of the interaction with text. Writers such as Luria (1976), Olson (1977, 1978, 1980, 1986), Scribner and Cole (1981), and Vygotsky (1978) have considered the impact on cognitive development. Fishman (1990), Heath (1982, 1983, 1986a, 1986b, 1986c), Klassen (1988) Street (1984, 1990), and others have discussed how the interaction with text helps shape the socialization of the individual. Nothing I had read, however, prepared me for the individual emotional impact of this learning experience.

I found the first two months of my Chinese literacy study very stressful. In earlier chapters, I describe how I was unable to recognize the progress that I was making and consequently how troubled I was by what I perceived as my failure to proceed adequately. I have recounted how I strengthened my efforts to succeed using strategies that had previously been reliable for me, not recognizing that those very strategies would impede my progress. So that the harder I tried the more unsuccessful I was. The result was a welter of emotional and physical distress.

My dreams were full of Chinese learning, which invariably manifested itself as a struggle to perform some intricate task that was beyond my capabilities. My childhood asthma returned and my excema flared. I found it difficult to discuss the experience I was undergoing because I did not have a way of framing what was happening to me in any acceptable story. I felt uncomfortable criticizing my teacher, but I was also reluctant to admit to personal failure.

The study was obviously not my first learning experience, which leads me to ask why this particular experience was perceived as being so stressful. There have been other learning tasks that I have found difficult without having such a reaction. I think of my attempts to learn windsurfing, for example, at which I was never successful, despite a number of tries. I was disappointed and mildly frustrated by my poor performance at the time but essentially forgot the issue in between visits to the beach.

I also questioned why the stress was related to the literacy learning, rather than the oral classes. Had the stress related simply to my concerns over being a successful learner, one might have expected that the protected environment of the literacy tutorials would have been less stressful than the competitive public forum of the oral Cantonese course.

I think the difference lay in the kind of difficulties that I was encountering. My oral language learning certainly involved difficulties and failures, but such problems came in essentially predictable areas and fulfilled my expectations. I had expected that tones would be difficult to hear and they were. Presented with long vocabulary lists, I was pleased to find that I remembered eighty per cent of them and did not berate myself for the ones that were forgotten.

In my literacy classes, however, what I was being asked to learn was so different from what I had anticipated, that I could not at first conceive of what was being asked of me. As a learner I was frustrated by what I saw as my slow progress. I was devoting large amounts of time to activities that I thought were critical but that were, in retrospect, irrelevant to what my teacher was asking me to learn. I was unable to recognize the goals that she had for the process, and consequently I could not make any reasonable assessment of progress.

Essentially the story I am telling is a story of bafflement. I thought I knew what literacy was, and I couldn't recognize what I was being taught as literacy. Because I was baffled by the process, not recognizing where I was going wrong, I felt that I had no control over the experience. I did not understand why this situation was stressful and consequently I did not know how to resolve it.

Literacy, I came to understand, is not merely a skill like windsurfing that a person can acquire as an added extra to be called on when useful. Literacy provides the external display of the self, so that a new literacy is like looking in the mirror with a new face. My sense of self, I discovered, is tied up closely with the language that I speak and the literacy that I use. Literacy can function merely as the channel through which the language command is displayed, but for many societies it is also the main educational, shaping force. We exemplify in literacy the skills, attributes, character traits and thinking patterns that our society prizes, so that literacy becomes a reflection of achievement and status. I was to discover that the aspects of self and character to be displayed through Chinese literacy for status were different from those with which English language literacy is associated.

In my Spoken Cantonese classes, I was not being taught a new way of thinking about myself. I was being taught how to express the same thoughts I had in English, via a different set of words. No doubt if I had become sufficiently fluent, the oral language would also have led me eventually into a consideration of the kind of thought that it was appropriate to express, as Fan's (1989) work suggests, but as a beginner I seemed to be learning new symbols for familiar concepts.

Had I learned Chinese literacy simply as an alternate set of symbols with which to encode Western thoughts, it is unlikely that the process would have had such a dramatic effect on me. However, I was being taught a literacy in which a philosophical approach to learning and communicating was inherent. I was being asked for a side of myself that I did not know I possessed, one that was so buried or undeveloped that I did not recognize it as part of my make-up. My sense of self as a communicator, as authoritative, as literate, and as a good learner were all challenged in the process of attempting to understand literacy in the traditional Chinese way. To learn what Cindy was trying to teach me, demanded not just the storage of new information or the acquisition of new physical skills, but a change in the way I understood literacy and learning and a change in the way I understood myself.

The effects that this process had are not easy for me to put into words, especially within an academic genre. Essentially, the experience was one of discovering that my "story of how things are" no longer fitted the events I was experiencing. Being forced to rethink my understandings was a difficult and painful process that I initially resisted so that, when I was finally forced to readjust my thinking, the accumulated resistance aggravated the stress.

An image that helped me to explain how it felt is one drawn from plate tectonics. The plates of the earth's crust are constantly being pressured in particular directions, just as we are constantly being faced by changes in our environment. Sometimes the plates slide gently by each other and the effects of the move are barely noticed. Sometimes and in some places, however, the plates do not slide smoothly to accommodate the relentless pressures, but instead the forces of change build and build until eventually the plates rip apart, producing an earthquake in the process.

In the same way, I suspect, we resist constantly revising our understanding of the world. Instead we attempt to impose a fixed frame on experience, a set of assumptions and stories that seem to function well to allow us to make sense of the world. During this experience of attempting to become literate in Chinese, I clung to a number of stories about myself, and about language and literacy. Initially I refused to change those stories. I interpreted everything that happened to me in the framework of the stories with which I began the study. As the changes accumulated it became harder and harder to make sense of what was happening to me, until finally I was forced to write a new story. The process of coming to recognize that I needed a new story was personally stressful because, as I was to discover, the nature of literacy was so bound up in my image of myself, that what I had to rewrite was not something "out there" but the way in which I saw myself.

A large part of how we see ourselves is in the reflections of the ways others see us, so our ability to express ourselves to others, to use language and literacy, is perhaps particularly relevant to our sense of self. However, I was also forced to think again what the character is of the person I know as myself, to rethink myself as a learner, and as a mature adult with authority and expertise.

I think right from the beginning Cindy must have been aware that identity and literacy are closely bound up, since one of the first questions she asked me related to my name. I had mentioned to her at an earlier meeting that my name had been transliterated into characters while I was in Singapore but I no longer had the transliteration to hand, and could not remember the characters that had been used. Before the first class, Cindy suggested that we might begin with my name.

Cindy	And the next question I was going to ask you was, "If you had a choice what would you do first." For instance, the thing you might think of is numbers. Or your name. If you wanted to find it somewhere, on a piece of paper or something…or whether you feel it is necessary for you to have a name in Chinese? Is it necessary for you to know what my name is in Chinese? Those are the questions I have. Some people, the first thing they ask is, "I want to know my English name."
Jill	I hadn't thought of it, but I think that would be nice. I think the routines of heading your paper with the name and the date, even if they're not the things you need to write very critically, because you can get hold of them and you feel like you're making progress and I would like that.

My response to the idea of working with my name doesn't suggest that I saw the name as being particularly related to my identity. I wasn't quite sure what Cindy meant when she asked me if it was necessary for me to have a name in Chinese, and consequently I was unsure how to respond. When we began the lesson proper, later that day, Cindy returned to this topic.

Cindy	Now the first thing we are going to do is see if you can find your name.
Jill	Okay. I will look. I don't think I am going to be able to find it.
Cindy	Did you like the name you had?

This question threw me. I had not thought of a transliterated name as something that I would have any feelings about. My identity was located in the name Jill—people could transcribe that in any way they wished, without affecting what I thought of as my real name. At that point it seemed unimportant to me which way they chose to write it. Presumably I was thinking in terms of phonetic transcriptions and had no sense that the words would be meaningful and consequently would suggest an identity along with a name. I answered Cindy's question by saying,

Jill	I never understood what was going on with my name.
Cindy	And nobody told you what it meant?
Jill	Not really. It was simply a matter of my business card. They were running around to get my name done for it. They eventually decided that what they could produce wasn't good

enough to be of any use to anybody so it never appeared on the back of the business card. They weren't linguists who were doing it. It was a Hakka speaker who was doing it. Now what language he—he would probably have done it into Mandarin, which was the official dialect. And in fact it was only much later that I was able to put...to realize that the reason he didn't work with Jill, the reason that he said, "Oh Jillian, oh that's better," was probably that he could break it down into *Ji* or *chi-lian*. At the time I didn't have a clue. I think he said it was jasmine blossom or some kind of blossom but I was quite baffled as to what—and certainly when I showed this to people and said could you read that out to me, what they read out didn't sound anything like Jillian Bell. So I never quite understood what was going on, so if you could re-transliterate it I would be very happy.

Cindy Yeah, well, Jill is very difficult by itself. I mean I have thought about it and how to use your last name as well, which is bell, which sounds like "white," *ba'*, and then something like *zi* for Jill, which would sound a lot like your name but would have absolutely no meaning. In fact it would sound very much like idiot, [laughter] so I really don't think we should use that one. So if we were to use Jillian because of the *lian* at the end we could use the word *lien*, which means lotus. Then you're another kind of flower, so...there are possibilities if you don't want to stick with what you have. I will try. [pause] Speaking of names—you know that Cindy has nothing to do with my Chinese name?

A later annotation on this section of the transcript notes, "Cindy had obviously put some real thought into this, and yet we never proceeded with it. Did she pick up that while interesting for me, it was essentially irrelevant? I am Jill, not *Chi Lien*."

Looking back at these exchanges now, I find it difficult to recapture the sense of surprise I felt when Cindy asked whether I liked the name I had been given. Was I really so ignorant of the meaning-based nature of Chinese characters that I thought of a name simply as a sound, and not as suggestive of the person bearing the name?

No doubt if I consulted appropriate texts, I could discover the original meaning for "Jill," but for me the meaning of the name is not in its etymological derivation, but in its personal and social use through my life. There is a social meaning to "Jill," which draws on the sort of families who choose to name their daughters so, the age group for which that name is popular, the type of character given that name in the media, and so on.

There is a personal meaning to "Jill," which is drawn largely from the people who call me that, rather than the "Jilly" favoured by close family, or the "Jillian," which is still associated with childhood discipline in my mind. I was prepared to see my name rewritten but I was reluctant as a grown adult to take on a new name, which suggested a new identity. Cindy and I never referred again to the issue of a Chinese name for me, but I was to find that other challenges to my sense of self would be less easy to shrug off.

I began this study with a sense of myself that was more or less unquestioned. There are obviously aspects of my personality that could stand improvement, but I accept these deficiencies and they do not trouble me on a day-to-day basis. Essentially, at the start of this study, I was happy with myself and the way I interact with people and situations. Over the years I have developed experiences, approaches, skills and other attributes that allow me to handle, to my satisfaction, most situations I encounter. I have built up a sense of myself as a competent adult who, for the most part, expects success within those situations that I select as being within my capabilities. My sense of self is confirmed with each success that I achieve and is vested in continuing to achieve success within a variety of areas that I have marked out for myself as my key interactions—in fulfilling the demands of everyday life, for instance, in maintaining a solid marriage and raising good kids, in having friends whose company I enjoy, in writing books that sell, in performing well at work, and so on.

Thus there are many aspects to my sense of self. I see myself in the varied roles I fulfill, as mother, professor, and so on and I see myself in the tasks I do, be it driving, cooking, or writing. These are external demonstrations of a sense of self that is held internally. I judge myself on these roles and tasks according to whether I feel emotional satisfaction or distress in relation to my performance, but my sense of what deserves emotional approval was no doubt determined as a child and continues to be determined by the feedback, either explicit or implicit, from others. When I feel distressed as a result of my own actions, or when I get negative feedback from others, I begin to question myself.

When I started this study, I had confidence in myself as a competent adult, and as a good learner. I assumed I was knowledgeable about my own personality, so that I knew my strengths and weaknesses and could work from my strengths to achieve success in new tasks. As I struggled to become literate in Chinese, I found myself in a state of emotional distress, which was aggravated by the negative feedback of my friends, and by what I perceived as the negative feedback from my teacher. As a result, I was forced to confront some of my assumptions about myself.

Sense of self as expert

It became apparent during the study that I was ambivalent about assuming the role of neophyte, and that my reluctance to lose my "expert status" was impeding my learning. My image of myself appeared to be vested in part in a sense of being knowledgeable and it was difficult and stressful to let go of that image. Although, in one way, my background in second language education would predispose me more than most learners to lay claim to having a sense of authority when approaching a second language study, this sense of being unwillingly turned into a neophyte is potentially significant for all adult learners who have developed an image of themselves as being in control of their own lives and as being adequate for whatever task they may set themselves.

When I explore the ways in which this image of self as knowledgeable is demonstrated, it does not become evident as a simply held position. Rather there is a conflicting sense of genuine expertise contrasted with an external image of "expert," which both covers and provokes an internal fear of being discovered to be ignorant.

There is self as known to self as knowledgeable, and self as known to world as knowledgeable, while simultaneously known to self as inexpert. The different aspects of this part of image of self appear throughout the study of Chinese, with the two components affecting each other, so that a challenge to expertise in one area would provoke a clinging to status in another. It is this interplay that suggests that my previous work in second language learning is less critical in producing this reaction to the learning process than my sense of self as adequate adult. Although my need to demonstrate adequacy arises at least in part from my personal story, I shall try to show that there is also a cultural element in this reaction, which lies in the ways in which I strove to show expertise, adequacy and knowledgeability.

When I came to begin the study of Chinese, I did not imagine that this issue of expert status would be significant in my learning experience, although I was conscious to some extent that my background in second language work made me a slightly unusual learner. I was aware, for instance, that the teacher's performance in the Spoken Cantonese course would be evaluated by people with whom I have been friendly for a number of years. Had I voiced any injudicious criticism, it might have had a more serious effect than criticism coming from another student. It was possible that the teacher also taught ESL to Cantonese speakers, in which case he might have read articles or books I had written and recognize my name. However, I was more concerned that the teacher would be inhibited by the knowledge that one of his students was using the course as part of a learning study, rather than being present simply to learn Cantonese. This stems perhaps from my own experiences, when colleagues drop in unexpectedly on workshops designed for a different audience. Knowing that they are present not for the informational content, but for ideas about presentation prior to doing their own workshops, I become painfully self conscious about technique and organization, to the detriment of the general atmosphere. With this in mind, I was doubtful about even telling the teacher of my primary purpose, and only a sharp reminder of the ethics of the situation made me inform him.

At the beginning of these oral classes my sense of myself as expert was very evident from my annotations on the class transcripts. I was critical, for instance, when an exercise on the nine Cantonese tones gradually shifted over to focus on detailed explanations of the vocabulary items selected to demonstrate the tones. I claimed that I lost my ability to hear the differences between the tones because, instead of being presented in contrast, they were widely separated by the discussion of the meaning. It is probably also true that I lost my ability to hear tone because I was concentrating on a criticism of the methodology, not the matter under discussion.

This was an issue that became less significant as the classes proceeded. It became obvious that the teacher's methodology, although different from my own sometimes, was in fact effective and I gradually relaxed and participated in much the same way as the other students. As I have described earlier, once the teacher became known as a person, a sense of loyalty developed, which became more important than adherence to particular tenets of methodology.

In these oral classes then, I began the study conscious that my background might affect my interaction with the learning. However, I did not foresee a similar situation in my private literacy tutorials. My tutor came with considerable experience in the ESL field and with a warm personal recommendation from a mutual friend. I had had no prior exposure of any significance to Chinese literacy or to Chinese patterns of learning and had someone suggested that I was holding any claims to being an authority I would have reacted with skepticism.

However, in retrospect, there were two areas in which I still maintained a position of authority. The first related to my general knowledge of the second language education field. Cindy was obviously aware that the study was being conducted for my Ph.D, as part of an ongoing programme of second language education. Further, in contrast to the usual teacher-learner contracts, the parameters of the study had been determined by me rather than the teacher.

Another area in which I held an unconscious sense of expertise, related to my knowledge of my own learning patterns and abilities. As the study progressed, it became gradually apparent that Cindy and I had a different view of what I was trying to learn and how I might learn it. I have described elsewhere my surprise at Cindy's reaction to my suggestion of studying characters on the subway. In my journal at the time I commented:

> My attitude [to her response] was a little ambivalent. I recognize that the character is supposed to be both beautiful in appearance and communicative, and that the first demand will not be easy to achieve in the subway, but I find myself thinking that I can begin by conquering the shape of the character, then work on improving its form.

The phrase, "I find myself thinking," is key here. I am already challenging the guidance she is giving me, before the study has even begun. As we continued with the study, this pattern of resistance became entrenched. I displayed similar resistance to the use of squared paper, and to the provision of a good writing surface and quiet surroundings for my practice sessions.

Sometimes I even seemed to resist listening to Cindy. There are a number of occasions in the transcripts where she gave me important information but I did not seem to hear or understand it. I have cited earlier my excitement at discovering the significance of the placement of units within the square. Cindy's explanation of that point begins, "Actually I showed you this a while ago, and I'll show it to you again." She was correct. The transcripts show that the information had been given earlier, but I had not then been ready to hear her.

When I came to transcribe our interactions I was always struck by how much I talked. As she would review my assignments, I would be rattling off explanations, apologies and justifications, rather than listening carefully to what she had to say to me. It didn't strike me then that I was busy asserting myself, but I was concerned that as a simple time waster, this might be having an effect on my progress. By early November, my journal notes that I, "went into the lesson with C determined to shut up. Silent, (self-consciously so) as she views assignments."

It is difficult to measure the significance of this shift, but over the next few weeks, I made a real effort to work on the characters in the way in which Cindy had asked from the beginning. I bought new pens especially for character writing, worked only at my desk and used only squared paper. Undistracted, I found that I approached the characters differently. No longer was I actively trying to commit the individual pieces to memory, using mnemonics to help me. Nor was I daydreaming about other matters while mindlessly copying. Instead I accepted that my task was to write the pages of copies without being concerned with whether or not I could already recognize and read them but to focus on the shapes I was producing.

As I spent more and more time working in this way, I found myself in something closely approaching a trance state in which I was tightly focused on the characters I was producing. When I played back the tape recordings I was making of what was supposed to have been a think-aloud process, I found long periods of silence that I had not been aware of at the time. I realized what Cindy had meant when she referred to concentration, and was not surprised when she commented on the improvement in my work. I began to recognize too that in addition to learning how to produce more acceptable characters, I was also learning them at a deeper level. Analyzing some homework I had done in late November, I discuss a grammatical error I made and then comment:

> Actually when I look back on it, it seemed my hand knew better than my brain—only one mistake and that was almost a forced 'better use the new literary version.' Good—I'm glad all that homework isn't invalidated.

Once again this learning gave physical impact to a position that I had previously only understood in a cognitive way. I had read Johnson's (1987) *The Body in the Mind* and paid lip service to the notion of bodily knowledge. Suddenly I was confronted with a demonstration that my hand knew things that my brain did not. An article on dancer, Edward Villella, helped me understand this.

> Villella also has 'muscle memory'— the thing most dancers rely on to remember a role. Muscle memory fades with inactivity. Villella says that the Prodigal [a role he made famous] is still in his body but he can feel the moment approaching when it will start to fade. (Croce, 1988.50)

I had been aware that literacy involved small muscle activity, but I had thought of it only in terms of training the muscles to be under firm control, not of teaching them complete patterns of movement that would live on in the muscle after the conscious brain had forgotten the pattern. I began to understand a little more why Cindy urged me to practice only at my very best level of production.

My pleasure at discovering that I was finally producing characters that met with Cindy's approval was compounded when it became evident that my assumption that three new characters per week would mean one hundred and fifty characters in a year was erroneous. It became evident that I had in fact been learning some of the basic components of characters, which would combine in different pieces to make more and more new characters. As I moved on to more complex ideographs, I found to my pleasure that I was learning them comparatively rapidly, thanks to my solid grounding with many of the basic strokes. It was fairly easy to produce these characters well immediately on being introduced to them. What was difficult was to commit them to long term memory. Here again the long hours of practice, often completing two hundred or three hundred repetitions of a single character before attempting to use the word in a sentence, suggested that I was training the body as much as the mind.

However, this is only a part of what Cindy saw as our task. I once suggested, "I begin to think tracing would be a really valuable activity," but Cindy responded, "It's only done with brushwork. I've always thought that its effectiveness is limited. How did you feel about copybooks when you were younger?—But motor skills are important , I suppose."

The experience of a change in consciousness obviously produced a change in my attitude towards Cindy and her methods of teaching, and I made a conscious effort for a time to do exactly what she asked of me. As I made progress in the subject, her praise and encouragement played a role in keeping me working within the defined framework. In a few areas, I began searching for a success determined by her standards of what was praiseworthy, rather than my own—in this case, in the area of presenting perfect work to the teacher. In late November, I discussed with Cindy one of my first attempts to create sentences within a provided framework and described how my need to succeed interferes with my role as researcher.

Jill   My failures are much richer sources of data than my successes...and yet even though I know this, I could kick myself when I make a mistake. I cringe, and you know—I really wanted to—I wanted to throw away this page so badly, I was just mortified to have to bring this page to you.

Cindy   Oh, I see, and you crossed it out,

Jill   ...All I thought was,"I've missed out the particle, ruined my nice page," and then I come back, I did that yesterday, then I come back today and think, "I've got those particles mixed up," but even though—I know this is good data, but I don't bring second class work to the teacher. If this were not a study I'd toss the whole page and recopy with the correct sentence. I find myself doing that all the time, I guess its my, er, my narrative of myself as a good learner keeps winning out over my student wish for a good study.

Cindy   If it were me, I'd probably do the same thing. If I weren't doing a study, it's true I would not show anybody anything that to me was less than perfect or that was beyond the acceptable, so I understand that.

This is not to suggest that I had moved away from a position of authority entirely though. On the contrary, the change appeared to be restricted to that particular area of study—the development of expertise with characters. As we moved onto a wider vocabulary, where items were chosen not for their appearance but for their semantic value, the task shifted to one where syntax played a large part. Cindy herself had been taught written sentence structure [which differs from oral Cantonese] by dint of copying sample sentences, gradually substituting personally chosen words within the defined framework. The transcripts show that she began to teach me by this same method.

In my impatience, however, and without any consultation with Cindy, I enlarged my homework assignments from straight copying of provided models to attempts to communicate my own material. This entirely self-imposed task, I saw at the time as a sign of my progress, not as another rebellion against the teaching methodology. It is an article of faith in current ESL methodology that one has learners writing personally significant text at the earliest possible moment. It did not occur to me then that such a premise might not work within a different learning system.

Sometimes I regretted having committed myself to such a difficult task as I struggled each week to find some event in my week that I had sufficient vocabulary to write about. I used all the resources I had to pull together these pieces. I did not have an English-Cantonese dictionary that I could use, so I could not simply look up unknown words. The back of my oral text, however, had a small glossary of Cantonese words transcribed in Yale Romanization. These were translated into both English and Chinese characters. If I knew the oral form of the word I wanted, I could thus track down some new characters, although there was no guarantee that the oral form and the written form were the same. Inevitably, this activity changed the focus of our lessons as Cindy was faced by grammatically incorrect pieces of work on which I required feedback. Because I was trying to express ideas that were important to me, I attempted a great variety of sentence structures, frustrating her attempts to build up from simple base patterns.

When I produced my first attempt at original communication it is difficult to tell from the transcript how Cindy viewed this innovation. She commented that the work was a "good try" and passed on a discussion of the grammar involved. My own attitude is fairly well indicated by the annotations on the transcript.

> I like the idea of trying to create a piece of text in Chinese, to write something with meaning, even if fairly trivial and I find it frustrating to be able to write only a small piece of what I can say. A few verbs like 'go,' 'see,' 'like' might be valuable, or perhaps Cindy and I could agree on a journal where I simply write unknown characters in pinyin, or English; a sort of *hai ngoh dik garden sih hou douh fa* type of thing. Otherwise it's hard to make much use of the vocabulary.

As I got more adventurous, the calibre of my characters dropped as I worked with new characters that I had never been taught. Typeset characters are stylized in ways that are not always appropriate for handwriting, and it is sometimes difficult to recognize the component parts of complex characters, and hence to produce the strokes in the appropriate order and direction.

When I asked Cindy how I could tell whether a square component in the printed text was developed from one of two possible patterns, she replied uncompromisingly, "You can't. You have to have seen it done." Locked into my own view of things, I failed to pick up on her implicit warning that the route I was following was not the most fruitful one for me, given the task at hand.

My own frustration at my progress could perhaps have given me some warning here. In early March, I wrote that I was not working as well as I would have liked.

> Homework has also been neglected. In part this is because I am setting myself a tougher target than merely writing individual characters. I am finding that I am reluctant now to write simple random sentences.

I go onto to acknowledge that what I am trying to do is to assert my personality.

> I am not sure whether I am pleased that I have constructed a more

or less true piece of information, or self-conscious and irritated that I can only express myself so meagrely—this despite the fact that I can use English to elaborate my meanings to Cindy and that I have, in effect, long ago presented whatever personality credentials I have to offer.

Cindy's comments on my attempts to write journal-type pieces were more positive than anything she had suggested earlier. At a later date, she wrote, "Did I tell you? I was impressed, I was proud of you. I'm glad you took the initiative. I was getting so used to our meetings that I kept thinking we had all the time in the world to get to compositions." She demonstrates here, I think, the split between ESL teacher and Chinese teacher. Instinctively, she knew that I required more time before I would be ready for Chinese composition, but her ESL training, like mine, led her to feel that student-generated language had to be seen as a positive move.

In a journal entry written some five months after the completion of the study, I noted that the new characters I had tried so hard to use and to teach myself, were no longer remembered. "I cannot read them, much less reproduce them. They [are] in fact the dead end that Cindy instinctively saw them as."

The same is true, though to a lesser extent, of many of the new characters she tried to teach me during this period. I would do perhaps a page of practice on a new character, which given my newly achieved command of the basic strokes was sufficient to allow me to produce a relatively attractive form. Then I would rush into an attempt to "use" the character within a meaningful context, not recognizing that the character had not been learned by the body. Inevitably in these text pieces, my attention would shift to meaning rather than form to the detriment of what I produced.

Looking back on the study now, some years later, the parts of the language that have remained with me are the parts that I was taught by the traditional methods that I fought so hard in the beginning. The early characters are thoroughly learned and can still be produced more or less effortlessly. Just this last week, I had call to use them in an exchange with an elderly Chinese lady in an ESL class I was visiting and I found that not only could I produce them, but their form was good enough to provoke surprised praise from her and explicit comments on my sense of balance.

It was noticeable, however, that the only characters that I could recall were ones that I was taught in the early part of my Chinese study, when the learning method was one of simple and constant repetition. The apparent oral fluency of which I was so proud at the end of the study also seems to have disappeared and the complex text pieces I crafted at that time are no longer intelligible to me. I can, however, still spot errors of accuracy, proportion and form in written characters. I can see balance within individual character and within overall text. That lesson, which was so hard to learn, has stayed with me and become part of me.

Sense of self as a learner

When I attempted to describe myself as a learner, prior to the beginning of this study, I focused on the ways in which I had noted differences in my learning from those of other people I had studied with. I commented on my preference for visual input, my fondness for working with words, my relative success at academic tests, examinations and so on. In the course of the study I was to become aware that these features are fairly superficial manifestations of much more basic assumptions about what learning is and how it is made manifest. My story of myself as a learner was so unconsciously held that even when specifically attempting to describe myself as a learner, I did not consider probing my understanding of what learning is, or how one functions as a good learner.

One aspect of this unconscious story related to the way one approaches knowledge. I became aware that, at least within a formal learning environment, my common approach was to break knowledge down into tiny pieces, and to gain complete control of those pieces before I tried to reassemble them. The transcripts of my lessons with Cindy show many occasions when I pushed her to break down the knowledge she was giving me. Rather than allowing her to simply model a sound for me to repeat, I would push her to break the overall sound down into individual phonemes. When shown a character, I would ask her to tell me exactly how long one line should be in proportion to another, or define the point at which the two intersected, as being at, above or below the midpoint.

I did not find this behaviour strange at the time and, when I first became conscious of this pattern in myself, initially I assumed that this was the way in which I learn most things and consequently demonstrated an essentially individual preference. However, when I think of my behaviour in non-academic learning, it is obvious that I do not follow this pattern. I do not become familiar with a new acquaintance's face by deciding that her nose is exactly one and one third times as long as her eye. Nor do I pick up a commercial jingle by studying the notes in a score. It appears that it is only within an academic context that I feel such analysis is the appropriate learning method, which suggests that it is a pattern that I developed in response to the way I was taught in school.

Analysis, I discovered, was only part of this learning pattern. The purpose of the analysis was largely an attempt to find generalizability. Ideally, having broken the input down into minute pieces, I would discover a rule that governed the way in which the pieces were reconstructed, and that rule would then be applicable to other related situations.

In search of such generalizability, I pushed Cindy, for instance, to tell me that the order of strokes in a character went from left to right and from top to bottom, and then plagued her for subsets of rules, as to whether a curved stroke in the bottom left would come before or after a slanted line at top right. When I encountered anomalies, I found myself irritated that the language failed to conform to the system I was trying to impose on it. This pattern can be seen in my interactions with Cindy at all levels of language learning, including character formation, pronunciation, syntax, and morphology. In searching for these rules I demonstrate my unquestioned assumption that the language was system-governed and that the best way to approach it was to recognize the pieces and the rules by which those pieces could be manipulated.

The following is a typical interaction. Cindy begins with a general instruction. I immediately respond with an attempt to analyze the difference between her work and mine. Then I begin to chatter :

Cindy   Watch me do this. [pause]

Jill   You're more vertical. I'm going off the vertical. When I look at my learners and they are copying an "A" and it's all over the page and it's so obvious to me where their "A" diverges from the perfect mental "A" in my head, that I wonder that they can't see it, yet you don't see it yourself. I can't see it at all.

	And there are so many ways…
Cindy	Even if you could see it you probably couldn't reproduce it.
Jill	Well that's true but surely seeing it is half way to being able to reproduce it. If you can't see it you can be wasting all your energies…
Cindy	There. This one's much better.

My remark that, "If you can't see it you can be wasting all your energies," is, I think, probably very typical of the way I thought of learning at this stage. Unlike Cindy, I saw no value to the act of practicing in itself. Instead my role was to note features such as the relative amount of verticality, and reduce the task to a set of rules to be followed.

There were some advantages for me in such a learning style. I would not have relied on such a system for many years had it not given me some rewards. I seemed to remember these fragments of knowledge according to the relationships that I assigned them. My chances of remembering pieces depended on how well connected they were to other firmly rooted pieces of knowledge. If there was a rule available that would have some generic application, I obviously made use of that. Most characters incorporating the symbol 十 丿 had some relation to plant life, for example. Failing a specific rule, I used any sort of mnemonic hook that I could develop as a way of trapping errant pieces of information.

As I write this I am struggling, as an example, to recreate the word for pumpkin. I find I cannot remember it as a sound or as a visual, but I know analytically that it broke down into the word for melon, *gwa*, preceded by one of the points of the compass, north, south, east or west. There are many such examples I could cite where the Cantonese words have faded from my memory but the rationale by which I was able to produce them still remains.

When I was studying Cantonese I wished many times for pattern tables that would allow me to manipulate pieces of language to create new phrases and sentences. I was impatient waiting for control of the language to come to me, and did not recognize the progress I was making.

As I have suggested earlier, Cindy was not teaching according to the analytic methods I expected. She did not break material down into tiny units for me; on the contrary, she stressed the unity of material. She would often comment that she could not produce a good character when she tried to go very slowly and demonstrate the individual strokes. To produce it properly, she needed to address it as a whole entity. Similarly, she found it difficult breaking her utterances down into individual sounds.

One of the shifts that I had to make in the course of this study was to realize that my patterns of analysis were not appropriate in this learning context. This was not as easy to do as it is to write. When I found I was not making the progress I would have wished, my tendency was to cling more strongly to the patterns that have been successful in previous learning opportunities, and to become more analytical rather than less.

Related to this was my sense of how a good learner behaves. It became evident over the course of the study that I felt my role was to be active, questioning, and participating. I showered Cindy with comments, interrupting her presentation to predict the likely outcome, drawing parallels with other material she had taught me, or that I had met outside of the class.

Some of this was perhaps personal volubility but another part was my attempts to fulfill what I saw as the role of an interested, committed learner. It was also an attempt to demonstrate to her how hard I was trying and how much I was learning. When I said something like, "Oh, so *neui* doesn't follow the stroke pattern," I was perhaps partly verbalizing my disappointment at the inconsistency, but I think I was also trying to show off to my teacher that I had absorbed the rules of stroke order well enough to recognize when they were being broken.

Such behaviours had limited value in impressing Cindy. Her judgments on my work were drawn far more from my performance in writing and speaking Chinese, not in my ability to verbalize the underlying system. She both taught me and assessed me through a more global performance.

Another issue that seemed to be integral to my notion of the good language learner related to the speed of performance. Cindy told me many times that speed was unimportant to her—that what mattered was how well a task was performed, not the speed at which it was performed. However, I did not seem able to take in such feedback, and continued to rush to answer her questions, to repeat, and to write and generally to move the focus of the lesson from her to me.

Learning from Cindy, I was reminded of a remark that a Eurasian friend had made to me some years earlier in Singapore. He had commented on how talkative he had found people on a trip to the States, adding that even taxi drivers talked his head off. He felt this national volubility was a direct result of Western educational methods, where children are constantly exhorted to "ask if you don't understand," and where one learns to think by talking an issue out.

He contrasted this with the way he had been raised and educated. Essentially, he said, he had been told that when he was young his role was to observe, and to listen. He was not to question, but to watch and perhaps to repeat. If he did not understand, he did not ask. He observed and he listened until he did understand. Eventually, when he was grown, he would come to understand, and if he lived long enough he might reach the point where he would be ready to build on the wisdom he had been taught.

The idea of sitting silently observing and listening and soaking up the words of the master is attractive in principle but difficult to enact when one has been raised in a different educational system. In particular, it is difficult when one has imposed a certain time frame on the learning. I had set myself a data collection period of one year, within which I wanted results. I found it hard at first to credit that I could make sufficient progress in the language simply by sitting and observing.

Again this brings me back to my notion of progress; when progress is measured in terms of gaining control of so many units, one becomes locked into an acquisition timetable. When one sees progress as a process of gradually coming to understand something more and more clearly, then the artificially demarcated time zones of an imposed time frame are less relevant.

The Shift

I cannot claim that I moved completely from an active, analytical learner with a need to demonstrate personal expertise into someone who was prepared to submerge herself in holistic learning, but I did change over this period. I found this change very difficult to discuss at the time. I had spent the early part of the study very unhappy and unable to pinpoint what was causing my distress other than a generalized dissatisfaction with my progress. The breakthrough into an understanding of a totally different learning style was difficult for me either to comprehend or to describe. I did not appear to have a vocabulary that would explain what I had learned. I toyed with words like mystical, holistic and meditative, all of which suggested something of the experience but none of which seemed to describe it in a way that felt right.

I had not previously seen myself as a person who described experience in such terms. I felt pretentious and out of my depth to be calling on a terminology that was foreign to me, and that seemed to come from a world and a group of people with which I had never identified myself. Trying to describe my discovery to others involved what seemed then to be a dramatic shift in the aspect of self I chose to make public. I struggled to find a way to express what I felt without having to readjust my public self. I looked at other aspects of my life that had similarities with the new experience. In some ways the trance-like work on the characters was akin to the feeling I sometimes have when I sketch: a feeling of withdrawing totally from the world around me and entering some part of my mind that works with space and shape rather than language, so that if I am interrupted I feel as if I have to journey back to the real world before I can communicate.

This feeling is fairly well documented in writings on art (Edwards, 1979, 1986), which suggest the use of terms such as "right brain experience." Although this terminology did not fully describe my experience, I found that I was at least prepared to discuss what had happened when I could describe it in this way.

Some twelve months later, in a presentation to other graduate students, I described how this period felt:

> When people were saying, 'How are you doing?' and I was giving progress reports, I didn't have a vocabulary for describing this. Part of the self- image that was so hard to accept was that, here I was, I'd had this experience that was very rich and meaningful for me, but it didn't fit with the character I had for myself. I couldn't find words to describe this that didn't jar with the personality in the story I told of myself. Eventually I started describing it as a 'right brain experience.'. It was the only way of explaining it within the kind of academic persona I held for myself. It took quite a long time

to work through this and to simply be able to come out and get to the point of being able to use my tutor's words of concentration, balance and discipline—to be able to say, 'Oh yes, well, I concentrated,' and not feel that it was strange that I concentrated so hard that 45 minutes of so-called 'think-aloud' [tape recording] had gone by in silence and I hadn't been conscious of the fact that I wasn't talking. To simply accept that as part of me—to accept that, 'Hey—I can be disciplined.' It was that sense of finding a harmony within myself that I didn't know was there; that was what the change was. I still find it embarrassing to talk about, so I haven't fully lived it, I guess, or I wouldn't be sitting here blushing right now.

I found also that the shift in the image of self has affected me in other contexts outside of the study. While this study of Chinese was ongoing, I was also attending a graduate seminar in an area that interested me considerably. In the early weeks of the seminar, I operated with the patterns described in the early part of this paper. I felt it was necessary to demonstrate my understanding of the texts under study and entered forcefully into discussions that allowed me to demonstrate this knowledgeable position. I drew my "knowledgeable position" from close analysis of the text to support my position and I expected my performance to be judged according to the power, clarity and analytical quality of my contributions.

About half way through the course on narrative, I found that I was approaching the classes differently. The change was not quite as clear-cut as taking a learning from my Cantonese and applying it wholesale to the graduate course. Rather the challenges that the Cantonese literacy posed for me made me more open to other possibilities, so that I reacted differently to an incident in the graduate course where some of the participants disagreed strongly about appropriate ways to approach a text.

I became aware that by racing to say my piece I was cutting myself off from the opportunity to hear others, and to think through issues. Quite consciously, I decided to sit quietly and listen to the discussion, contributing only when I felt I had something of genuine originality to offer. This change of behaviour was due in part to a growing awareness of my competitive patterns of behaviour in the classroom, which became evident during the thesis study. It was also, however, an offshoot of my discovery that I could learn in a number of ways, and that the highly active way in which I had previously seen learning was by no means the only route that could be followed.

It was not really a surprise to me to discover that I found the seminars to be more fruitful when approached in this way. What I had not expected, however, was the tremendous sense of relief I experienced once I had decided that I was not going to be a key participant in the discussions. I had not previously been aware that in order to maintain that image of self as knowledgeable, I had laid an obligation on myself to lead the discussion and to find an answer for every question posed.

Around the same time, I was becoming conscious of a related change in my interactions with texts and concepts. Prior to this experience, when I was introduced to a new term I would search for a definition and try to pin down exactly what the term meant. In the early days of graduate work I remember struggling with dictionary definitions of terms such as "hermeneutics" and "phenomenology." I was irritated when the professor who used these terms refused to define them for me, and felt I was being fobbed off with his comment that I needed to come to understand them for myself.

During this later period, towards the end of my Chinese study, I became aware that terms such as these had found their way into my vocabulary, without my ever having heard them formally defined. I would still have found it difficult to offer a one or two sentence definition of them but I no longer felt that the ability to summarize them in a context-free mode was indicative of understanding. New terms that we met through the narrative course no longer troubled me in the same way, and I was content to read and to discuss and to allow them to take shape for me in their own time. Something similar took place in relation to philosophical texts, which I began to approach more as whole entities to be gradually understood in increasing depth, in contrast with my earlier patterns where I began with the specifics of the individual sentence.

This experience with Cantonese literacy taught me that I have skills as a learner that I never previously credited. It gave me increased faith in my tolerance for what I might call the "fuzzy image"—the half recognized face, the slightly familiar song, or the poorly understood concept. I have come to believe that time will clarify fuzzy images for me, and that the process of taking the images into tiny pieces to make sense of them is not always fruitful.

Conclusion

Change does not come overnight, nor do we completely reverse ourselves. Some of the change of which I am conscious in myself may well have its roots in the long period of graduate study as much as in the attempt to become literate in Chinese. I cannot say, for instance, exactly where my increased interest in form originated. I know only that I now struggle to find the exact word in situations where previously I would have used the first to come to mind. Other "changes" are perhaps better described as being more tolerant and encouraging of aspects of my personality that were always present.

Although I present myself as being surprised, for example, by the inner balance and control I discovered as a result of this study, I am aware that I used exactly those powers to handle the process of childbirth many years ago. What has changed is the way I am prepared to talk about these feelings. Having accepted the possibility of seeing myself as having balance, I am now consciously striving to develop that aspect of self through the study of yoga. What is changing is not only the self, but the story of self, which is a vital precondition for change to occur.

In a discussion of elements in the narrative method, Clandinin and Connelly (1991) comment:

> As we worked with teachers..., we discovered a collection of rather obvious matters that alternatively, like the figures in figure-ground exercises, either strike us as prosaic and unworthy of attention or significant and fundamental to the understanding of curriculum. We see ourselves turning these matters into subjects of inquiry while at the same time straining to keep the magic in the foreground and the prosaic in the background. We expect that the principal difficulty for those who may imagine themselves interested in narrative is not so much in understanding the subtlety of the ideas, which are mostly commonplace, as it is to be excited by the taken-for-granted. (p. 260)

In the course of this inquiry, I was frequently taken by surprise. New revelations would seem immensely powerful or immensely shocking. Soon, however, I would rewrite my story to accommodate the new insight, and then it would become difficult to remember the sense of power that the insight had previously held. I described in the introduction to this book my sense of surprise when Cindy first demonstrated an understanding of literacy based on a notion of personal harmony. As I comment there, it is difficult now to remember how strange that conversation seemed at the time and I have to struggle to remember my sense of excitement and the magic of the new ideas that I encountered over the course of my encounter with Chinese literacy.

My understanding of the changes that this study wrought in me produces a similar sense of shifting between the truly new and the long-familiar but unrecognized. When I look at the impact that the *Process* of attempting a culturally different literacy has had on this *User*, I recognize that this study has allowed me to look at the relationships between literacy, culture and identity in a new way. I find myself eager to work with other learners and other literacies, to see whether what I experienced will be reflected in the experiences of others. In Clandinin and Connelly's words, I look forward with enthusiasm to the ongoing excitement of the taken-for-granted.

References

Adler, M. J. & van Doren, C. (1940, 1967). *How to read a book.* New York, NY: Simon and Schuster.

Alden, H. (1982). *Illiteracy and poverty in Canada: Toward a critical perspective.* Unpublished master's thesis. University of Toronto.

Anderson, A. B. & Stokes, S. J. (1984). Social and institutional influences on the development and practice of literacy. In H. Goelman, A. Oberg, and F. Smith, (Eds.), *Awakening to literacy* (pp. 24-37). Exeter, NH: Heinemann.

Aristotle. (1947). Topica. In R. McKeon (Ed. and Trans.), *The basic works of Aristotle.* New York, NY: Random House.

Bailey, K.M. & Ochsner, R. (1983). A methodological review of the diary studies: Windmill tilting or social science? In K. M. Bailey, M. H. Long, & S. Peck, (Eds.), *Second language acquisition studies* (pp. 188-198). Rowley, MA: Newbury House.

Bell, J. & Burnaby, B. (1984). *A handbook for ESL literacy.* Toronto, ON: Hodder and Stoughton/OISE Press.

Bell, J. S. [Ed.] (1990). *TESL Talk: Special issue on ESL literacy.* Toronto, ON: Ontario Ministry of Citizenship.

____ (1993). The teacher as link between program and practice: A response to Kerfoot and Wrigley. *TESOL Quarterly, 27. 3,* 467-476.

____ (1995). The relationship between first and second language literacy: Some complicating factors. *TESOL Quarterly, 29. 4,* 687-704.

____ (1997). The author responds... Comments on Hilder. *TESOL Quarterly, 31.1.*

____ (1997). Shifting stories: shifting frames. In C. Pearson Casanave & S. Schecter (Eds.) *On becoming a language educator.* Hillsdale, NJ: Lawrence Erlbaum Associates.

Bereiter C. & Scardamalia, M. (1983). Does learning to write have to be so difficult? In A. Freedman, I. Pringle & J. Yalden (Eds.), *Learning to write: First language/second language* (pp. 20-23). New York, NY: Longman.

Bransford, J. (1983). Schema activation—schema acquisition. In R.C. Anderson, J. Osborne and R. Tierney, (Eds.), *Learning to read in American schools* (pp. 259-272). Hillsdale, NJ: Erlbaum.

Brewer, W. F. & Lichtenstein, E. H. (1981). Event schemas, story schemas, and story grammars. In J. Long & A. Baddley (Eds.), *Attention and performance* (pp. 363-379). Hillsdale, NJ: Erlbaum.

Bruner, J. S. (1966). On cognitive growth. In J. S. Bruner, R. R. Olver, & P. M. Greenfield, (Eds.), *Studies in cognitive growth* (pp. 1-67). New York, NY: John Wiley and Sons.

_____ (1972). *The relevance of education.* Harmondsworth, UK: Penguin Press.

_____ (1986). *Actual minds, possible worlds.* Cambridge, MA: Harvard University Press.

_____ (1987). *Forms of self-report: Autobiography and its genres.* Paper presented at International Conference on Orality and Literacy. McLuhan Centre, University of Toronto, June 1987.

_____ & Weisser, S. (1990). The invention of self: Autobiography and its forms. In D. Olson, & N. Torrance (Eds.), *Literacy and orality* (pp. 129-148). Cambridge, UK: Cambridge University Press.

Calamai, P. (1987). Literacy in Canada: A special report. *The Toronto Star*, September 12, 1987.

Canale, M. & Swain, M. (1980). Theoretical bases of communicative approaches to second language teaching and testing. *Applied Linguistics 1*, 1-47.

Carr, D. (1986). *Time, narrative and history: Studies in phenomenology and existential philosophy.* Bloomington, IN: Indiana University Press.

Carrell, P. L. (1983). Evidence of formal schema in second language comprehension. *Language Learning, 34. (2),* 87-112.

_____ (1985). Facilitating ESL reading by teaching text structure. *TESOL Quarterly, 19,* 727-751.

_____ & Eisterhold J. C. (1983). Schema theory and ESL reading pedagogy. *TESOL Quarterly, 17,* 553-573.

Chafe, W. L. (1985). Linguistic differences produced by differences between speaking and writing. In D. Olson, N. Torrance & A. Hildyard (Eds.), *Literacy, language, and learning* (pp. 105-123). Cambridge, UK: Cambridge University Press.

Chall, J. (1983a). *Stages of reading development.* New York, NY: McGraw-Hill.

_____ (1983b). *Learning to read: The great debate.* New York, NY: McGraw-Hill.

_____ (1984). *New views on developing basic skills with adults.* Paper presented at the National Conference on Adult Literacy, Washington, DC, Jan. 1984.

Chik Hon Man. (1985). *Everyday Cantonese.* Hong Kong: Department of Extra Mural Studies, The Chinese University of Hong Kong; Radio Television Hong Kong.

Clandinin, D. J. (1986). *Classroom practice: Teacher images in action.* London, UK: Falmer Press.

_____ & Connelly, F. M. (1986). Rhythms in teaching: The narrative study of teachers' personal knowledge of classrooms. *Teaching and Teacher Education, 2,* 377-387.

_____ & Connelly, F. M. (1991). Narrative and story in practice and research. In D. Schon (Ed.), *The reflective turn: Case studies in and on educational practice* (pp. 258-281). New York, NY: Teachers' College Press.

Clay, M. M. (1979). *Reading: The patterning of complex behaviour.* London, UK: Heinemann Educational Books.

Cochrane Smith, M. (1986). Reading to children: A model for understanding texts. In B. Schieffelin & P. Gilmore (Eds.), *The acquisition of literacy: Ethnographic perspectives. Advances in Discourse Processes XXI.* Norwood, NJ: Ablex.

Connelly, F. M. & Clandinin, D. J. (1988a). Narrative meaning: Focus on teacher education. *Elements 19, (2),* 15-18.

_____ & Clandinin, D. J. (1988b). *Teachers as curriculum planners: Narratives of experience.* New York, NY: Teachers College Press.

_____ & Clandinin, D. J. (1990). Stories of experience and narrative inquiry. *Educational Researcher, 19*, (5) 2-14.

Creative Research Group. (1987). *The Southam Literacy Survey*. Ottawa, ON: Southam News, Inc.

Crites, S. (1971). The narrative quality of experience. *Journal of the American Academy of Religion 39*, (3), 291-311.

Crites, S. (1979). The aesthetics of self-deception. *Soundings, 62*, 107-129.

Croce, A. (1988). Profiles: The Prodigal II. An interview with Edward Villella. *New Yorker*. Nov. 28, 1988.

Curtis, J. K. (1986). *The development of graphic sense: Pre-literate children's knowledge about written language.* Unpublished doctoral dissertation, University of Toronto.

D'Andrade, R. (1987). A folk model of the mind. In D. Holland, & N. Quinn (Eds.), *Cultural models in language and thought* (pp. 112-148). Cambridge, UK: Cambridge University Press.

de Castell, S., Luke, A. & MacLennan D. (1986). On defining literacy. In S. de Castell, A. Luke, & K. Egan (Eds.), *Literacy, society and schooling* (pp. 3-14). Cambridge, UK: Cambridge University Press.

Delgado-Gaetan, C. (1996) *Protean literacy: Extending the discourse on empowerment.* Bristol, PA: Falmer Press.

Dewey, J. (1938). *Experience and education.* New York: Collier Macmillan.

Draper, J. A. (Chairman). (1985). *Concerning policies and priorities for dealing with literacy and occupational health and safety.* Seventh Annual Report of the Advisory Council on Occupational Health and Safety. Toronto, ON: Ontario Ministry of Labour.

Edwards, B. (1979). *Drawing on the right side of the brain.* Boston, MA: Houghton Mifflin.

Edwards, B. (1986). *Drawing on the artist within.* Boston, MA: Houghton Mifflin.

Eisenstein, E. (1979). *The printing press as an agent of change.* Cambridge, UK: Cambridge University Press.

Elbaz, F. (1983). *Teacher thinking: A study of practical knowledge*. London, UK: Croom Helm.

Enns, R. (1982). *Crisis research in curriculum policy making*. Unpublished Ph.D. dissertation, University of Toronto.

Erbaugh, M. S. (1990). Taking advantage of China's literary tradition in teaching Chinese students. *The Modern Language Journal, 74.(1)*, 15-27.

Estes, T. H., Gutman, C., & Estes, J. T. (1989). Cultural literacy: Another view from the University of Virginia. *Curriculum Inquiry, 19*, 309-326.

Fan, S. (1989). The classroom and the wider culture: Identity as a key to learning English composition. *College Composition and Communication, 40.4*, pp. 458-466.

Ferreiro, E. & Teberosky, A. (1982). *Literacy before schooling*. Portsmouth, NH: Heinemann.

Fishman, A. (1988). *Amish literacy: What and how it means*. Portsmouth, NH: Heinemann.

Fisiak, J. (Ed.) (1981). *Contrastive linguistics and the language teacher*. Oxford, UK: Pergamon Press.

Flower, L. & Hayes, J. R. (1980). The cognition of discovery: Defining a rhetorical problem. *College Composition and Communication, 31*, 21-32.

Fondacaro, R. & Higgins, E. T. (1985). Cognitive consequences of communication mode: A social psychological perspective. In D. Olson, N.Torrance & A. Hildyard (Eds.), *Literacy, language and learning* (pp. 73-101). Cambridge, UK: Cambridge University Press.

Freire, P. & Macedo, D. (1987). *Literacy: Reading the word and the world*. South Hadley, MA: Bergin and Garvey.

Gee, J. P. (1990) *Social linguistics and literacies: Ideology in discourses*. Bristol, PA: Falmer Press.

Gee, J. P. (1991) What is literacy? In C. Mitchell & K. Weiler (Eds.) *Rewriting literacy: Culture and the discourse of the other* (pp. 3-11). Toronto, ON: OISE Press.

Geertz, C. (1983). *Local knowledge: Further essays in interpretive anthropology.* New York, NY: Basic Books.

Gillette, B. (1987). Two successful language learners. In C. Faerch & G. Kasper (Eds.), *Introspection in second language research* (pp. 267-279). Clevedon, UK: Multilingual Matters.

Gillooly, W. B. (1973). The influence of writing system characteristics on learning to read. *Reading Research Quarterly, 8,* 167-199.

Goody, J. (1977). *The domestication of the savage mind.* Cambridge, UK: Cambridge University Press.

____ & Watt, I. (1963). The consequences of literacy. *Comparative Studies in Society and History, 5,* 305-345.

Graff, H. J. (1979). *The literacy myth: Literacy and social structure in the 19th century.* New York, NY: Academic Press.

____ (1981). *Literacy and social development in the West.* Cambridge, UK: Cambridge University Press.

____ (1986). The legacies of literacy: Continuities and contradictions in Western society and culture. In S. de Castell, A. Luke, & K. Egan, *Literacy, society and schooling* (pp. 61-86). Cambridge, UK: Cambridge University Press.

Gray, W. S. (1956). *The teaching of reading and writing: An international survey.* Paris: UNESCO.

Hamilton, M. & Stasinopoulos, M. (1987). *Literacy, numeracy and adults: Evidence from the National Child Development Study.* London, UK: Adult Literacy and Basic Skills Unit.

Hardy, B. (1968). Towards a poetics of fiction: An approach through narrative. *Novel, 2,* 5.

Hardy, B. (1977). Narrative as a primary act of mind. In M. Meek, A. Warlow, & G. Barton (Eds.), *The Cool Web* (pp. 12-23). London, UK: Bodley Head.

Harste, J., Woodward, V. A. & Burke, C. L. (1984). *Language stories and literacy lessons.* Portsmouth, NH: Heinemann.

Havelock, E. (1963). *Preface to Plato.* Cambridge, MA: Harvard University Press.

Havelock, E. (1987). *The oral-literate equation: A formula for the modern mind.* Paper presented at the International Conference on Orality and Literacy, McLuhan Centre, University of Toronto, June 1987.

Heath, S. B. (1982). What no bedtime story means: Narrative skills at home and at school. *Language in Society, 2,* 49-76.

____ (1983). *Ways with words.* Cambridge, UK: Cambridge University Press.

____ (1986a). Functions and uses of literacy. In S. de Castell, A. Luke, & K. Egan (Eds.), *Literacy, society and schooling* (pp. 15-26). Cambridge, UK: Cambridge University Press.

____ (1986b). The book as narrative prop in language acquisition. In B. Schieffelin, & P. Gilmore (Eds.), *The acquisition of literacy: Ethnographic perspectives. Advances in discourse processes, XXI* (pp. 16-34). Norwood, NJ: Ablex Publishing.

____ (1986c). *Sociocultural contexts of language development. Beyond language: Social and cultural factors in schooling language minority students.* Los Angeles, CA: Evaluation, Dissemination and Assessment Center, California State University.

Herriman, M. (1986). Metalinguistic awareness and the growth of literacy. In S. de Castell, A. Luke and K. Egan (Eds.), *Literacy, society and schooling* (pp. 159-174). Cambridge, UK: Cambridge University Press.

Herron, M.D. (1971). The nature of scientific enquiry. *School Review, 79,* 171-212.

Hildyard, A. & Hidi, S. (1985). Oral-written differences in the production and recall of narratives. In D. Olson, N. Torrance & A. Hildyard (Eds.), *Literacy, language, and learning* (pp. 285-306). Cambridge, UK: Cambridge University Press.

Hirsch, E. D. (1987). *Cultural literacy: What every American needs to know.* Boston, MA: Houghton Mifflin.

Hoggart, R. (1957). *The uses of literacy.* Harmondsworth, UK: Pelican Books.

Hudson, T. (1982). The effects of induced schemata on the "short-circuit" in L2 reading: Non-decoding factors in L2 reading performance. *Language Learning, 32 (1),* 1-31.

Hunter, C. & Harman, D. (1979). *Adult illiteracy in the United States: A report to the Ford Foundation.* New York, NY: McGraw-Hill.

Innis, H. A. (1951). *The bias of communication.* Toronto, ON: University of Toronto Press.

James, C. (1980). *Contrastive analysis.* London, UK: Longman.

Johnson, J. N. (1985). *Adults in crisis: Illiteracy in America.* National Adult Literacy Project, Far West Laboratory.

Johnson, M. (1987). *The body in the mind: The bodily basis of meaning, imagination and reason.* Chicago, IL: University of Chicago Press.

Johnson, P. (1981). Effects on reading comprehension of language complexity and cultural background of a text. *TESOL Quarterly, 15,* 169-181.

Johnson, P. (1982). Effects on reading comprehension of building background knowledge. *TESOL Quarterly, 16,* 503-516.

Just, M. A. & Carpenter, P. A. (1980). A theory of reading: From eye fixations to comprehension. *Psychological Review, 4,* 329-354.

Kaplan, R. B. (1983). Contrastive rhetorics: Some implications for the writing process. In A. Freedman, I. Pringle and J. Yalden (Eds.), *Learning to write: First language/second language* (pp. 139-161). London, UK: Longman.

Kintsch, W. & Greene, E. (1978). The role of culture-specific schemata in the comprehension and recall of stories. *Discourse Processes, 1,* 1-13.

_____ & Van Dijk, T. (1978). Toward a model of text comprehension and production. *Psychological Review, 85,* 363-394.

Klassen, C. (1988). *Non-literate adults in ESL classrooms.* Unpublished master's thesis. University of Toronto.

Kohn, J. (1992). Literacy strategies for Chinese university learners. In F. Dubin & N. Kuhlman (Eds.), *Cross-cultural literacy: Global perspectives on reading and writing.* New Jersey: Prentice Hall.

Kozol, J. (1985). *Illiterate America.* New York, NY: Plume, New American Library.

Krashen, S. D. (1981). *Second language acquisition and second language learning.* Oxford, UK: Pergamon Press.

Kulick D. & Stroud, C. (1993). Conceptions and uses of literacy in a Papua New Guinean village. In B. Street, (Ed.) *Cross-cultural approaches to literacy* (pp. 30-61). Cambridge, UK: Cambridge University Press.

Lado, R. (1957). *Linguistics across cultures: Applied linguistics for language teachers.* Ann Arbor, MI: University of Michigan.

Lakoff, G. & Johnson, M. (1980). *Metaphors we live by.* Chicago, IL: University of Chicago Press.

Langer, J. A. (1987). A socio-cognitive perspective on literacy. In J. Langer (Ed.), *Language, literacy and culture: Issues of society and schooling* (pp. 1-20). Norwood, NJ: Ablex.

Levine, K. (1986). *The social context of literacy.* London, UK: Routledge & Kegan Paul.

Lord, A. B. (1960). *The singer of tales.* Cambridge, MA: Harvard University Press.

Luria, A. R. (1976). *Cognitive development: Its cultural and social foundations.* Cambridge, MA: Harvard University Press.

MacIntyre, A. (1981). *After virtue: A study in moral theology.* Notre Dame, IN: University of Notre Dame.

Mandler, J. & Johnson, N.W. (1977). Remembrance of things parsed: Story structure and recall. *Cognitive Psychology, 9,* 111-151.

Mason, J. M. & Au, K. H. (1986). *Reading instruction for today.* Glenview, IL: Scott Foresman.

McLuhan. M. (1962). *The Gutenberg galaxy: The making of typographic man.* Toronto, ON: University of Toronto Press.

McKay. S. L. (1993). *Agendas for second language literacy.* New York, NY: Cambridge University Press.

Mink, L. O. (1978). Narrative form as a cognitive instrument. In R.H. Canary, & H. Kozicki (Eds.), *The writing of history.* Madison,WI: University of Wisconsin Press.

Molinsky, S. J. & Bliss, B. (1983). *Side by Side.* Englewood Cliffs, NJ: Prentice Hall.

Naiman, N., Froehlich, M., Stern, H. H. & Todesco, A. (1978). *The good language learner.* Research in Education Series, No. 7. Toronto, ON: OISE.

Narasimhan, R. (1987). *Literacy: Its characterisation and implications.* Paper presented at the International Conference on Orality and Literacy, McLuhan Centre, University of Toronto, June 1987.

Neilsen, L. (1989). *Literacy and living: The literate lives of three adults.* Portsmouth, NH: Heinemann.

Ninio, A. & Bruner, J. S. (1978). The achievements and antecedents of labelling. *Journal of Child Language, 5,* 5-15.

Oakeshott, M. (1962). *Rationalism in politics and other essays.* London, UK: Methuen.

Olson, D.R. (1977). From utterance to text: The bias of language in speech and writing. *Harvard Educational Review, 47,* 257-281.

_____ (1978). The language of instruction: On the literate bias of schooling. In R.C. Anderson, R.J., Spiro, & W. E. Montague (Eds.), *Schooling and the acquisition of knowledge* (pp. 65 98). Hillsdale, NJ: Erlbaum.

_____ (1980). *The social foundations of language and thought.* New York, NY: W.W. Norton.

_____ (1986). The cognitive consequences of literacy. *Canadian Psychology, 27,(2),* 109-121.

Ong, W. J. (1977). *Interfaces of the word.* Ithaca, NY: Cornell University Press.

_____ (1982). *Orality and literacy: The technologizing of the word.* London, UK: Methuen.

Pennycook, A. (1996). TESOL and critical literacies: Modern, post, or Neo? *TESOL Quarterly, 30.1,* pp. 163-171.

Peshkin, A. (1988). In search of subjectivity—one's own. *Educational Researcher, 17, (7),* 17-22.

Polanyi, M. (1959). *The study of man.* Chicago, IL: University of Chicago Press.

_____ (1962). *Personal knowledge: Towards a post-critical philosophy.* (2nd ed.) Chicago, IL: University of Chicago Press.

Ross, D. P. (1981). *The working poor.* Toronto, ON: James Lorimer.

Rubin, J. (1975). What the good language learner can teach us. *TESOL Quarterly, 9,* 41-51.

Rumelhart, D. E. (1980). Schemata: The building blocks of cognition. In R. J. Spiro, B. C. Bruce, & W. E. Brewer, (Eds.), *Theoretical issues in reading comprehension* (pp. 34-58). Hillsdale, NJ: Erlbaum.

Sampson, G. P. (1979). *New routes to English.* Don Mills, ON: Collier MacMillan.

____ (1990). Teaching English literacy using Chinese strategies. In J. Bell (Ed.), *TESL Talk: Special issue on ESL literacy* (pp.126-138). Toronto, ON: Ontario Ministry of Citizenship.

Savignon, S. J. (1983). *Communicative competence: Theory and classroom practice. Texts and contexts in second language learning.* Reading, MA: Addison Wesley.

Scardamalia, M. & Bereiter, C. (1983). The development of evaluative, diagnostic, and remedial capabilities in children's composing. In M. Martlew (Ed.), *The psychology of written language: A developmental approach.* London, UK: John Wiley.

____ & Bereiter, C. (1985). Development of dialectical processes in composition. In Olson, D., Torrance, N.and Hildyard, A. (Eds.) *Literacy, language, and learning* (pp. 307-329). Cambridge, UK: Cambridge University Press.

____ Bereiter, C. and Steinbach, R. (1984). Teachability of reflective processes in written composition. *Cognitive Science, 8,* 173-190.

Schieffelin, B. & Cochrane-Smith, M. (1984). Learning to read culturally: Literacy before schooling. In H. Goelman, A. Oberg, and F. Smith, (Eds.), *Awakening to literacy* (pp. 3-23). Exeter, NH: Heinemann.

____ & Gilmore, P. (1986). The acquisition of literacy; Ethnographic perspectives. *Advances in Discourse Processes, XXI.* Norwood, NJ: Ablex.

Schumann, F. M. & Schumann, J. H. (1977). Diary of a language learner: An introspective study of second language learning. In H. D. Brown et al. (Eds.) *On TESOL '77, Teaching and learning English as a second language* (pp. 241-249). Washington, DC: TESOL.

Schutz, A., & Luckmann, T. (1973). *The structures of the life-world.* Chicago, IL: Northwestern University Press.

Scollon, R., & Scollon, S. (1981). *Narrative, literacy and face in interethnic communication. Advances in Discourse Processes, VII.* Norwood, NJ: Ablex.

____ & Scollon, S. B. K. (1982). Face in interethnic communication. In J. C. Richards & R. W. Schmidt (Eds.), *Language and Communication* (pp. 156-188). London, UK: Longman.

Scribner, S. (1984). Literacy in three metaphors. *American Journal of Education, 93,* 6-21.

____ & Cole M. (1981). *The psychology of literacy.* Cambridge, MA: Harvard University Press.

Seliger, H. W. (1983). Learner interaction in the classroom and its effect on language acquisition. In H. W. Seliger, & M. H. Long, (Eds.), *Classroom oriented research in second language acquisition* (pp. 246-267). Rowley, MA: Newbury House.

Smith, D. M. (1986). The anthropology of literacy acquisition. In B. Schieffelin & P. Gilmore (Eds.), *The acquisition of literacy: Ethnographic perspectives. Advances in Discourse Processes, XXI* (pp. 261-275). Norwood, NJ: Ablex.

Smith, F. (1985). A metaphor for literacy: Creating worlds or shunting information. In D. Olson, N. Torrance and A. Hildyard (Eds.), *Literacy, language and learning* (pp. 195-213) Cambridge, UK: Cambridge University Press.

Snow, C. & Goldfield, B. (1982). Building stories: The emergence of information structures from conversation. In D. Tannen (Ed.), *Analyzing discourse. Text and talk* (pp. 127-141). Washington, DC: Georgetown University Press.

Steffenson, M. S. & Joag-Dev, C. (1984). Cultural knowledge and reading. In J. C. Alderson & A.H. Urquhart (Eds.), *Reading in a foreign language* (pp. 48-61). London, UK: Longman.

Sticht, T. G. (1984). *Strategies for adult literacy development.* Applied Behavioural and Cognitive Sciences, Inc. ERIC ED240300.

Stock, B. (1983). *The implications of literacy: Written language and models of interpretation in the 11th and 12th centuries.* Princeton NJ: Princeton University Press.

Street, B. V. (1984). *Literacy in theory and practice.* Cambridge, UK: Cambridge University Press.

____ (Ed.) (1990). *Discourse, context and ideology: Essays in the anthropology of literacy*. Cambridge, UK: Cambridge University Press.

____ (1993). *Cross-cultural approaches to literacy*. New York, NY: Cambridge University Press.

Stubbs, M. (1980). *Language and literacy: The sociolinguistics of reading and writing*. London, UK: Routledge & Kegan Paul.

Szwed, J.F. (1981). The ethnography of literacy. In M.F. Whiteman, (Ed.), *Writing: The nature, development, and teaching of written communication. Volume I: Variation in writing: Functional and linguistic cultural differences*. Baltimore, MD: Erlbaum.

Tannen, D. (Ed). (1982a). *Analyzing discourse: Text and talk*. Washington, DC: Georgetown University Press.

____ (1982b). *Spoken and written language: Exploring orality and literacy. Advances in Discourse Processes, IX*. Norwood NJ: Ablex.

Taylor, D. (1989). Toward a unified theory of literacy learning and instructional practices. *Phi Delta Kappan*, (Nov. 1989.)

Taylor, I. (1981). Writing systems and reading. In G. E. MacKinnon and T.G. Waller (Eds.), *Reading Research: Advances in Theory and Practice, Volume 2* (pp. 1-51). New York, NY: Academic Press.

____ & Taylor, M. M. (1995) *Writing and literacy in Chinese, Korean and Japanese*. Philadelphia, PA: John Benjamins.

Taylor, M. C. & Draper, J. A. (1989). *Adult literacy perspectives*. Toronto, ON: Culture Concepts Inc.

Thomas, A. M. (1976). *Adult basic education and literacy activities in Canada*. World Literacy Council.

____ (1983). *Adult illiteracy in Canada: A challenge*. Occasional paper, 42. Ottawa, ON: Canadian Commission for UNESCO.

____ (1989). Definitions and evolution of the concepts. In M.C. Taylor & J. A. Draper (Eds.), *Adult literacy perspectives* (pp. 3-14). Toronto, ON: Culture Concepts Inc.

US Department of Justice. (1983). *Report to the nation on crime and justice*. Washington, DC.

Venezky, R. L. (1973). The letter-sound generalizations of first, second, and third grade Finnish children. *Journal of Educational Psychology, 64*, 288-292.

Vygotsky, L. S. (1978). *Mind in society: The development of higher psychological processes.* Cambridge, MA: Harvard University Press.

Wells, G. (1986). *The meaning makers.* Portsmouth, NH: Heinemann.

―――― (1990). Talk about text: Where literacy is learned and taught. *Curriculum Inquiry, 20,* 369-405.

White, H. (1973a). The value of narrativity in the representation of reality. In W. J. T. Mitchell, (Ed.), *On Narrative.* Chicago, IL: University of Chicago Press.

White. H. (1973b). *The historical imagination in nineteenth century Europe.* Baltimore, MD: Johns Hopkins Press.

Wigfield, J. (1982). *First steps in reading and writing.* Rowley, MA: Newbury House.

Jill Sinclair Bell is Associate Dean in the Faculty of Education at York University, Toronto, Canada. She has published a variety of articles in professional journals, classroom materials for adult learners of English and four books for teachers including, *Teaching Multilevel Classes in ESL* and *A Handbook for ESL Literacy*. She is currently co-editor of *The Canadian Modern Language Review*.